THE
PHAEDRA
OF
SENECA

Stage of Roman Theater at Sabratha,
N. Africa, ca. 180 A.D. Photo: R. Schoder, S.J.

THE
PHAEDRA
OF
SENECA

Second Edition

LATIN TEXT • FACING VOCABULARY
STUDY QUESTIONS • ANALYSIS
STAGE DIRECTIONS • ILLUSTRATIONS

New Translation of the *Hippolytus of Euripides*

INTERMEDIATE

GILBERT AND SARAH LAWALL
AND GERDA KUNKEL

Bolchazy-Carducci Publishers, Inc.
Mundelein, Illinois USA

Cover Design
Adam Phillip Velez

The Phaedra of Seneca

Gilbert and Sarah Lawall
and Gerda Kunkel

© 1982 Bolchazy-Carducci Publishers, Inc.
All rights reserved.

Bolchazy-Carducci Publishers, Inc.
1570 Baskin Road
Mundelein, IL 60060 USA
www.bolchazy.com

Printed in the United States of America
2009
by BookSurge

ISBN 978-0-86516-016-3

TABLE OF CONTENTS

Phaedra and Nurse Plotting
Painting from Pompeii, Photo: R. Schoder, S.J.

About this Book

The purpose of this book is to make one of the influential masterworks of Roman tragic poetry readily accessible to students in their second or third year of college Latin. The Latin text of Seneca's play is here presented unaltered except for the addition of full stage directions in English. Each page of the text is accompanied by running vocabularies, translation aids, and identifications of mythological allusions. Part II contains additional study materials. It begins with notes on the meters used in the play and continues with full and detailed study questions and comments on each speech, scene, and choral ode. These questions and comments are intended more to prompt close observations and thoughtful reading than to provide a ready-made interpretation of the play. They are extensive and detailed in the belief that a close and active reading and interrogation of the text will amply reward the reader by revealing the complex interplay of words, characters, and dramatic events that makes this play come alive as a compelling piece of literature. These study questions and comments are followed by a new translation of Euripides' *Hippolytus*. This Greek play provided one of the models for Seneca's tragedy, and it deserves careful study alongside of the Latin play.

Reading and study of the play with the materials contained in this volume should be accompanied by study projects on related topics such as the following:

The Neronian age,
Seneca Rhetor (the father of our Seneca),
Seneca Philosophus (our tragic poet),
The Roman theater,
Rhetoric in Latin literature,
Stoicism,
Epicureanism,
Euripides (who wrote two plays on the Hippolytus theme, one of which
    has survived and is included in this volume),
Sophocles (who wrote a *Phaedra*, which is no longer extant), and
The Greek theater.

Later adaptations may be read alongside of the Senecan and Euripidean versions contained here. Of special interest will be Racine's *Phèdre*, Robinson Jeffers' *The Cretan Woman*, and Eugene O'Neill's *Desire Under the Elms*. These are conveniently available in *Phaedra and Hippolytus: Myth and Dramatic Form* by James L. Sanderson and Irwin Gopnik (Houghton Mifflin Company, Boston, 1966).

The Latin text of Seneca's play is (with a few minor changes) that of Giardina (Bologna, Editrice Compositori Bologna, 1966). Pierre Grimal's edition of the play (*L. Annei Senecae Phaedra: Sénèque Phèdre: Edition, introduction et commentaire;* Paris, Presses Universitaires de France, 1965) and Bernd Seidensticker's study of the poetry of Seneca's plays (*Die Gesprächsverdichtung in den Tragödien Senecas;* Heidelberg, Carl Witner Universitätsverlag, 1969) have influenced much of the stage directions, the commentary, and the study questions. The translations of Euripides' *Hippolytus* is based on Barret's Greek text and commentary (*Euripides Hippolytus: Edited with Introduction and Commentary by W.S. Barrett;* Oxford, Clarendon Press, 1964).

Venus Born, Arriving at Paphos

Painting at Pompeii in House of Venus Marina, Photo: R. Schoder, S.J.

PART I

THE PHAEDRA OF SENECA:

LATIN TEXT WITH STAGE DIRECTIONS

AND RUNNING VOCABULARIES

DRAMATIS PERSONAE:

Hippolytus
Phaedra
Nutrix
Chorus
Theseus
Nuntius

1 ite...Cecropii: imperative and vocative.
   cingo, -ere -- to surround.
2 iugum -- summit or ridge of a mountain.
   Cecropii, -orum, m. pl. -- Cecropians = Athenians. Cecrops was the
        first king of Athens.
3 planta -- sole of the foot, foot.
   lustro, 1 -- to go around, wander over, traverse.
   vagus -- roaming, wandering.
4 quae saxoso loca... = loca quae saxoso Parnethi subiecta iacent.
   Parnes, -ethis, m. -- mountain range separating Attica from Boeotia.
5 subiectus -- lying under or near + dat.
   quae... = et loca quae...amnis...verberat.
   Thriasius -- of Thria, an area north of Eleusis (a city to the west of
        Athens, famed for the mysteries of Ceres-Demeter).
6 amnis, -is, m. -- river.
7 verbero, 1 -- to lash, beat.
   scando, -ere -- to climb.
8 Riphaeus -- of or belonging to the Riphean mountains located in
        northern Scythia. The adjective is purely ornamental here.
9 hac, hac...qua...qua...qua...: "here, here...where...where...where..."
   Hippolytus indicates places where groups of hunters should go.
   Supply the imperative *ite* from line 1.
10 texo, -ere -- to weave, compose, interweave.
   alnus, -i, f. -- the alder tree. Note the gender.
   pratum -- meadow.
11 rorifer, -fera, -ferum (ros-fero) -- dew-bringing.
   mulceo, -ere -- to stroke, touch lightly, caress.
12 Zephyrus -- the West Wind.
   vernus (ver) -- of or belonging to spring.
13 gracilis, -e -- thin. graciles...agros: "meager" (as opposed to
        rich) "fields." Here used as a technical agricultural term.
   levis, -e -- light, slight, gentle.
   Ilisos (Greek nominative) -- a river flowing from the slopes of Mt.
        Hymettus, past Athens, and into the Bay of Phaleron.
16 malignus -- stingy, scanty.
   rado, -ere -- to scrape, scratch, graze, touch in passing.
17 vos...: again, supply *ite*.
   trames, -itis, m. -- foot-path.
   laevus -- on the left.

*Scene: Before the royal palace on the Acropolis in Athens.
A statue and altar of Diana, goddess of the hunt, stand in
front of the palace. Time: dawn. On stage as the curtain
rises is Hippolytus dressed for the hunt and surrounded by
his companions who carry spears, nets, and snares and hold
hunting dogs by their leashes. Hippolytus sings as he
addresses his companions.*

HIPPOLYTUS	Īte, umbrōsās cingite silvās	1 anapestic
	summaque montis iuga, Cecropiī.	2
	celerī plantā lustrāte vagī	3
	quae saxōsō loca Parnēthī	4
	subiecta iacent, quae Thrīasiīs	5
	vallibus amnis rapidā currens	6
	verberat undā; scandite collēs	7
	semper cānōs nive Rīphaeā.	8

to one group of his companions

Hāc, hāc aliī quā nemus altā	9
texitur alnō, quā prāta iacent	10
quā rōriferā mulcens aurā	11
Zephyrus vernās ēvocat herbās,	12
ubi per gracilēs levis Īlisos	13 (14)
lābitur agrōs piger et sterilēs.	15
amne malignō rādit harēnās.	16

to other groups of hunters

Vōs quā Marathōn trāmite laevō	17

18   saltus, -us, m. -- woodland, woodland-pasture.
     qua comitatae... = qua fetae comitatae gregibus parvis nocturna pabula
          petunt.
     comitatus -- accompanied.
19   grex, gregis, m. -- flock.   greges parvi = lambs.
20   pabulum -- food.   nocturna pabula: sheep are put out to pasture very
          early in the morning or even while it is still dark in order to
          take advantage of the dew on the grass.
     feta -- technical agricultural term for a ewe that has just given
          birth to its young.
21   subditus (subdo) -- lying beneath, exposed to.
     auster, -tri, m. -- the south wind.
     frigus, -oris, n. -- cold, the cold of winter, winter.
     mollio, -ire -- to soften.
22   Acharnae -- a mountain range in the deme of Acharne in Attica.
23   rupes, -is, f. -- rock.
     Hymettus -- a mountain range to the south-east of Athens, famous for
          its bees and honey; hence, *dulcis*.
24   calco, 1 -- to tread under foot, to pass over.
     Aphidnae, -arum, f. pl. -- a small place to the north of Athens.
25   vaco, 1 -- to be empty, vacant.
     immunis, -e -- free or exempt from taxes or public service. Hippoly-
          tus thinks of each region as owing him game.   diu vacat immunis:
          i.e., it has long been exempt from providing game.
27a Sunion (Greek nominative) -- a promontory in south-east Attica.
     urget: the weight of the elevated cape appears to crush or push out
          (*urget*) the shore (*litora*) that curves (*curvati*) around it.
27b si quem = si aliquem.
28   Phyle (Greek nominative) -- a place in Attica.
29   versor, 1 dep. -- to dwell, live.
30   aper, -pri, m. -- wild boar.
31   laxus -- loose.
32   mitto, -ere -- to let go, let loose.
     habena -- leash.
33   lorum -- thong, leash.
     Molossi (sc., canes) -- Molossian dogs from Epirus; a very fierce
          breed (thus, *acres*).
34   tendo, -ere -- to stretch.
     Cretes (sc., canes) -- Cretan dogs, greyhounds.   Subject of *tendant*.
     tritus -- rubbed, bruised, worn.

saltūs aperit, quā comitātae   18

gregibus parvīs nocturna petunt   19

pābula fētae; vōs quā tepidīs   20

subditus austrīs frīgora mollit   21

dūrus Acharneus.   22

to individual hunters

Alius rūpem dulcis Hymettī,   23

parvās alius calcet Aphidnās.   24

musing to himself as he looks toward the east

Pars illa diū vacat immūnis,   25

quā curvātī lītora pontī   26

Sūnion urget.   27a

addressing his companions again

      Sī quem tangit   27b

glōria silvae, vocat hunc Phȳlē: 28

hīc versātur, metus agricolīs,   29

vulnere multō iam nōtus aper.   30

giving instructions for care of the dogs

At vōs laxās canibus tacitīs   31

mittite habēnās; teneant acrēs   32

lōra Molossōs et pugnācēs   33

tendant Crētēs fortia trītō   34

34b vinculum -- rope, cord, fetter, leash.
36 avidus -- eager for + gen.
    fera -- wild beast.
    nodus -- knot.
    cautus -- cautious.
37 propior, -ius -- nearer, tighter.
    ligo, 1 -- to tie, bind.
38 latratus, -us, m. (latro) -- barking.
39 demissus (demitto) -- drooping, with head hanging down.
    naris, -is, f. -- nostril.
    sagax, -acis -- keen-scented.
40 capto, 1 -- to seize, catch.
    lustrum -- a haunt or den of wild beasts.
41 rostrum -- snout.
42 roscidus (ros) -- dewy.
43 impressa: with *signa*.
44 raras...plagas: "loosely woven hunting nets."
    cervix, -icis, f. -- neck.
45 teretes...laqueos: "tightly woven snares."
46 properet: the structure of 44-46 is as follows: alius...portare...
        alius... (portare) properet. "Let one hasten to carry _____,
        let another hasten to carry _____."
    pictus -- painted, colored.
47 pinna -- feather. linea picta rubenti pinna: a line colored or
        adorned with red feathers was used to frighten the prey into
        nets.
    cludo, 1 = claudo -- to shut, shut in, enclose.
48 tibi: used here in place of *a te*.
    vibro, 1 -- to brandish, shake. "Let it be brandished by you!" =
        "Brandish it!"
    missilis, -e (mitto) -- that may be thrown.
49 simul -- at the same time, together.
50 robur lato...ferro: "oak (spear) with broad iron (tip)."
    dirigo, -ere -- to hurl straight ahead.
51 praeceps, -cipitis -- headlong, swift.
52 subsessor, -oris, m. (subsido) -- one who lies in wait for the prey.
53 solvo, -ere -- to loosen, remove.
    viscera, -um, n. pl. -- the inner parts of the animal.
    culter, -tri, m. -- knife.

vincula collō.   34b

At Spartānōs — genus est audax   35

avidumque ferae — nōdō cautus   36

propiōre ligā: veniet tempus,   37

cum lātratū cava saxa sonent;   38

nunc dēmissī nāre sagācī   39

captent aurās lustraque pressō   40

quaerant rostrō, dum lux dubia est,   41

dum signa pedum roscida tellūs   42

impressa tenet.   43

assigning tasks to be carried out by the hunters

Alius rārās cervīce gravī   44

portāre plagās, alius teretēs   45

properet laqueōs. picta rubentī   46

līnea pinnā vānō clūdat   47

terrōre ferās.   47b

Tibi vibrētur missile tēlum,   48

tū grave dextrā laevāque simul   49

rōbur lātō dīrige ferrō,   50

tū praecipitēs clāmōre ferās   51

subsessor agēs; tū iam victor   52

curvō solvēs viscera cultrō.   53

54 en (interj.) -- come, behold.
    comes, -itis, m. or f. -- companion.
    diva virago: i.e., Diana.
55 cuius regno...vacat: lit.,"to whose rule...lies open." I.e., "you
        who alone rule over the solitary parts of the world."
56 secretus -- solitary, not inhabited.
57 gelidus -- icy cold.
58 Araxes, -is, m. -- the Aras river in Armenia.
    stanti...in Histro: "on the frozen Hister" (= the lower Danube).
59 Gaetulus -- of or belonging to Gaetulia, the modern Morocco.
61 sequitur = persequitur -- pursues.
    cerva -- hind.
62 figo, -ere -- to fix, pierce.
    damma -- deer.
63 variae...tigres: "striped tigers."
    pectora...terga: "chests...backs." Two explanations have been
        offered for these lines. (1) Tigers resist (*tibi dant pectora*),
        while the horned beasts flee (*tibi dant terga*). (2) Both kinds
        of animals offer themselves spontaneously to the death blow as if
        being sacrificed. The tiger is killed with a blow to the chest,
        while the horned beasts are killed as were bulls in sacrifices by
        a blow at the jointure of the back and the neck.
64 villosus -- hairy, shaggy.
    bison, -ontis, m. -- a species of northern wild ox.
65 ferus -- wild.
    urus -- a wild ox. Both the *bisontes* and the *uri* inhabited the
        forests of Germany.
66 solis...arvis: "in deserted, lonely fields."
    pascor, 3 dep. -- to feed, graze.
67 Arabs -- an Arab.
    divite silva: "in his rich forest(s)."
68 inops, -opis -- destitute, needy.
    Garamans -- a Garamantian, member of a tribe of the interior of
        Africa, beyond the Gaetulians.
71 Sarmata, -ae, m. -- a Sarmatian, a Slavic people dwelling between the
        Vistula and the Don.
69 iugum -- summit or ridge of a mountain.
    Pyrene, -es, f. -- the Pyrenees. Pyrene was originally the name of a
        woman, who was raped by Hercules. She bore a serpent and fled in
        terror to the mountains where she was devoured by beasts. Hence,
        Seneca's adjective *ferox*.
70 Hyrcani...saltus: "the forests (*saltus*) on the Caspian (Hyrcanian)
        Sea."
    celo, 1 -- to conceal.
73 gratus...cultor: "a worshiper pleasing (to you)."
    numen, -inis, n. -- divine will, power, favor.
74 retium -- a net.

*turning to the statue of the goddess Diana
and praying*

Ades ēn comitī, dīva virāgō,   54

cuius regnō pars terrārum   55

sēcrēta vacat, cuius certīs   56

petitur tēlīs fera quae gelidum   57

pōtat Araxēn et quae stantī   58

lūdit in Histrō. tua Gaetulōs   59

dextra leōnēs, tua Crētaeās   60

sequitur cervās; nunc vēlōcēs   61

fīgis dammās leviōre manū.   62

tibi dant variae pectora tigrēs,   63

tibi villōsī terga bisontēs   64

lātīsque ferī cornibus ūrī.   65

Quidquid sōlīs pascitur arvīs,   66

sīve illud Arabs dīvite silvā   67

sīve illud inops nōvit Garamans   68

vacuīsque vagus Sarmata campīs,   71

sīve ferōcis iuga Pyrēnēs   69

sīve Hyrcānī cēlant saltūs,   70

arcūs metuit, Diāna, tuōs.   72

Tua sī grātus nūmina cultor   73

tulit in saltūs, rētia vinctās   74

75 tenuere = tenuerunt: the perfect tense is sometimes used instead of
       the present to state a general truth.
    laqueum -- a snare.
76 rupere = ruperunt.
    pedes: i.e., of animals caught in the snares.
    plaustrum -- wagon.
77 gemo, -ere -- to groan, creak.
    rostrum -- snout.
78 rubicundus -- red.
79 longo...triumpho: "in a long triumph(al procession)."
81 argutus -- clear, shrill-sounding.
82 misere = miserunt.
83 pergo, -ere -- to proceed, go forward.
84 compenso, 1 -- to shorten.

tenuēre ferās, nullī laqueum   75

rupēre pedēs: fertur plaustrō   76

praeda gementī; tum rostra canēs   77

sanguine multō rubicunda gerunt   78

repetitque casās rustica longō   79

turba triumphō.   80

The dogs, impatient for the hunt, bark.

Ēn, dīva, favēs: signum argūtī   81

mīsēre canēs.   82a

turning to leave

                    Vocor in silvās.   82b

hāc, hāc pergam quā via longum   83

compensat iter.   84

Exeunt Hippolytus, companions, and dogs.

85 fretum -- the sea.
86 cuius: antecedent is *Creta*; modifies *rates* -- "whose ships..."
    litus, -oris, n. -- shore, coast. ratis, -is, f. -- ship.
87 tenuere - tenuerunt: perfect used to state a general truth.
    quidquid: neuter pronoun in apposition to the masculine *pontum*
        = *quidquid ponti* "whatever of sea" = "the sea which..."
    tenus, w. abl. -- as far as. Assyrian = Syrian.
88 Nereus -- son of Oceanus and Tethys, god of the sea; the sea.
    pervius (per-via) -- passable, crossable.
    rostrum -- the curved end of a ship's prow; its beak. Compare lines
        41 and 77 where the word is used in another sense.
    seco, 1 -- to cut. Lines 87-88 define the extent of the Cretan mari-
        time empire.
89 penates, -ium, m. pl. -- household gods; the household or home itself.
    obses, -idis, m., f. -- a hostage. invisus -- hated.
90 degere aetatem: "to lead my life." dego, -ere (de-ago) -- to spend,
        pass.
91b profugus -- a fugitive from one's country.
92 praestat...fidem: "he keeps faith." *Theseus* is subject. Word order:
        Theseus nuptae fidem praestat quam (praestare) solet. "Theseus
        keeps faith with his wife such as he is accustomed to keep."
        Phaedra is thinking of Theseus' abandonment of Ariadne and kill-
        ing of Antiope, his two former wives.
93 Word order: per altas tenebras invii retro lacus (gen.).
    invii retro: "that has no way (*via*) back." retro (adv.) -- back.
    lacus, -us, m. -- lake; here used poetically of the river Styx.
94 vado, -ere -- to go. tenebrae, -arum, f. pl. -- darkness.
    procus -- a suitor, wooer. The reference is to Pirithous, who went to
        the underworld to woo Persephone, its queen. Theseus accompanied
        him (some say out of love for Pirithous) in this amorous "mili-
        tary expedition" (thus, *miles*).
95 solium -- throne.
    revello, -ere, revelli, revulsum -- to pull or tear away. revulsam:
        sc., Proserpinam.
96 pergo, -ere -- to go.
    furor, -oris, m. -- madness. furoris socius: abstract for concrete =
        a companion of Pirithous' mad scheme to carry off the queen of
        the underworld.
97 tenuit = retinuit: "held back."
    stuprum -- dishonor, disgrace, debauchery, lewdness. Again, abstract
        for concrete. stupra = adultery with the queen of the underworld.
    illicitus -- not allowed, forbidden. torus -- bed.

*Scene: the same. Time: slightly later. Enter
Phaedra (dressed in a royal purple and gold robe,
wearing earrings, her hair impressively arranged
on the top of her head) and the nurse from the
palace. Phaedra looks southward towards her home
across the sea and soliloquizes.*

PHAEDRA	Ō magna vastī Crēta dominātrix fretī,	85 iambic
	cuius per omne lītus innumerae ratēs	86
	tenuēre pontum, quidquid Assyriā tenus	87
	tellūre Nēreus pervius rostrīs secat,	88
	cūr mē in penātēs obsidem invīsōs datam	89
	hostīque nuptam dēgere aetātem in malīs	90
	lacrimīsque cōgis?	91a
	Profugus ēn coniunx abest	91b
	praestatque nuptae quam solet Thēseus fidem.	92
	fortis per altās inviī retrō lacūs	93
	vādit tenebrās mīles audācis procī,	94
	soliō ut revulsam rēgis infernī abstrahat;	95
	pergit furōris socius, haud illum timor	96
	pudorque tenuit -- stupra et illicitōs torōs	97
	Acheronte in īmō quaerit Hippolytī pater.	98

99   incubo, 1 -- to lie upon, weigh down, burden.
     maestus -- sad, unhappy, gloomy. Supply *mihi* with *maestae*:   dat. with
          incubat.
101 solvere = solverunt.   solvo, -ere, solvi -- to free, release.
     alo, -ere -- to feed.
102 Aetnaeo...antro: the volcanic mouth of Mt. Aetna in Sicily.
          antrum -- cave.
     vapor, -oris, m. -- steam, vapor. Word order: malum intus (*adv.*)
          ardet qualis vapor Aetnaeo antro exundat.
103 Pallas, -adis, f. -- a name of the Greek goddess Athena = Minerva; she
          taught women how to work and spin wool.
     tela -- the threads in the loom, the warp.
     vaco, 1 -- to be empty, vacant.
104 pensum -- the wool weighed out (*pendo*) to spin in a day.
106 Atthidum...choris: "in choral dances of Athenians." Atthis, -idis--
          Attic or Athenian.
     mixtam: supply *me*.
107 conscius: here -- "the torches (*faces*) that are conscious (*conscias*)
          of the secret rites (*tacitis...sacris*)." The secret rites are
          the Eleusinian mysteries.
108 prex, precis, f. -- prayer.
109 adiudico, 1 -- to grant or award to. Both Athena and Poseidon laid
          claim to Athens, and in a contest between them the other gods
          decided to award the city to Athena.
     praeses, -idis, m. or f. -- protector, guardian.
110 excito, 1 -- to arouse, awaken, excite (here of wild animals, *feras*,
          driven from their lairs).
111 gaesum -- javelin.
112 saltus, -us, m. -- woodlands.
113 malum: "curse."
114 pecco, 1 -- to sin.
115 miseret + acc. and gen. (impersonal verb) -- it makes one feel pity or
          compassion for someone. tui me miseret: "I feel pity for you."
     infandus (for) -- unspeakable, unnatural, abominable.

Sed māior alius incubat maestae dolor.   99

nōn mē quiēs nocturna, nōn altus sopor   100

solvēre cūrīs: alitur et crescit malum   101

et ardet intus quālis Aetnaeō vapor   102

exundat antrō. Palladis tēlae vacant   103

et inter ipsās pensa lābuntur manūs;   104

looking toward the temples and altars on the
Acropolis

nōn colere dōnīs templa vōtīvīs libet,   105

nōn inter ārās, Atthidum mixtam chorīs,   106

iactāre tacitīs consciās sacrīs facēs,   107

nec adīre castīs precibus aut rītū piō   108

adiūdicātae praesidem terrae deam: 109

looking off in the direction in which Hippolytus
has just departed; gesturing and speaking wildly

iuvat excitātās consequī cursū ferās   110

et rigida mollī gaesa iaculārī manū.   111

recalling herself to her senses

Quō tendis, anime? quid furens saltūs amās?   112

fatāle miserae mātris agnoscō malum: 113

peccāre noster nōvit in silvīs amor.   114

looking back toward Crete

Genetrix, tuī mē miseret: infandō malō   115

116 corripio, -ere, -ripui, correptum -- to seize, snatch up.
     pecus, -oris, n. -- herd.
     efferus -- very wild, fierce, savage.
117 torvus -- wild, fierce.
     impatiens, -entis (patior) -- that refuses to bear + gen.
118 indomitus -- untamed.
119 Word order: quis deus aut quis Daedalus meas flammas miserae ("of
         wretched me") iuvare queat? The interrogative pronoun *quis* is
         used where we would expect the interrogative adjective *qui*.
120 iuvo, 1 -- to help. Daedalus helped Pasiphae in her love for the bull
         by constructing a wooden cow within which Pasiphae concealed her-
         self so that she could mate with the bull.
     queo -- to be able. queat: potential subjunctive.
121 remeo, 1 -- to come back, return.
     Mopsopius -- Attic, Athenian (Mopsopia was an old name for Attica).
         arte Mopsopia: i.e., Daedalus' craftsmanship or skill in making
         the wooden cow for Pasiphae.
122 nostra...monstra: i.e., the Minotaur, born from the union of
         Phaedra's mother, Pasiphae, with the bull (115-118).
     caeca...domo: the "blind house" is the Labyrinth, built by Daedalus
         to hide the Minotaur.
123 promitto, -ere -- to promise, hold out, assure.
     casus, -us, m. -- misfortune.
124 stirps, -is, f. -- stock, race, family.
     perodi, -odisse, -osus -- to hate greatly, detest. *Perosus* often has
         a present meaning: "hating."
     invisus -- hated, detested. The sun-god (who sees all) told
         Hephaestus (Vulcan) that his wife, Aphrodite (Venus), was sleep-
         ing with Ares (Mars), the god of war. Hephaestus forged a net of
         thin chains and caught Aphrodite and Ares in the act the next
         time they made love. Aphrodite thus came to hate the sun-god,
         and she takes out her hatred by punishing his descendants --
         Pasiphae, Ariadne, and Phaedra -- by making them experience
         unnatural or unlawful loves.
125 catena -- chain(s).
     vindico, 1 -- to avenge.
126 probrum -- disgrace, unchastity, adultery.
     omne Phoebeum genus: all the descendants of Phoebus, the sun-god.
127 onero, 1 -- to burden.
     nefandus -- unspeakable, impious, abominable.
     Minois, -idis, f. -- daughter, wife, or female descendant of Minos,
         king of Crete.
     levis, -e -- light, gentle.
128 defungor, -i, -functus -- to get away with, get off with + abl.
     nefas, n. (indecl.) -- sin, crime.
129 progenies, -ei, f. -- offspring, descendant.
130 nefanda, -orum, n. pl. -- unspeakable, impious, abominable things or
         deeds.
     pectus, -oris, n. -- breast, heart.
     exturbo, 1 -- to drive or thrust out.
     ocius (comparative adverb, used for positive) -- quickly, speedily.

correpta pecoris efferum saevī ducem   116

audax amastī; torvus, impatiens iugī   117

adulter ille, ductor indomitī gregis --   118

sed amābat aliquid. quis meās miserae deus   119

aut quis iuvāre Daedalus flammās queat?   120

nōn sī ille remeet, arte Mopsopiā potens,   121

quī nostra caecā monstra conclūsit domō,   122

prōmittet ullam cāsibus nostrīs opem.   123

looking up toward the sun

Stirpem perōsa Sōlis invīsī Venus   124

per nōs catēnās vindicat Martis suī   125

suāsque, probrīs omne Phoebēum genus   126

onerat nefandīs: nulla Mīnōis levī   127

dēfuncta amōre est, iungitur semper nefās.   128

NUTRIX *to Phaedra*

Thēsea coniunx, clāra prōgeniēs Iovis,   129

nefanda castō pectore exturbā ōcius,   130

extingue flammās nēve tē dīrae speī   131

132 praebeo, -ere -- to hold forth, offer.
    obsequens, -entis -- yielding, compliant + dat.
    obsisto, -ere, -stiti, -stitum -- to set one's self before or against,
        oppose, resist.
134 blandior, 4 dep. -- to be agreeable, favorable towards; to flatter.
    dulce...malum: love (as bitter-sweet).
135 sero (adv.) -- late, too late.
    subeo, -ire, -ii, -itum -- to go under; to take upon one's self.
136 insolens, -entis -- unaccustomed to + gen.
137 ad recta: "towards things upright" = towards virtue or the good.
    flecto, -ere -- to bend. The infinitive here may be translated as
        middle or reflexive = "to bend itself."
    tumor, -oris, m. -- a swelling; the state of being swollen with pride;
        pompousness.
138 exitus, -us, m. -- outcome.
    casus, -us, m. -- chance, fortune.
139 vicina libertas: the nurse is old, and the nearness of death liber-
        ates her from fear of being punished for giving unwanted advice
        and makes her bold (*fortem*).
140 primum est: "The first thing to do is to..." "The most important
        thing is..."
    honesta...velle: predicate to *primum est*. honesta: neut. pl.
141 pudor, -oris, m. -- modesty, decency. "Second (best) is the decency
        to know (*nosse*) a limit (*modum*) of one's sinning (*peccandi*)."
142 pergo, -ere -- to go.
    aggravo, 1 -- to make heavier, oppress, burden.
143 monstrum (moneo) -- a divine omen indicating misfortune, an evil omen,
        portent; an unnatural thing or event; a monstrosity, monster.
        The allusion is to the Minotaur, the offspring of Phaedra's
        mother after mating with the bull.
    nefas, n. (indecl.) -- sin.
144 mores, -um, m. pl. -- character, morals.
    scelus, -eris, n. -- sin, crime.
    imputo, 1 -- to credit or attribute something to someone or something.
145 superus -- upper. supera...loca: this earth as opposed to the under-
        world.
146 facinus, -oris, n. -- deed, act; misdeed, crime.
147 Lethaeo...profundo -- the Lethean deep = Hades with the stream of
        Lethe (forgetfulness).
    abdo, -ere, -idi, -itum -- to put away, hide, conceal.
149 quid ille...pater? "What (about) that one...(your) father" (i.e.,
        Minos)?
151 lateo, -ere -- to be hidden, concealed.
    occultus -- hidden, concealed.

praebē obsequentem: quisquis in prīmō obstitit   132

pepulitque amōrem, tūtus ac victor fuit;   133

quī blandiendō dulce nūtrīvit malum,   134

sērō recūsat ferre quod subiit iugum.   135

aside

Nec mē fugit, quam dūrus et vērī insolens   136

ad recta flectī rēgius nōlit tumor.   137

quemcumque dederit exitum cāsus feram: 138

fortem facit vīcīna lībertās senem.   139

to Phaedra

Honesta prīmum est velle nec lābī viā,   140

pudor est secundus nosse peccandī modum.   141

Quō, misera, pergis? quid domum infāmem aggravās 142

superāsque mātrem? māius est monstrō nefās: 143

nam monstra fātō, mōribus scelera imputēs.   144

Sī, quod marītus supera nōn cernit loca,   145

tūtum esse facinus crēdis et vacuum metū,   146

errās; tenērī crēde Lēthaeō abditum   147

Thēsea profundō et ferre perpetuam Styga: 148

quid ille, lātō maria quī regnō premit   149

populīsque reddit iūra centēnīs, pater?   150

latēre tantum facinus occultum sinet?   151

152   sagax, -acis -- of quick perception, keen-scented, acute, shrewd.
153   astus, -us, m. -- craft, cunning.
      dolus -- guile, trickery.
      tegere: i.e., "that we might be able to cover..."
155   matris parens: the sun-god, Phoebus.
      quatio, -ere -- to shake.
156   vibro, 1 -- to brandish, shake, hurl.
      coruscus -- waving, vibrating; flashing, gleaming.
      fulmen Aetnaeum: the Cyclopes on Mount Aetna made thunderbolts
            (*fulmina*) for Jupiter.
157   sator, -oris, m. -- father.
158   Word order: inter avos videntes omnia. Translate *ut lateas* after *hoc*
            157.
      lateo, -ere -- to be hidden, concealed.
159   sed ut...: "but even if..."
      secundus -- favoring, favorable.
      numen, -inis, n. -- divine will; pl. the gods.
      abscondo, -ere -- to conceal.
160   coitus, -us, m. -- sexual intercourse.
      contingo, -ere -- to happen, fall to + dat. *Fides* is subject.
      stuprum -- debauchery, adultery. "But even if your adultery meets
            with loyalty (i.e., secrecy) which is always denied to great
            crimes..."
162   conscius -- conscious (of wrong doing), guilty.
163   semet: emphatic form of *se*.
164   securus -- free from care or anxiety.
165   compesco, -ere -- to hold in check, repress, curb.
167   Getae -- Thracian tribesmen on the Danube.
168   Scythes -- a Scythian, a member of a nomadic tribe of northern Europe
            and Asia, beyond the Black Sea.
169   castificus -- pure; made pure again.
      concubitus, -us, m. -- lying together, copulation.
171   thalamus -- bed-room; marriage-bed.
      gnatus = natus -- son.
172   proles, -is, f. -- offspring.
      capere = concipere -- to conceive.
173   pergo, -ere -- to go.
      verte = subverte.
      ignibus: here metaphorical of the fires of love.
174   aula -- palace. Here = the labyrinth. fratris: i.e., of the
            Minotaur.
175   prodigium -- an unnatural event portending a disaster; a monstrous,
            unnatural creature.
      insuetus -- to which one is not accustomed, unusual.
176   cedet = decedet -- to depart from, swerve from + abl.

sagax parentum est cūra. crēdāmus tamen   152

astū dolōque tegere nōs tantum nefās;   153

quid ille rēbus lūmen infundens suum,   154

mātris parens? quid ille, quī mundum quatit   155

vibrans coruscā fulmen Aetnaeum manū,   156

sator deōrum? crēdis hoc posse efficī,   157

inter videntēs omnia ut lateās avōs?   158

sed ut secundus nūminum abscondat favor   159

coitūs nefandōs utque contingat stuprō   160

negāta magnīs sceleribus semper fidēs: 161

quid poena praesens, conscius mentis pavor   162

animusque culpā plēnus et sēmet timens?   163

scelus aliqua tūtum, nulla secūrum tulit.   164

Compesce amōris impiī flammās, precor,   165

nefāsque quod nōn ulla tellūs barbara   166

commīsit umquam, non vagī campīs Getae   167

nec inhospitālis Taurus aut sparsus Scythēs;   168

expelle facinus mente castificā horridum   169

memorque mātris metue concubitūs novōs.   170

miscēre thalamōs patris et gnātī apparās   171

uterōque prōlem capere confūsam impiō?   172

perge et nefandīs verte natūram ignibus.   173

cūr monstra cessant? aula cūr frātris vacat?   174

prōdigia totiens orbis insuēta audiet,   175

natūra totiens lēgibus cēdet suīs,   176

177a Cressa -- a Cretan woman.
179 vado, -ere -- to go, rush.
     praeceps, -cipitis, n. -- a steep place, a precipice; great danger,
          extremity.
180 remeo, 1 -- to come back, return.
     frustra (adv.) -- in vain, vainly.
181 adversa...unda: "against opposing wave(s)."
     ratis, -is, f. -- boat.
182 vanum -- nothingness, naught.
183 pronus -- downward (rushing).
     puppis, -is, f. -- the stern of a ship; a ship.
     vadum -- a shallow part of a river; a river.
185 dominor, 1 dep. -- to rule, reign.
186 hic volucer (sc., deus) = Cupido. volucer, -ucris, -ucre -- flying,
          winged.
     polleo, -ere -- to be strong, powerful.
     impotens, -entis -- not master of himself, violent, furious.
187 laedo, -ere, -si, -sum -- to wound.
     torreo, -ere -- to burn.
     indomitus -- unrestrained, fierce. Word order: torret Iovem laesum
          indomitis flammis.
188 Gradivus = Mars.
     fax, facis, f. -- torch (here the torches of Cupid).
189 opifex, -icis, m. -- a maker. Here = Vulcan, the blacksmith-god who
          lives on Mount Aetna.
     trisulcus (tres-sulcus "furrow") -- three pointed.
190 et qui: further description of Vulcan.
191 verso, 1 -- to turn; to stir up, poke up (the fires in the *caminus*).
     caminus -- furnace.
     igne tam parvo: i.e., the torch of Cupid.
     caleo, -ere -- to be hot, glow.
192 nervus -- bowstring.
193 figo, -ere -- to fix, pierce.
     sagitta: with *missa* "sent," "shot."
     certior: with surer aim (than even Apollo, the god of archery, has).
     puer: i.e., Cupid.
194 pariter -- equally.
     gravis, -e -- heavy, burdensome, troublesome, painful.
195 vitio favens: "that favors vice."
196 fingo, -ere, finxi, fictum -- to make. "...has made love to be a
          god."
     libido, -inis, f. -- lust.
     quoque = et ut -- and so that...
     liberior: "freer" in being less open to reproach and censure. *Libido*
          is still the subject. foret = esset.
197 titulum...numinis falsi: "the title (i.e., name) of a false god."
     furori: "to the madness (of love)."
198 natum: Venus' son, Cupid.
     scilicet -- to be sure (often sarcastic).

quotiens amābit Cressa?   177a

PHAEDRA   Quae memorās sciō   177b

vēra esse, nūtrix; sed furor cōgit sequī   178

pēiōra. vādit animus in praeceps sciens   179

remeatque frustrā sāna consilia appetens.   180

sīc, cum gravātam nāvita adversā ratem   181

prōpellit undā, cēdit in vānum labor   182

et victa prōnō puppis aufertur vadō.   183

Quid ratio possit? vīcit ac regnat furor,   184

potensque tōtā mente dominātur deus.   185

hic volucer omnī pollet in terrā impotens   186

laesumque flammīs torret indomitīs Iovem;   187

Gradīvus istās belliger sensit facēs,   188

opifex trisulcī fulminis sensit deus,   189

et quī furentēs semper Aetnaeīs iugīs   190

versat camīnōs igne tam parvō calet;   191

ipsumque Phoebum, tēla quī nervō regit,   192

fīgit sagittā certior missā puer   193

volitatque caelō pariter et terrīs gravis.   194

NUTRIX   Deum esse amōrem turpis et vitiō favens   195

finxit libīdō, quōque līberior foret   196

titulum furōrī nūminis falsī addidit.   197

nātum per omnēs scīlicet terrās vagum   198

199 Erycina: Venus as the goddess of Eryx, a mountain in the northwestern
         part of Sicily where a temple of Venus stood.
200 protervus -- violent, wanton, impudent.
     molior, 4 dep. -- to wield (weapons). *Tenera* modifies *manu*.
201 superi, -orum, m. pl. -- the gods above.
202 vana ista: "these vain, false things," "lies."
     ascisco, -ere, -ivi, -itum -- to approve, accept as true. sibi: "for
         itself."
203 fingo, -ere, finxi, fictum -- to make, invent.
204 secundis rebus: "in favorable circumstances."
     exulto, 1 -- to exult, rejoice excessively.
     nimis (adv.) -- too much.
205 fluit = diffluit. diffluo, -ere -- to flow away, dissolve; to be
         dissolved in, abandoned to + abl.
     luxus, -us, m. -- luxury, extravagance. insolitus -- unusual.
206 dirus -- fearful, awful, dreadful.
     comes, -itis, m. -- companion.
207 suetus -- accustomed.
     daps, dapis, f. -- feast, banquet.
208 tectum -- roof; house.
     mos, moris, m. -- manner, custom, habit.
     vilis, -e -- cheap, paltry, poor.
     scyphus (Greek word) -- cup.
209 penates...tenues: "a modest household." tenuis, -e -- thin, trifl-
         ing, poor. penates -- the household gods; the household. The
         subject of *subit* ("enters") is *haec...pestis* ("this plague,"
         i.e., unbridled *libido*).
210 delicatas...domos: "luxurious, voluptuous homes."
     eligo, -ere -- to choose.
212 medium...vulgus: "the middle classes." vulgus, -i, n. -- multitude,
         people, public.
     affectus, -us, m. -- a state of mind.
213 coerceo, -ere -- to restrain.
     modicus -- moderate, ordinary. "And moderate things (i.e., people)
         restrain themselves."
     contra (adv.) -- but, on the other hand.
     dives, -itis -- rich.
214 fultus (fulcio) -- propped up, supported.
     fas est -- is right.
216 quid deceat: "what befits..." + acc. *Deceat* is subjunctive in an
         indirect question.
     praeditus -- endowed, provided with. alto preditam solio: "a woman
         endowed with a lofty throne."
217 remeo, 1 -- to return.
219 reditus, -us, m. -- return.
     amplius -- more. umquam amplius: "ever again."
220 convexa...supera: "the convex (regions) above," i.e., the earth with
         the sky above.
     mergo, -ere, -si, -sum -- to sink, overwhelm, cover, bury.
     semel -- once.

Erycīna mittit, ille per caelum volans   199

proterva tenerā tēla molītur manū   200

regnumque tantum minimus ē superīs habet: 201

vāna ista dēmens animus ascīvit sibi   202

Venerisque nūmen finxit atque arcūs deī.   203

Quisquis secundīs rēbus exultat nimis   204

fluitque luxū, semper insolita appetit.   205

tunc illa magnae dīra fortūnae comes   206

subit libīdō: nōn placent suētae dapēs,   207

nōn tecta sānī mōris aut vīlis scyphus.   208

cūr in penātēs rārius tenuēs subit   209

haec dēlicātās ēligens pestis domōs?   210

cūr sancta parvīs habitat in tectīs Venus   211

mediumque sānōs vulgus affectūs tenet   212

et sē coercent modica? contrā dīvitēs   213

regnōque fultī plūra quam fās est petunt?   214

Quod nōn potest vult posse quī nimium potest.   215

Quid deceat altō praeditam soliō vidēs: 216

metue ac verēre sceptra remeantis virī.   217

PHAEDRA   Amōris in mē maximum regnum ferō,   218

reditūsque nullōs metuo: nōn umquam amplius   219

convexa tetigit supera quī mersus semel   220

221 Word order: domum silentem perpetua nocte: i.e., Hades.
222 Dis, -itis, m. -- Pluto, god of the underworld.
     licet -- although + subjunctive. clauserit: subject is *Dis*.
225 venia -- mercy, pardon.
     forsitan -- perhaps.
226 immitis, -e -- not soft; harsh.
227 experior, 4 dep. -- to experience. *Experta* with *est*: perfect tense.
     Antiope: Amazon wife of Theseus; killed by Theseus because of his new
             love for Phaedra.
     manum: i.e., of Theseus.
228 flecto, -ere -- to bend; prevail upon, soften, appease.
229 huius: i.e., of Hippolytus.
     intractabilis, -e -- not to be handled; rough, wild.
230 exosus -- hating, detesting.
231 caelebs, -libis -- unmarried, single.
     dico, 1 -- to dedicate.
232 conubium -- marriage.
     vito, 1 -- to avoid, shun.
233 nivosus (nix, nivis) -- snowy.
     haereo, -ere -- to hold fast, cling, be fixed, remain.
234 calco, 1 -- to tread.
235 placet (sc., mihi) -- it pleases me; I wish to.
236 resisto, -ere -- to stop.
     mulceo, -ere -- to stroke, caress.
237 ritus, -us, m. -- custom, manner, way.
     exuo, -ere -- to put off, lay aside.
238 pono, -ere -- to put aside.
239 omnes: sc., feminas.
     prex, precis, f. -- prayer.
     haud -- not at all.

	adiit silentem nocte perpetuā domum.	221
NUTRIX	Nē crēde Dītī. clauserit regnum licet	222
	canisque dīrās Stygius observet forēs:	223
	sōlus negātās invenit Thēseus viās.	224
PHAEDRA	Veniam ille amōrī forsitan nostrō dabit.	225
NUTRIX	Immītis etiam coniugī castae fuit:	226
	experta saevam est barbara Antiopē manum.	227
	Sed posse flectī coniugem īrātum putā:	228
	quis huius animum flectet intractābilem?	229
	exōsus omne fēminae nōmen fugit,	230
	immītis annōs caelibī vītae dicat,	231
	cōnubia vītat: genus Amāzonium sciās.	232
PHAEDRA	Hunc in nivosī collis haerentem iugīs,	233
	et aspera agilī saxa calcantem pede	234
	sequī per alta nemora, per montēs placet.	235
NUTRIX	Resistet ille sēque mulcendum dabit	236
	castōsque rītus Venere nōn castā exuet?	237
	tibi pōnet odium, cuius odiō forsitan	238
	persequitur omnēs? precibus haud vincī potest.	239
PHAEDRA	Ferus est? amōre dīdicimus vincī ferōs.	240

242a memento (imperative): "remember!"
243a genus: sc., muliebre.
243b paelex, -icis, f. -- a mistress.
244b nempe -- indeed, to be sure, certainly (often sarcastic).
245b mitis, -e -- mild, gentle.
246 senecta -- old age.
     splendidus -- bright (of her white hair, *comas*).
247 uber, -eris, n. -- breast.
248 sisto, -ere -- to stop, arrest, check.
249 fuit: perfect tense used instead of present in a maxim; translate as
          present.

NUTRIX   Fugiet.   241a

PHAEDRA   Per ipsa maria sī fugiet, sequar.   241b

NUTRIX   Patris mementō.   242a

PHAEDRA   Meminimus mātris simul.   242b

NUTRIX   Genus omne profugit.   243a

PHAEDRA   Paelicis careō metū.   243b

NUTRIX   Aderit marītus.   244a

PHAEDRA   Nempe Pīrithoī comes?   244b

NUTRIX   Aderitque genitor.   245a

PHAEDRA   Mītis Ariadnae pater.   245b

NUTRIX   Per hās senectae splendidās supplex comās   246
          fessumque cūrīs pectus et cāra ūbera   247
          precor, furōrem siste tēque ipsa adiuvā: 248

          pars sānitātis velle sānārī fuit.   249

250 ingenuus -- noble.
251 altrix, -icis, f. = nutrix.
252 maculo, 1 -- to spot, stain, defile.
254 praeverto, -ere -- to forestall, prevent.
255 moderor, 1 dep. -- to moderate, restrain. moderare: imperative.
     alumna -- a foster daughter.
     effrenus (frenum) -- unbridled.
     impetus, -us, m. -- impetus, force, fury (acc. pl. here).
256a coerceo, -ere -- to hold back, restrain.
256b dignam: supply *te*. dignam...vita: "worthy of life."
     reor, 2 dep. -- to believe, think, judge.
257 temet = emphatic form of *te*.
     autumo, 1 -- to affirm, assert.
     nex, necis, f. -- death.
258 fati genus: "the kind of death." fatum -- fate, death.
259 laqueus -- snare; noose.
260 praeceps, -cipitis -- headlong.
     arce Palladia: "the citadel of Pallas" (Athena) = the Acropolis.
261 proin -- just so, hence, accordingly (monosyllabic here).
     vindex, -icis, m. or f. -- a defender, protector. With *castitatis*.
262 praecipiti...leto: "in a headlong death."
263 furibundus -- raging, mad, furious.
265 nulla ratio: "no reasoning," "no argumentation."
266 ubi qui: "when someone..."
     constituo, -ere, -ui, -utum -- to fix, determine, decide.

PHAEDRA   Non omnis animo cessit ingenuo pudor.   250

           paremus, altrix. qui regi non vult amor   251

           vincatur. haud te, fama, maculari sinam.   252

           pausing briefly, then

           Haec sola ratio est, unicum effugium mali: 253

           virum sequamur, morte praevertam nefas.   254

NUTRIX   *frightened by Phaedra's decision to commit*
           suicide

           Moderare, alumna, mentis effrenae impetus,   255

           animos coerce.   256a

                              Dignam ob hoc vita reor   256b

           quod esse temet autumas dignam nece.   257

PHAEDRA   *determined*

           Decreta mors est: quaeritur fati genus.   258

           laqueone vitam finiam an ferro incubem?   259

           an missa praeceps arce Palladia cadam?   260

           proin castitatis vindicem armemus manum.   261

NUTRIX   Sic te senectus nostra praecipiti sinat   262

           perire leto? siste furibundum impetum.   263

           haud quisquam ad vitam facile revocari potest.   264

PHAEDRA   Prohibere nulla ratio periturum potest,   265

           ubi qui mori constituit et debet mori.   266

267   solamen, -inis, n. -- a comfort, solace, consolation. In apposition
        to *era* (= *domina* -- mistress).
268   protervus -- violent, vehement.
269   contemno, -ere -- to consider as unimportant, despise.
      vix (adv.) -- scarcely, hardly.
270   Word order: (fama) melior est peius merenti ("for the person who
        deserves worse") et peior est bono ("for a good person").
271   tempto, 1 -- to make an attempt upon; to attack, assail.
      animum: i.e., of Hippolytus.
      tristis, -e -- sad; morose, ill-humored; stern, harsh, severe.
272   aggredior, 3 dep -- to approach; to attack.

NUTRIX   Solāmen annīs ūnicum fessīs, era,   267

si tam protervus incubat mentī furor,   268

contemne fāmam. fāma vix vērō favet,   269

pēius merentī melior et pēior bonō.   270

pauses, then

Temptēmus animum tristem et intractābilem.   271

meus iste labor est aggredī iuvenem ferum   272

mentemque saevam flectere immītis virī.   273

Exeunt into palace.

274 mitis, -e -- mild, calm, gentle.
275 geminus Cupido: twin- or double-natured Cupid, who is often thought
        of as bittersweet. Cf. Cupid as *impotens* and *renidens* in the
        next lines.
276 impotens, -entis -- not master of himself; violent, furious; who mis-
        uses something (his torches and arrows).
     simul -- at the same time.
277 lascivus -- wanton, sportive, playful; lewd, lustful, lascivious.
     renideo, -ere -- to beam with joy, be glad, cheerful; to smile.
278 moderor, 1 dep. -- to guide, direct.
279 medulla -- the marrow of the bones.
280 populor, 1 dep. -- to ravage, devastate, lay waste.
281 latus -- wide, broad.
     plaga -- wound. data plaga: i.e., the wound caused (by Cupid).
282 tectus -- covered, concealed.
     penitus (adv.) -- inwardly, inside.
284 spargo, -ere -- to hurl or throw about; to scatter.
     effundo, -ere, -fudi, -fusus -- to pour out.
     agilis, -e -- nimble, quick; active, busy.
285 Word order: ora quae nascentem solem videt = the eastern boundary,
        shore, or region of the world.
286 meta -- a boundary marker. ad Hesperias...metas: "at the western
        boundaries" (of the world). Hesperus: the evening star in the
        western sky.
287 si qua = si aliqua (with *ora* supplied): "if any region" = "the region
        which..."
     subicio, -ere, -ieci, -iectum -- to throw under, to place under.
        subiecta est: "lies beneath."
     cancer, -cri, m. -- crab; the Crab -- the sign of the zodiac in which
        the sun is found at the time of the summer solstice (hence,
        ferventi); designates the southern hemisphere.
288 Parrhasius: Arcadian, referring to Callisto, who was raped by Jupiter
        and transformed into a bear, then elevated to become the Great
        Bear (= Big Dipper) in the sky (in the north: hence, *glacialis*).
     ursa -- bear. *Glacialis* modifies qua (ora). *Parrhasiae...ursae* is a
        second dative after *subiecta...est* (287).
289 colonus -- farmer; here simply "inhabitant." errantes...colonos =
        nomadic Scythian tribes in Northern Europe.
290a novit: subject is *quaeque...ora* (285), etc.
     aestus, -us, m. -- fire, heat, passion (of love).
291 concito, 1 -- to stir up, rouse.
292 calor, -oris, m. -- warmth, heat, glow; passion.
293 ferio, -ire -- to strike.
294 superi, -orum, m. pl. -- the gods above.
295 vultus, -us, m. -- face, features, appearance.

*Enter chorus of Cretan women, who sing the
following song.*

CHORUS Dīva nōn mītī generāta pontō,   274 sapphic

quam vocat mātrem geminus Cupīdō,   275

impotens flammīs simul et sagittīs,   276

iste lascīvus puer et renīdens   277

tēla quam certō moderātur arcū!   278

lābitur tōtās furor in medullās   279

igne furtīvō populante vēnās.   280

nōn habet lātam data plāga frontem,   281

sed vorat tectās penitus medullās.   282

Nulla pax istī puerō: per orbem   283

spargit effusās agilis sagittās;   284

quaeque nascentem videt ōra sōlem,   285

quaeque ad Hesperiās iacet ōra metās,   286

sī qua ferventī subiecta cancrō est,   287

sī qua Parrhasiae glaciālis ursae   288

semper errantēs patitur colonōs,   289

nōvit hōs aestūs.   290a

                    Iuvenum ferocēs   290b

concitat flammās senibusque fessīs   291

rursus extinctōs revocat calorēs,   292

virginum ignōtō ferit igne pectus   293

et iubet caelō superōs relictō   294

vultibus falsīs habitāre terrās.   295

296 Phoebus (Apollo) was condemned by Jupiter to spend a year in servitude
     to a mortal; he fulfilled his obligation by shepherding the herds
     of Admetus, king of Pherae in Thessaly. The version Seneca fol-
     lows here implies that Apollo served Admetus because he had
     fallen in love with him.
     pecus, -oris, n. -- cattle, herd.
297 armentum -- cattle, herd.
     plectrum -- a plectrum for striking the cords of a lyre; the lyre
     itself.
298 impari...calamo: "with unequal reed." I.e., with a shepherd's pipe,
     made from several reeds of unequal length fastened together side
     by side.
299 induo, -ere, -ui, -utum -- to put on, to assume.
301 ales, alitis, m. or f. -- bird. Jupiter disguised as a swan had a
     love affair with Leda.
302 vocem: acc. of respect with *dulcior.* cygnus -- swan.
303 torvus -- fierce, savage. petulans, -antis -- impudent, wanton.
     iuvencus -- a young bull. Jupiter disguised as a bull carried off
     Europa.
304 sterno, -ere, stravi, stratum -- to spread out, stretch out. Jupiter,
     disguised as the bull, lay down and offered his back for Europa
     and her companions to play on. When Europa got on, Jupiter car-
     ried her off over the sea.
305 fraternos...fluctus: the sea is ruled by Jupiter's brother, Neptune.
     nova regna: in apposition to *fraternos fluctus.* The sea is not
     Jupiter's accustomed kingdom; he is lord of the sky.
306 ungula -- hoof.
     lentos...remos: the oars are *lenti* because they are slightly pliant
     and bend when being pulled. lentus -- pliant, flexible.
307 adverso: i.e., turned against (the sea).
     domo, -are, -ui, -itum -- to tame, overcome.
     profundum -- the deep, the sea.
308 vector, -oris, m. (veho) -- a carrier.
     rapina: with *pro sua.* rapina -- plunder, booty; i.e., Europa.
309 ardeo, -ere, arsi, arsum -- to take fire, burn, blaze.
     dea clara: Diana, goddess of the moon, in love with Endymion.
310 nitidus -- shining, bright. fratri: i.e., Apollo, god of the sun.
311 aliter -- in another manner (than that in which they were accustomed
     to being guided by Diana).
312 ille: i.e., the sun-god.
     bigae, -arum, f. pl. -- a two-horsed chariot.
313 gyrus -- circle, course.
     flecto, -ere -- to bend, turn. The passive (*flecti*) makes the transi-
     tive verb intransitive, with the same meaning. "To turn in a
     smaller circuit" -- the circuit of the moon being shorter than
     that of the sun.
314 tenuere = tenuerunt.
315 remeo, 1 -- to return.
316 axis, axis, m. -- the axle tree about which the wheel turns.
     graviore curru: the axles tremble beneath the weight of the chariot
     which is heavier with Phoebus driving it than it is with its
     usual driver, Diana.

Thessalī Phoebus pecoris magister   296

ēgit armentum positōque plectrō   297

imparī taurōs calamō vocāvit.   298

Induit formās quotiens minōrēs   299

ipse quī caelum nebulāsque dūcit: 300

candidās āles modo mōvit ālās,   301

dulcior vōcem moriente cygnō;   302

fronte nunc torvā petulans iuvencus   303

virginum strāvit sua terga lūdō,   304

perque frāternōs nova regna fluctūs   305

ungulā lentōs imitante rēmōs   306

pectore adversō domuit profundum,   307

prō suā vector timidus rapīnā.   308

Arsit obscurī dea clāra mundī   309

nocte dēsertā nitidōsque frātrī   310

trādidit currūs aliter regendōs: 311

ille nocturnās agitāre bīgās   312

discit et gȳrō breviōre flectī;   313

nec suum tempus tenuēre noctēs   314

et diēs tardō remeāvit ortū,   315

dum tremunt axēs graviōre currū.   316

317 natus Alcmena: the son of Alcmena is Hercules, usually armed with bow
       and lion skin; he was sold to Omphale, queen of Lydia, and served
       as her slave; in love with her and eager to please her, he wore
       effeminate dress and jewelry and performed women's work.
     pharetra -- quiver.
318 minax: modifies *spolium*. The "threatening spoils of the lion" are
       the lion's skin, including the head with its mouth open.
319 passus (est): "he endured."
     apto, 1 -- to fit, put on.
     smaragdus -- emerald.
320 capillus -- hair.
321 crus, -uris, n. -- leg.
     distinctus -- decorated, adorned.
     religo, 1 -- to bind.
322 luteus -- golden-yellow.
     planta -- sole of the foot; foot.
     cohibeo, -ere -- to hold together, confine.
     soccus -- slipper.
323 clava -- club.
     qua: follows *manu*: "and with the hand *in which* he used to hold..."
324 filum -- thread.
     fusus -- spindle.
325 Persis, -idis, f. -- Persia.
     dis, ditis -- rich.
     ferax, -acis -- fruit-bearing, fruitful, fertile. "Lydia fertile with
       its rich kingdom" (*diti...regno*).
327 umerisque: "and on his shoulders."
328 regia -- a royal palace. alti regia caeli = the heavens with the
       palaces of the gods.
329 Tyrius -- Tyrian (here with reference to the purple dye for which Tyre
       was famous).
     stamen, -inis, n. -- thread.
330 sacer, sacra, sacrum -- holy, sacred; accursed, wicked.
     laedo, -ere, -si, -sum -- to wound. With *laesis* supply *nobis*:
       "(believe) us who have been wounded."
331 qua -- where.
     salum -- the sea.
335 spiculum -- dart, arrow.
336 caerulus -- blue.
     grex, gregis, m. -- flock, company, band.
     Nereis, -itis, f. -- a daughter of Nereus, a Nereid, a sea-nymph.
337 relevo, 1 -- to lift up; to lighten; to alleviate.
338 aliger, -gera, -gerum -- bearing wings, winged; (as noun) a bird.
339 instinctus -- instigated, incited, urged on.
341 timuere = timuerunt.

Nātus Alcmēnā posuit pharetrās   317

et minax vastī spolium leōnis,   318

passus aptārī digitīs smaragdōs   319

et darī lēgem rudibus capillīs;   320

crūra distinctō religāvit aurō,   321

lūteō plantās cohibente soccō;   322

et manū, clāvam modo quā gerēbat,   323

fīla dēduxit properante fūsō.   324

vīdit Persis dītīque ferax   325   anapestic

Lȳdia regnō dēiecta ferī   326

terga leōnis, umerīsque, quibus   327

sēderat altī rēgia caelī,   328

tenuem Tyriō stāmine pallam.   329

Sacer est ignis -- crēdite laesīs --   330

nimiumque potens. quā terra salō   331

cingitur altō, quāque per ipsum   332

candida mundum sīdera currunt: 333

haec regna tenet puer immītis,   334

spīcula cuius sentit in īmīs   335

caerulus undīs grex Nēreidum,   336

flammamque nequit relevāre marī.   337

ignēs sentit genus āligerum;   338

Venere instinctus suscipit audax   339

grege prō tōtō bella iuvencus;   340

sī coniugiō timuēre suō,   341

342 poscunt...proelia: "ask for battles" = challenge to war.
     cervus -- stag, deer.
343 mugitus, -us, m. -- lowing, bellowing.
     concepti...furoris: "of the madness that has taken possession of
          them." Lit., "that has been taken up (by them)."
344 virgatus -- striped.
345 decolor, -oris -- discolored, swarthy.
346 acuo, -ere -- to sharpen.
347 spumeus -- foaming, frothing.
348 Poenus -- Carthaginian.
     quatio, -ere -- to shake.
351 belua -- beast, monster.
     Luca bos: "Lucanian cow" = elephant. The Romans first saw elephants
          in Lucania (in southern Italy) in the army of Pyrrhus.
352 vindico, 1 -- to lay claim to.
     natura: (here) the power of love, the reproductive power of nature.
353 immunis, -e -- free from, exempt from.
355 ignibus: i.e., the fires of love; love.
356-357 cura -- care, concern; love.
     noverca -- step-mother.

poscunt timidī proelia cervī,   342

et mūgītū dant conceptī   343

signa furōris. tunc virgātās   344

India tigrēs dēcolor horret   345

tunc vulnificōs acuit dentēs   346

aper et tōtō est spūmeus ōre;   347

Poenī quatiunt colla leōnēs   348

cum mōvit amor. tum silva gemit   349

murmure saevō. -- amat insānī   350

bēlua pontī Lūcaeque bovēs.   351

Vindicat omnēs natūra sibi.   352

nihil immūne est, odiumque perit   353

cum iussit Amor; veterēs cēdunt   354

ignibus īrae. quid plūra canam?   355

vincit saevās cūra novercās.   356-57

358 altrix, -icis, f. = nutrix.
     profar, 1 dep. -- to speak out. profare: imperative.
359 ecquis, ecquid -- any.
360 lenio, 4 -- to soften, calm.
362 torreo, -ere -- to roast, bake, scorch, burn.
     aestus, -us, m. -- heat, passion.
363 tego, -ere -- to cover.
     prodo, -ere -- to betray.
364 lassus -- tired, exhausted.
     gena -- a cheek; pl. cheeks, eyelids, eyes.
365 nil idem...placet: "the same thing doesn't please her (long)."
     dubius -- wavering, uncertain, irresolute. Supply *ei* with *dubiae*.
366 artus, -us, m. -- limb (of the body).
     incertus -- uncertain, unsettled. Here of a pain (*dolor*) that cannot
          be localized in any one part of her body.
367 ut: with *moriens* = *sicut moriens*, "as if dying."
     soluto...gradu: "with loosened or faltering footstep."
368 vix (adv.) -- scarcely.
370 querela -- a complaint.
371 poni = reponi -- to be put back (to bed).
372 fingo, -ere -- to form, fashion, shape, arrange.
     impatiens, -entis -- unable to bear + gen.
373 habitus, -us, m. -- condition, habit, deportment, nature, character.
     Ceres, -eris, f. -- goddess of agriculture; grain, food, bread.
375 defectus (deficio) -- weak, worn out, enfeebled.
376 tinguo, -ere -- to wet, moisten; to dye, color.
     nitidus -- shining, bright.
377 populor, 1, dep. -- to ravage, devastate, lay waste.
     gressus, -us, m. -- a stepping, a going, a step.
378 decor, -oris, m. -- elegance, grace, beauty.
379 ferebant = referebant. refero, referre -- to bear or give back,
          return; to represent, reproduce.
     fax, facis, f. -- a torch. "The torch of Phoebus" = the sun.
          Phaedra's mother, Pasiphae, was a daughter of Phoebus, the god
          of the sun, and Phaedra inherited bright, radiant eyes from her
          grandfather.

*Enter the nurse from the palace. The
chorus-leader questions her in normal
spoken iambics.*

CHORUS-
LEADER   Altrix, profāre quid ferās; quōnam in locō est   358

         regīna? saevīs ecquis est flammīs modus?   359

NUTRIX   Spēs nulla tantum posse lēnīrī malum,   360

         fīnisque flammīs nullus insānīs erit.   361

         torrētur aestū tacitō et inclūsus quoque,   362

         quamvīs tegātur, prōditur vultū furor;   363

         ērumpit oculīs ignis et lassae genae   364

         lūcem recūsant; nīl idem dubiae placet,   365

         artūsque variē iactat incertus dolor.   366

         nunc ut solūtō lābitur moriens gradū   367

         et vix labante sustinet collō caput,   368

         nunc sē quiētī reddit, et, somnī immemor,   369

         noctem querēlīs dūcit; attollī iubet   370

         iterumque pōnī corpus et solvī comās   371

         rursusque fingī: semper impatiens suī   372

         mutātur habitus. nulla iam Cereris subit   373

         cūra aut salūtis; vādit incertō pede,   374

         iam vīribus dēfecta: nōn īdem vigor,   375

         nōn ōra tinguens nitida purpureus rubor;   376

         populātur artūs cūra, iam gressūs tremunt,   377

         tenerque nitidī corporis cecidit decor.   378

         et quī ferēbant signa Phoebēae facis   379

380 gentilis, -e -- belonging to the family, hereditary.
     mico, 1 -- to sparkle, glitter, flash.
381 assiduus -- continual, incessant.
382 ros, roris, m. -- dew; moisture.
     qualiter -- just as.
383 madesco, -ere -- to become moist or wet.
     percutio, -ere, -cussi, -cussum -- to strike through; to strike.
384 patesco, -ere -- to open.
     fastigium -- the top of a gable, pediment; roof of a house.   regiae
          fastigia: poetic, "the lofty palace."
385 reclinis, -e -- leaning back, reclining.
     sedes, -is, f. -- a seat, bench, throne.
     torus -- a couch, bed; a bolster, cushion.
386 amictus, -us, m. -- clothing.
     abnuo, -ere -- to deny, refuse, decline.
387 famula -- maid-servant, handmaiden.
     inlitus -- spread over with, decorated with.
388 murex, -icis, m. -- purple dye (from Tyre).
     rubor, -oris, m. -- redness. Here of red or purple clothes.
389 filum -- thread. With *quae fila* (= *fila quae*), repeat *procul sint*.
          "Away with the threads which..." (threads = the silk of which her
          clothes are made = her silken clothes).
     Seres, -um, m. pl. -- a people of Eastern Asia; the Chinese.
390 expeditus -- unimpeded, unencumbered.
     zona -- belt, girdle.
     constringo, -ere -- to draw together, bind, tie up.
     sinus, -us, m. -- the hanging fold of the upper part of the toga. She
          wants her toga to be tucked up so that its folds will not impede
          the movement of her limbs as she runs in the chase.
391 monile, -is, n. -- a necklace.
393 odore...Assyrio: perfume.
     spargo, -ere, -si, -sum -- to scatter. Here of her hair "scattered"
          or "spread out."
     vaco, 1 -- to be without + abl.
394 temere -- at random, casually.
395 citus -- swift, rapid.
396 laeva: sc., manus.
397 hastile, -is, n. -- a spear, javelin.
     vibro, 1 -- to shake, brandish.

oculī nihil gentīle nec patrium micant.   380

lacrimae cadunt per ōra et assiduō genae   381

rōre irrigantur, quāliter Taurī iugīs   382

tepidō madescunt imbre percussae nivēs.   383

The doors of the palace open, and Phaedra
is visible as she reclines on a golden couch.
She is surrounded by her handmaids, who are
attentive to her every wish.

Sed ēn, patescunt rēgiae fastīgia: 384

reclīnis ipsa sēdis aurātae torō   385

solitōs amictūs mente nōn sānā abnuit.   386

The nurse and chorus silently watch and listen
as Phaedra gives orders to her handmaids.

PHAEDRA   Removēte, famulae, purpurā atque aurō inlitās   387

vestēs, procul sit mūricis Tyriī rubor,   388

quae fīla rāmīs ultimī Serēs legunt: 389

brevis expedītōs zōna constringat sinūs,   390

cervix monīlī vacua, nec niveus lapis   391

dēdūcat aurēs, Indicī dōnum maris;   392

odōre crīnis sparsus Assyriō vacet.   393

sīc temere iactae colla perfundant comae   394

umerōsque summōs, cursibus mōtae citīs   395

ventōs sequantur. laeva sē pharetrae dabit,   396

hastīle vibret dextra Thessalicum manus: 397

399 Pontus: the Black Sea.
     plaga -- region, quarter, tract.
400 caterva -- a troop, company of soldiers.
     pulso, 1 -- to push, strike, beat; to attack.
401 Tanaitis, -idis, f. -- an Amazon living on the river Tanais, now the
         Don.
     Maeotis, -idis, f. -- an Amazon living on Lake Maeotis. The geni-
         tives depend on *catervas* (400).
     nodus -- a knot.
402 cogo, -ere, coegi, coactus -- to drive together, collect.
     emitto, -ere, -misi, -missus -- to send out, let out. Translate the
         perfect tenses here as presents.
     lunatus -- half-moon shaped.
     latus: acc. of respect ("protected with respect to her flanks by a
         crescent-shaped shield").
403 pelta -- a small, light shield.
     feror (*pass. of* fero) -- to hasten, rush.
404 sepono, -ere -- to lay aside.
     questus, -us, m. -- complaining, complaint, expression of grief.
     levo, 1 -- to lift up, raise; to lighten, relieve, ease. I.e., cease
         complaining about Phaedra as you were doing (360-383); your
         grief (*dolor*) will not alleviate (*levat*) her misery (*miseros*).
405 agrestis, -e -- of or pertaining to land, fields, the country; rural,
         rustic. The chorus recommends that the nurse pray to Diana as
         goddess of the fields to aid Phaedra, who is delirious for the
         chase.
     placo, 1 -- to quiet, soothe, appease, pacify (often through prayer).
406 nemus, -oris, n. -- woods.
     colo, -ere -- to cultivate, tend; to dwell in, inhabit; to honor,
         reverence, worship.
408 tristes ominum...minas: "gloomy threats of omens" = "the threats of
         these gloomy omens."
     in melius: with *converte*.
409 lucus -- a wood, grove.
410 sidus, -eris, n. -- a star, heavenly body; the moon. Diana is
         addressed as goddess of the moon.
     decus, -oris, n. -- splendor, glory.
411 vicis, *abl.*, vice, f. -- change, alternation.
412 triformis: the goddess appears in three forms, as Diana (goddess of
         the hunt), Luna (goddess of the moon), and Hecate (a chthonian
         goddess of black magic).
     coeptum -- an undertaking.
413 rigeo, -ere -- to be stiff or numb; to be inflexible, unbending.
414 mitigo, 1 -- to soften (make *mitis*).

tālis severī māter Hippolytī fuit.   398

quālis relictīs frīgidī Pontī plagīs   399

ēgit catervās Atticum pulsans solum   400

Tanaïtis aut Maeōtis et nōdō comās   401

coēgit ēmīsitque, lūnātā latus   402

protecta peltā, tālis in silvās ferar.   403

Phaedra disappears from sight within the
palace. The chorus-leader addresses the
nurse.

CHORUS–   Sēpōne questūs: nōn levat miserōs dolor;   404
  LEADER
                      agreste plācā virginis nūmen deae.   405

NUTRIX   *praying to the statue of Diana which Hippolytus*
                 had addressed earlier.

Rēgīna nemorum, sōla quae montēs colis,   406

et ūna sōlīs montibus coleris dea,   407

converte tristēs ōminum in melius minās.   408

Ō magna silvās inter et lucōs dea,   409

clārumque caelī sīdus et noctis decus,   410

cuius relūcet mundus alternā vice,   411

Hecatē triformis, ēn ades coeptīs favens.   412

animum rigentem tristis Hippolytī domā: 413

det facilis aurēs, mītigā pectus ferum: 414

416 innecto, -ere -- to tie, bind.
     torvus -- wild, stern, fierce, gloomy.
     aversus -- turned off or away; disinclined, alienated, opposed,
        hostile.
418 intendo, -ere -- to stretch forth, extend.
     sic te lucidi vultus ferant: "so may a bright face carry you" = "so
        may your face be bright."
419 nube rupta: "with the cloud (that now covers your face) broken or
        dispersed."
420 rego, -ere -- to guide, conduct, direct.
     frenum -- bridle, reins.
     aether, -eris, m. -- the upper air; heaven. frena nocturni aetheris =
        the chariot that Diana as moon-goddess drives through the heavens
        at night.
421 Thessali cantus: songs of Thessalian witches (who boasted that they
        could draw the moon down from the sky).
422 gloria -- glory; vainglory, vaunting, boasting. gloriam...ferat:
        "boast." de te: "at your expense." The allusion is to Endymion,
        a shepherd, who was so handsome that the goddess of the moon fell
        in love with him. See above, lines 309-316.
424 ipsum: i.e., Hippolytus.
     intuor, 3 dep. -- to look at, see.
425 comitor, 1 dep. -- to attend, follow, accompany.
426 casus, -us, m. -- chance
427 mando, 1 -- to commit or entrust to one's charge; order, command.
428 verum -- but. artibus: "wiles."
429 decus, -oris, n. -- honor.
430 minister, -tri, m. -- an attendant, servant, promoter.

amāre discat, mūtuōs ignēs ferat.   415

innecte mentem. torvus āversus ferox   416

in iūra Veneris redeat.   417a

                          Hūc vīrēs tuās   417b

intende: sīc tē lūcidī vultūs ferant   418

et nūbe ruptā cornibus pūrīs eās,   419

sīc tē regentem frēna nocturnī aetheris   420

dētrahere numquam Thessalī cantūs queant   421

nullusque dē tē glōriam pastor ferat.   422

Ades invocāta, iam favē votīs, dea.   423

*The nurse has finished her prayer to Diana,
and she moves away from the statue of the
goddess. As she does so, Hippolytus enters
alone, having returned from the hunt, and he
approaches the statue and prays silently to
the goddess. The nurse sees him and speaks
the following in an aside. She does not
disturb his veneration of the statue.*

Ipsum intuor sollemne venerantem sacrum   424

nullō latus comitante -- quid dubitās? dedit   425

tempus locumque cāsus: ūtendum artibus.   426

trepidāmus? haud est facile mandātum scelus   427

audēre, vērum iussa quī rēgis timet,   428

dēpōnat omne et pellat ex animō decus: 429

malus est minister rēgiī imperiī pudor.   430

431 molior, 1 dep. -- to set in motion.
433 sospes, -itis -- safe, unhurt; happy, lucky, fortunate.
434 stirps, stirpis, f. -- the stem, stalk; stock; family, offspring.
     iugum -- yoke, pair. The two children of Phaedra and Theseus, named
         Acamas and Demophon.
435 remitto, -ere -- to send back, relax.
     status, -us, m. -- posture, position, condition, state.
436 sors, -tis, f. -- lot, fate, fortune, condition.
     vigeo, -ere -- to thrive, flourish.
437 veni = es!
438 cura: with *tui*.
     sollicito, 1 -- to disturb.
439 infestus -- hostile, troublesome, dangerous.
440 venia -- forgiveness, pardon.
441 ultro -- of one's own accord, voluntarily.
442 torqueo, -ere -- to turn, twist; to rack, torture.
443a quis = quibus (ablative after *uti*).
443b potius -- rather.
     annorum memor: i.e., remembering that you are young.
444 facem: the torch to illuminate a celebration or a party.
445 Bacchus: the god of wine = wine.
     exonero, 1 -- to disburden, unload.
446 fruor, 3 dep. -- to enjoy, delight in + abl.
     fugit: subject is *aetas* "youth."
447 pectus, -oris, n. -- heart.
448 exulto, 1 -- to leap, jump up, rejoice.
     torus -- bed.
     viduus -- deprived of a wife or lover, mateless.
449 cursus rape: "take flight."
450 effundo, -ere -- to pour out, let loose.
     habena -- reins.
451a effluo, -ere -- to flow forth.

HIPPOLYTUS   *seeing the nurse and turning away from*
              the statue to address her.

              Quid hūc senīlēs fessa molīris gradūs,   431

              ō fīda nūtrix, turbidam frontem gerens   432

              et maesta vultū? sospes est certē parens   433

              sospesque Phaedra stirpis et geminae iugum?   434

NUTRIX   Metūs remitte. prosperō regnum in statū est   435

              domusque flōrens sorte fēlīcī viget.   436

              Sed tū beatīs mītior rēbus venī: 437

              namque anxiam mē cūra sollicitat tuī,   438

              quod tē ipse poenīs gravibus infestus domās.   439

              quem fāta cōgunt, ille cum veniā est miser;   440

              at sī quis ultrō sē malīs offert volens   441

              sēque ipse torquet, perdere est dignus bona   442

              quīs nescit ūtī.   443a

                              Potius annōrum memor   443b

              mentem relaxā: noctibus festīs facem   444

              attolle, cūrās Bacchus exoneret gravēs.   445

              aetāte fruere: mōbilī cursū fugit.   446

              nunc facile pectus, grāta nunc iuvenī Venus: 447

              exultet animus. cūr torō viduō iacēs?   448

              tristem iuventam solve; nunc cursūs rape,   449

              effunde habēnās, optimōs vītae diēs   450

              effluere prohibē.   451a

451b propria...officia: i.e, the occupations proper (to each period in a man's life).

452 aevum -- time, eternity; age, generation; lifetime.

454 coerceo, -ere -- to restrain, repress.

indoles, -is, f. -- inborn or native quality, nature.

455 seges, -itis, f. -- a wheatfield.

fenus, -oris, n. -- the proceeds of capital lent out, interest; gain, profit.

456 tenera: i.e., while still young.

sata, -orum, n. pl. -- standing wheat, crops.

457 celsus -- high, lofty.

vertex, -icis, m. -- top.

evinco, -ere -- to overcome completely; (here) to tower over.

458 malignus -- wicked, malicious.

reseco, 1 -- to cut back.

459 ingenium -- innate quality, nature, character.

460 vegetus -- vigorous, active.

461 truculentus -- savage, fierce, ferocious.

463 munus, -eris, n. -- a service, office, post, employment.

indictus -- appointed, fixed.

464 domito, 1 -- to break, tame.

466 provideo, -ere, -vidi, -visum -- to see forwards, to be provident, to take care.

467 Fatum -- fate, death.

468 damnum -- hurt, harm, damage, injury, loss.

suboles, -is, f. -- sprout, shoot, offspring.

469 agedum (interj.) -- well then, come now.

470 suppleo, -ere -- to fill up, make full, make good, repair.

471 situs, -us, m. -- neglect.

473 ales, -itis, m. or f. -- bird.

derit: fut. of *desum* -- to be away, be absent.

474 pervius -- passable; passed through by.

475 letum -- death.

     Propria descrīpsit deus 451b

officia et aevum per suōs duxit gradūs: 452

laetitia iuvenem, frons decet tristis senem. 453

quid tē coercēs et necās rectam indolem? 454

seges illa magnum fēnus agricolae dabit 455

quaecumque laetīs tenera luxuriat satīs, 456

arborque celsō vertice ēvincet nemus 457

quam nōn maligna caedit aut resecat manus: 458

ingenia melius recta sē in laudēs ferunt, 459

sī nōbilem animum vegeta lībertās alit. 460

truculentus et silvester ac vītae inscius 461

tristem iuventam Venere dēsertā colēs? 462

hoc esse mūnus crēdis indictum virīs, 463

ut dūra tolerent, cursibus domitent equōs 464

et saeva bella Marte sanguineō gerant? 465

prōvīdit ille maximus mundī parens, 466

cum tam rapācēs cerneret Fātī manūs, 467

ut damna semper subole reparāret novā. 468

excēdat agedum rēbus hūmānīs Venus, 469

quae supplet ac restituit exhaustum genus: 470

orbis iacēbit squālidō turpis sitū, 471

vacuum sine ullīs classibus stābit mare, 472

alesque caelō dērit et silvīs fera, 473

sōlīs et āer pervius ventīs erit. 474

Quam varia lētī genera mortālem trahunt 475

476   carpo, -ere -- to pick, pluck.
     turbam: i.e., the mass of living human beings.
     dolus -- deceit, treachery.
477   fata: here, the causes of violent death listed in line 476.
     sic: i.e., even in the natural course of life (i.e., without violent
        accidents and murders).
     ater, atra, atrum -- black.
478a ultro (adv.) -- of our own accord.
478b caelebs, -ibis -- unmarried, single.
     probo, 1 -- to approve. "Let sterile youth (i.e., let youth be
        sterile and) approve of the unmarried life; this will mean that
        whatever you see about you in the world will last for one life-
        time only and will tumble down upon itself."
480   semet = se.
     ruo, -ere -- to fall down, tumble down.
481   proinde -- just so, therefore.
     sequere: imperative.
482   frequento, 1 -- to visit, resort to frequently, frequent.
     coetus, -us, m. -- an assembling; a crowd, company.
483   Word order: non alia vita est magis libera et vitio carens et quae
        ritus priscos melius colat quam...
     vitium -- fault, defect, vice.
484   ritus, -us, m. -- a religious usage or ceremony, rite; a custom,
        manner, mode, way.
     priscus -- belonging to former times, ancient, primitive, venerable.
485   moenia, -ium, n. pl. -- city walls, ramparts.
486   avarae mentis furor: i.e., greed.
487   dico, 1 -- to dedicate, consecrate, devote.
     insons, -ntis -- guiltless, innocent.
488   aura -- air, breeze; (as a political term) the popular breeze, popu-
        lar favor (with *populi*).
     vulgus, -i, n. -- the multitude, the public, the people.
490   immineo, -ere -- to hang over; to strive eagerly after, to be eager
        for, intent upon.
491   fluxus -- flowing, fluid, fleeting, transient.
     opes, opum, f. pl. -- riches, wealth.
492   haud -- by no means.
493   edax, -acis (edo) -- voracious, gluttonous, devouring.
     livor, -oris, m. -- a black and blue spot; envy, spite, malice,
        ill-will.
     degener, -eris -- that departs from its race or kind, degenerate,
        ignoble, base.
494   Word order: scelera sata inter populos atque urbes.
     sero, -ere, sevi, satum -- to sow, plant.
495   conscius -- knowing of something; conscious of; conscious of one's
        self, of one's wrong deeds, conscience-stricken.
     strepitus, -us, m. -- noise.
496   verba fingit: "lies," "tells falsehoods."
     mille: with *columnis*.
497   trabs, trabis, f. -- a beam, timber (here of those that support the
        ceiling).
     insolens, -entis -- contrary to custom; haughty, arrogant, insolent.

carpuntque turbam, pontus et ferrum et dolī!   476

sed fāta credās desse: sīc ātram Styga   477

iam petimus ultro.   478a

                  Caelibem vītam probet   478b

sterilis iuventus: hoc erit, quidquid vidēs,   479

unīus aevī turba et in sēmet ruet.   480

Proinde vītae sequere natūram ducem: 481

urbem frequentā, cīvium coetum cole.   482

HIPPOLYTUS   Nōn alia magis est lībera et vitiō carens   483

ritūsque melius vīta quae priscōs colat,   484

quam quae relictīs moenibus silvās amat.   485

Nōn illum avārae mentis inflammat furor   486

quī sē dicāvit montium insontem iugīs,   487

nōn aura populī et vulgus infīdum bonīs,   488

nōn pestilens invidia, nōn fragilis favor;   489

nōn ille regnō servit aut regnō imminens   490

vanōs honorēs sequitur aut fluxās opēs,   491

speī metūsque līber, haud illum niger   492

ēdaxque līvor dente dēgenerī petit;   493

nec scelera populōs inter atque urbēs sata   494

nōvit nec omnēs conscius strepitūs pavet   495

aut verba fingit; mille nōn quaerit tegī   496

dīves columnīs nec trabēs multō insolens   497

498 suffigo, -ere -- to fasten, fix on, to affix with.
    cruor, -oris, n. -- blood.
499 frux, frugis, f. -- barley meal (used in sacrifices; it was sprinkled
    on the necks of sacrificial animals before they were slaugh-
    tered).
500 summitto, -ere -- to let down, lower, sink, drop.
501 potior, 4 dep. -- to become master of, get, obtain; possess, occupy +
    abl.
502a innocuus -- harmless, innocent; unharmed, uninjured.
502b callidus -- shrewd, expert, skillful; crafty, cunning, artful, sly.
    With *fraudes*.
503 struo, -ere, -xi, -ctum -- to arrange, construct, devise. Word
    order: callidas fraudes feris struxisse novit. Perfect infini-
    tive used *metri causa* in place of present.
    fraus, fraudis, f. -- a cheating, deceit, fraud. Here of snares or
    traps for catching wild animals (*feris*).
504 Ilisos (Greek nominative) -- a river flowing from the slopes of Mt.
    Hymettus, past Athens, and into the Bay of Phaleron.
    foveo, -ere -- to warm, keep warm; to cherish, caress, love, favor,
    support, assist, pamper.
505 Alpheus -- the chief river in the Peloponnesus, flowing past Olympia.
    lego, -ere -- to collect; to remove; to go, pass, wander through; to
    read.
506 metor, 1 dep. -- to measure, measure off; to traverse, pass through.
507 Lerna -- a river near Corinth.
    perluceo, -ere -- to shine through, be transparent.
    vadum -- stream.
508 sedes, -is, f. -- seat, dwelling.
    querulus -- complaining, querulous.
    fremo, -ere -- to make a low noise, murmur.
509 lene (adv.) -- gently.
    percutio, -ere, -cussi, -cussum -- to strike.
510 fagus -- beech-tree.
    iuvo, -are, iuvi, iutum -- to please. The perfect tense states a
    general truth.
511 caespes, -itis, m. -- turf, sod, grass.
512 duxisse = ducere. somnos ducere = dormire.
    citus -- swift, rapid.
514 rivus -- a brook. Word order: dulcis sonus fugiente rivo murmurat.
515 compesco, -ere -- to hold in check, repress, curb, restrain; (of
    hunger, *famem*) to satisfy.
516 fraga, -orum, n. pl. -- strawberries.
    vello, -ere, vulsi, vulsum -- to pluck, pull.
    dumetum -- thorn bush.
517b Word order: impetus est regios luxus procul fugisse (= fugere).
    luxus, -us, m. -- luxury.
    procul: with *fugisse* = "to flee far from..."
518 sollicitus -- troubled, disturbed, full of anxiety.
519 superbus -- proud, arrogant, domineering.
520 capto, 1 -- to seize, catch at, snatch. captasse = captavisse
    (again, perfect infinitive for present).
521 torus -- couch, bed.

suffīgit aurō; nōn cruor largus piās   498

inundat ārās, frūge nec sparsī sacrā   499

centēna niveī colla summittunt bovēs: 500

sed rūre vacuō potitur et apertō aethere   501

innocuus errat.   502a

            Callidās tantum ferīs   502b

struxisse fraudēs nōvit et fessus gravī   503

labōre niveō corpus Ilīsō fovet;   504

nunc ille rīpam celeris Alpheī legit,   505

nunc nemoris altī densa metātur loca,   506

ubi Lerna pūrō gelida perlūcet vadō,   507

sedēsque mūtat: hinc avēs querulae fremunt   508

rāmīque ventīs lēne percussī tremunt   509

veterēsque fāgī. iuvit aut amnis vagī   510

pressisse rīpās, caespite aut nūdō levēs   511

duxisse somnōs, sīve fons largus citās   512

dēfundit undās sīve per flōrēs novōs   513

fugiente dulcis murmurat rīvō sonus.   514

excussa silvīs pōma compescunt famem   515

et frāga parvīs vulsa dūmetīs cibōs   516

facilēs ministrant.   517a

           Rēgiōs luxūs procul   517b

est impetus fūgisse: sollicitō bibunt   518

aurō superbī; quam iuvat nūdā manū   519

captasse fontem! certior somnus premit   520

secūra dūrō membra versantem torō.   521

522 recessus, -us, m. -- a distant, retired, or secret spot; a nook,
        corner.
     furtum -- theft, robbery; a secret action, crafty deceit, trick;
        stolen or secret love, intrigue.
     obscuro: with *cubili* (523).
523 multiplex, -icis -- that has many folds, windings, or concealed
        places. Modifies *domo* (524).
     recondo, -ere -- to shut up, close, hide, conceal.
525a testis, -is, m. or f. -- a witness.
525b hoc: with *ritu*: "in this way."
526 ritus, -us, m. -- custom, manner, way.
527 profundo, -ere, -fudi, -fusum -- to pour forth, bring forth, produce.
     Word order: hoc equidem ritu reor vixisse eos quos prima aetas (the
        first Age of Man; the Golden Age) mixtos deis profudit. Men and
        gods lived together on earth in the Golden Age.
528 sacer...lapis: boundary stones were sacred.
529 arbiter, -tri, m. -- a judge, arbitrator. With *populis* (dat.); in
        apposition to *lapis*.
530 seco, -are -- to cut.
     credulae...rates: ships were *credulae* because they "trusted" the
        untrustworthy seas.
531 norat = noverat: "knew."
     agger, -eris, m. -- rampart.
532 creber, -bra, -brum -- frequent, numerous. We would expect plural
        forms here.
     cinxerant urbes latus: "cities had surrounded their sides."
533 apto, 1 -- to fit, put on, furnish. "Was not yet fitting weapons to
        his hand" (abl.).
534 tortus (torqueo) -- twisted. With *ballista* (535).
535 ballista -- a catapult.
     Word order: nec terra iussa dominum pati servitium iuncto bove
        ferebat.
536 iuncto...bove: "with the oxen yoked (to the plough)." Agriculture
        enslaved the earth to mankind: terra servitium ferebat.
537 arvum -- a field.
     fetus -- fruitful, productive. *Arva per se feta* is subject of *pavere*
        (= *paverunt*).
538 pasco, -ere, pavi, pastum -- to feed.
     gentes: modified by *poscentes nihil* (537).
539 opacus -- shady, dark.
540 rupere = ruperunt.
     foedus, -eris, n. -- a league, treaty, compact; a law; (here) the
        harmony of the world in the Golden Age with nature, men, and the
        gods living happily together.
     lucrum -- gain, profit, advantage.
     furor = furiosus amor.
541 praeceps, -cipitis -- headforemost, headlong; swift, rapid, rushing;
        violent; hasty, rash.
     succendo, -ere, -di, -sum -- to kindle, set on fire, inflame.
542 sitis, -is, f. -- thirst.
543 praeda -- spoils, booty. Word order: minor praeda maiori factus
        est. *Praeda maiori* is predicate.

nōn in recessū furta et obscūrō improbus   522

quaerit cubīlī sēque multiplicī timens   523

domō recondit: aethera ac lūcem petit   524

et teste caelō vīvit.   525a

                    Hōc equidem reor   525b

vīxisse rītū prīma quōs mixtōs deīs   526

profūdit aetās. nullus hīs aurī fuit   527

caecus cupīdō, nullus in campō sacer   528

dīvīsit agrōs arbiter populīs lapis;   529

nōndum secābant crēdulae pontum ratēs: 530

sua quisque nōrat maria; nōn vastō aggere   531

crēbrāque turre cinxerant urbēs latūs;   532

nōn arma saeva mīles aptābat manū   533

nec torta clausās frēgerat saxō gravī   534

ballista portās, iussa nec dominum patī   535

iunctō ferēbat terra servitium bove: 536

sed arva per sē fēta poscentēs nihil   537

pavēre gentēs; silva natīvās opēs   538

et opāca dederant antra natīvās domōs.   539

Rupēre foedus impius lucrī furor   540

et īra praeceps quaeque succensās agit   541

libīdo mentēs; vēnit imperiī sitis   542

cruenta, factus praeda maiōrī minor: 543

544 vires (pl. of *vis*) -- force, might. *Esse* (historical infinitive)
        instead of *erant*. "Might took the place of law."
545 rudis, -e -- unwrought, rough, raw.
546 vertere = verterunt.
547 cornus, -i, f. -- a cornel cherry tree; a javelin made of cornel
        wood. Note the gender. Word order: non erat levis cornus
        armata gracili ferro.
      ferrum -- iron; iron javelin tip.
548 mucro, -onis, m. -- a sharp point or edge. Word order: ensis
        cingens latus ("girding the side" of the soldier) longo mucrone.
      crista -- the crest of a helmet, the plume.
549 galea -- helmet.
      comans, -antis -- having long hair. *Crista comantes* describes the
        helmets with horse-hair plumes. *Procul* indicates that they are
        visible from far off.
550 Mavors = Mars, god of war.
551 cruor, -oris, m. -- blood.
552 inficio, -ere, -feci, -fectum -- to stain, dye.
553 demo, -ere, -mpsi, -mptum -- to take away, remove. dempto fine:
        "with no limits."
554 iere = ierunt.
555 gnatus -- son.
556 iacet: "lies (dead)."
557 perimo, -ere -- to kill, slay.
      fetus, -us, m. -- young, offspring.
558 noverca -- a step-mother.
      mitis, -e -- mild, kindly, gentle. mitius nil: "not more mild" =
        "more cruel." Subject is *noverca*. *Feris* is abl. of comparison.
560 obsideo, -ere, -edi, -essum -- to beset, besiege, blockade. The pf.
        tense states a general truth.
      incestus -- impure, polluted, defiled, sinful; unchaste, lewd,
        incestuous. huius incestae: i.e., of unchaste woman (we would
        prefer the plural).
      stuprum -- defilement, dishonor, disgrace; debauchery, lewdness.
561 fumant tot urbes: for example, Troy, destroyed by the Greeks in
        order to recover Helen, the wife of Menelaus.
562 versa ab imo regna: "kingdoms overturned from their foundations."
      premo, -ere -- to oppress.
563 sileo, -ere -- to keep silent. sileantur aliae: "let all others be
        kept silent." I.e., there is no need to mention any others.
      Aegeus: Theseus' father.
564 Medea: Medea attempted to kill Hippolytus' father, Theseus, in order
        to assure the succession of her own son, Medus, to the throne of
        Athens.
      reddo, -ere -- to give back; to make something appear something; to
        render, prove, make.
565 culpa -- blame, responsibility. *Scelus* is subject; *culpa* is predi-
        cate.
566 execror, 1 dep. -- to curse.

prō iūre vīrēs esse. tum prīmum manū   544

bellāre nūdā saxaque et rāmōs rudēs   545

vertēre in arma: nōn erat gracilī levis   546

armāta ferrō cornus aut longō latus   547

mucrōne cingens ensis aut cristā procul   548

galeae comantēs: tēla faciēbat dolor.   549

invēnit artēs bellicus Māvors novās   550

et mille formās mortis. hinc terrās cruor   551

infēcit omnēs fūsus et rubuit mare.   552

tum scelera demptō fīne per cunctās domōs   553

iēre, nullum caruit exemplō nefās: 554

ā frātre frāter, dexterā gnātī parens   555

cecidit, marītus coniugis ferrō iacet   556

perimuntque fētūs impiae mātrēs suōs.   557

Taceō novercās: mītius nīl est ferīs.   558

sed dux malōrum fēmina: haec scelerum artifex   559

obsēdit animōs, huius incestae stuprīs   560

fūmant tot urbēs, bella tot gentēs gerunt   561

et versa ab īmō regna tot populōs premunt.   562

sileantur aliae: sōla coniunx Aegeī,   563

Mēdēa, reddet fēminās dīrum genus.   564

NUTRIX   Cūr omnium fit culpa paucārum scelus?   565

HIPPOLYTUS   Dētestor omnēs, horreō fugiō execror.   566

567 ratio, -onis, f. -- reason.
569 ante: *ante* in lines 569 and 570 are not to be translated in their
        own clauses; rather, join with *quam* (573) = antequam. That is,
        all of these impossible things will happen before Hippolytus
        gives in to a woman.
     ratis, -is, f. -- ship.
     promitto, -ere -- to send forth; to promise, assure. Word order:
        incerta Syrtis promittet vada amica ratibus (sc., *esse* -- "that
        its waters will be friendly to ships").
570 Syrtis, -is, f. -- a dangerous sand-bank in the sea off the coast of
        North Africa, thus *incerta* "treacherous."
     sinus, -us, m. -- a curve, fold, hollow; a bay, gulf, sea. I.e.,
        from the sea at the farthest edge of the world (in the west).
571 Hesperius -- western.
     Tethys, -yos, f. (Greek declension) -- a sea-goddess, wife of
        Oceanus.
     lucidum attollet diem: i.e., dawn will come from the west instead of
        the east.
572 damma -- a deer, buck, doe.
     blandus -- flattering, fawning, caressing.
     praebeo, -ere -- to hold forth, reach out, offer.
573 mitis, -e -- mild, kindly, gentle.
574 obstinatus -- firmly set, fixed, resolved, stubborn.
     induo, -ere -- to put on (usually of clothes).
     freni, -orum, m. pl. -- a bridle, curb, bit.
575 regna materna: i.e., the Amazons. Hippolytus was the son of an
        Amazon, Antiope.
577 testor, 1 dep. -- to bear witness, give evidence; to prove.
     unicus gentis puer: the Amazons usually killed their male offspring
        at birth, in order to keep the tribe purely female. Antiope,
        however, submitted to the "yoke of Venus" (the phrase implies
        normal marriage as opposed to the transient affairs Amazons
        normally had with men) and spared the life of her son,
        Hippolytus.
578 solamen, -inis, n. -- a comfort, relief, solace, consolation.
     matris amissae: Theseus slew Antiope in order to marry Phaedra.
580 cautes, -is, f. -- a rough, pointed rock.
     intractabilis, -e -- not to be handled; rough, wild.
581 lacesso, -ere -- to excite, challenge, attack, assail.

sit ratio, sit nātūra, sit dūrus furor: 567

ōdisse placuit.   568a

               Ignibus iungēs aquās   568b

et amīca ratibus ante prōmittet vada   569

incerta Syrtis, ante ab extrēmō sinū   570

Hesperia Tēthys lūcidum attollet diem   571

et ōra dammīs blanda praebēbunt lupī,   572

quam victus animum fēminae mītem geram.   573

NUTRIX   Saepe obstinātīs induit frēnōs Amor   574

et odia mūtat. regna māterna aspice: 575

illae ferocēs sentiunt Veneris iugum;   576

testāris istud ūnicus gentis puer.   577

HIPPOLYTUS Solāmen ūnum mātris āmissae ferō,   578

ōdisse quod iam fēminās omnēs licet.   579

NUTRIX   *aside*

Ut dūra cautēs undique intractābilis   580

resistit undīs et lacessentēs aquās   581

longē remittit, verba sīc spernit mea.   582

*Phaedra, who has been observing the nurse
and Hippolytus from inside the palace, rushes
unexpectedly onto the stage, dressed as a
huntress. Her simple tunic is tucked up
under her bosom as that of Diana or an
Amazon. Her hair is scattered wildly over
her shoulders. The nurse continues to
speak, aside.*

583   praeceps, -cipitis -- headlong.
584   vergo, -ere -- to bend, turn, incline.
585   repente (adv.) -- suddenly, unexpectedly.
586   obduco, -ere, -xi, -ctum -- to draw over, cover.
      color: with *morti similis*.
587   dimove vocis moras: i.e., "speak!"
      mora -- delay.
588   alumna -- a foster-daughter.
      temet = te.
589   aestus: i.e., the seething of her emotion.
590   quam bene: "how nice it was to have..."
      excido, -ere, -cidi -- to fall down; to fail, faint, swoon.
591   munus, -eris, n. -- gift.
592   perago, -ere -- to carry through, accomplish.
      mandatum -- a charge, order, command.

Sed Phaedra praeceps graditur, impatiens morae.   583

quō sē dabit fortūna?   quō verget furor?   584

Phaedra faints and falls to the ground; the
nurse, shocked, describes the stricken Phaedra.

Terrae repentē corpus exanimum accidit   585

et ōra mortī similis obduxit color.   586

Hippolytus rushes forward and lifts Phaedra
to her feet. As he holds her in his arms,
she lowers her face in shame and remains
silent. The nurse addresses Phaedra.

Attolle vultūs, dīmovē vōcis morās: 587

tuus ēn, alumna, tēmet Hippolytus tenet.   588

Having regained her senses, Phaedra is
released from Hippolytus' arms and steps
away from him. She is still in a daze
as she speaks the following.

PHAEDRA   Quis mē dolōrī reddit atque aestūs gravēs   589

repōnit animō?   quam bene excideram mihi!   590

HIPPOLYTUS *to Phaedra*

Cūr dulce mūnus redditae lūcis fugis?   591

PHAEDRA   *ignoring Hippolytus' question and speaking*
            aside

Aude, anime, temptā, perage mandātum tuum.   592

intrepida constent verba: quī timidē rogat   593

docet negāre.   magna pars sceleris meī   594

595 olim -- in time past, already.
     perago, -ere, -egi, -actum -- to carry through, accomplish, complete.
596 nefanda, -orum, n. pl. -- impious, heinous, abominable deeds.
     coepta, -orum, n. pl. (coepi) -- undertakings, things begun.
597 forsan = forsitan -- perhaps.
     iugali...face: i.e., in marriage (which would be possible if Theseus
          were actually dead in the underworld).
     fax, facis, f. -- a wedding torch; wedding, marriage.
     abscondo, -ere -- to hide.
598 honesta: (neuter pl. "respectable") predicate to *quaedam sclera*,
          which is the subject of *facit*.
599b commodo, 1 -- to give, lend.
600 secretus -- in secret.
     si quis = si aliquis. With *comes*: "if any companion is present."
601 arbitrium -- a coming near, a being present, presence; a person
          present.
602 coeptis...verbis: "to the words (which I have) begun (to speak)."
     transitus, -us, m. -- a going over, passing over, passage.
604 testor, 1 dep. -- to call upon as a witness.
606 effor, 1 dep. -- to speak out, utter.
607 locuntur - loquuntur.
     stupeo, -ere -- to be struck senseless, to be stunned, dumbed,
          stupified.
610 affectus, -us, m. -- a state of mind, affection, mood.
611 vel...vel -- either...or.
     famula -- a servant, attendant.

olim peracta est; serus est nobis pudor: 595

amavimus nefanda. si coepta exequor,   596

forsan iugali crimen abscondam face: 597

honesta quaedam scelera successus facit.   598

en, incipe, anime!   599a

to Hippolytus

                          Commodes paulum, precor,   599b

secretus aures. si quis est abeat comes.   600

HIPPOLYTUS   En locus ab omni liber arbitrio vacat.   601

PHAEDRA   Sed ora coeptis transitum verbis negant;   602

             vis magna vocem mittit et maior tenet.   603

             vos testor omnes, caelites, hoc quod volo   604

             me nolle.   605

HIPPOLYTUS   Animusne cupiens aliquid effari nequit?   606

PHAEDRA   Curae leves locuntur, ingentes stupent.   607

HIPPOLYTUS   Committe curas auribus, mater, meis.   608

PHAEDRA   Matris superbum est nomen et nimium potens: 609

             nostros humilius nomen affectus decet;   610

             me vel sororem, Hippolyte, vel famulam voca,   611

612 potius -- rather.
614 piget -- it irks, troubles, displeases, disgusts.
    gelatus -- frozen.
    ingredior, 3 dep. -- to go into, enter; to walk on + dat.
    Pindus -- a mountain in Thessaly.
615 ire: supply *me...iubeas* from 613.
    infestus -- hostile.
    agmen, -inis, n. -- an army on the march.
616 cunctor, 1 dep. -- to delay, linger; to hesitate.
    paratis ensibus: i.e., the drawn swords of the enemy.
    pectus: i.e., my breast.
617 mando, 1 -- to commit to one's charge, to entrust.
618 Word order: te decet imperia regere... exequi = exsequi.
619 muliebre non est: "it is not a woman's (job)..."
    tutor, 1 dep. -- to guard, protect, defend.
620 primaevus -- in the first period of life; young.
    vigeo, -ere -- to thrive, flourish, bloom.
622 sinu: i.e., in your bosom, under your protection.
    receptam supplicem ac servam: supply *me*.
    tego, -ere -- to cover, shelter, protect.
623a misereor, 2 dep. -- to pity + gen. *Miserere* is imperative.
    viduus -- widowed. She speaks as if Theseus were dead.
623b omen, -inis, n. -- foreboding, sign, omen. The suggestion in
        Phaedra's word *viduae* that Theseus is dead is itself a bad omen,
        which Hippolytus prays may be averted.
624 sospes, -itis -- safe.
    actutum (adv.) -- immediately, instantly.
625 tenax, -acis -- holding fast, gripping, tenacious.
626 nullam...viam: i.e., no road for a return.
    relictos...ad superos: "to the rest of us who are left behind up
        here."
627 thalamus -- bedroom; marriage-bed; wife.
628 forte -- perhaps.
    amori placidus: i.e., looks kindly upon love affairs. placidus --
        gentle, quiet, still, peaceful, placid.
    et Pluton: "even Pluto" or "Pluto, too." I.e., in addition to
        Pluto's brother, Jupiter, who is notorious for being *amori
        placidus*.
    sedet: i.e., sits by and does nothing (even when his wife is being
        raped and carried off).
629 aequus -- even, favorable, kindly, fair. It is not Theseus, but
        Pirithous, who is trying to carry off Persephone; the gods, who
        are fair, will recognize Theseus' innocence and let him return
        alive to earth.
    caelites = di.
    illum...reducem dabunt = illum reducent. redux, -ucis -- returned.
630 vota: i.e., (our) prayers (for Theseus' return).
631 pietate: with *debita*: "with the piety that would be required or
        expected of me, or that I owe to them."

famulamque potius: omne servitium feram.   612

nōn mē per altās īre sī iubeās nivēs,   613

pigeat gelātīs ingredī Pindī iugīs;   614

nōn, sī per ignēs īre et infesta agmina,   615

cuncter parātīs ensibus pectus dare.   616

mandāta recipe sceptra, mē famulam accipe: 617

tē imperia regere, mē decet iussa exequī.   618

muliebre nōn est regna tūtārī urbium;   619

tū quī iuventae flōre prīmaevō vigēs,   620

cīvēs paternō fortis imperiō rege;   621

sinū receptam supplicem ac servam tege.   622

Miserēre viduae.   623a

HIPPOLYTUS   Summus hoc ōmen deus   623b

āvertat. aderit sospes actūtum parens.   624

PHAEDRA   Regnī tenācis dominus et tacitae Stygis   625

nullam relictōs fēcit ad superōs viam: 626

thalamī remittet ille raptōrem suī?   627

nisi forte amōrī placidus et Plūton sedet.   628

HIPPOLYTUS   Illum quidem aequī caelitēs reducem dabunt.   629

sed dum tenēbit vōta in incertō deus,   630

pietāte cārōs dēbitā frātrēs colam,   631

632 mereor, 2 dep. -- to deserve, merit; to behave. Word order: et
        merebor ne putes viduam te esse. "I'll behave (in such a way)
        that you will not think yourself widowed" = I'll take good care
        of you.
633 suppleo, -ere -- to fill up.
634 credulus -- that believes too easily; too confident.
        fallax, -acis, -- deceitful, deceptive.
635 admoveo, -ere, -movi, -motum -- to bring, move, conduct, lead.
        precibus admotis: "with my prayers brought to bear against him"
        (a military metaphor, as if her prayers were siege weapons).
        agam: "I will conduct" (the affair, business, matter).
636 tacitae mentis: "of my heart that does not dare speak."
639 perplexus -- tangled, involved, confused; ambiguous, obscure. With
        voce.
640a effor, 1 dep. -- to speak out.
640b vapor, -oris, n. -- warmth, heat.
641 intimus -- innermost.
642 penitus (adv.) -- inwardly, internally, within.
        medulla - the marrow of the bones.
        meo, 1 -- to go, pass.
643 viscus, -eris, n. -- the inner organs, the viscera.
        mersus...latens: "submerged...hidden."
644 trabs, trabis, f. -- a beam, timber.
645 nempe -- doubtless, certainly.
        furo, -ere -- to rage, rave.
646 vultus, -us, m. -- the countenance, visage, face.

et tē merēbor esse nē viduam putēs 632

ac tibi parentis ipse supplēbō locum. 633

PHAEDRA *aside*

Ō spēs amantum crēdula, ō fallax Amor! 634

satisne dixī? precibus admōtīs agam. 635

to Hippolytus

Miserēre, tacitae mentis exaudī precēs -- 636

libet loquī pigetque. 637a

HIPPOLYTUS   Quodnam istud malum est? 637b

PHAEDRA   Quod in novercam cadere vix crēdās malum. 638

HIPPOLYTUS   Ambigua vōce verba perplexā iacis. 639

effāre apertē. 640a

PHAEDRA   Pectus insānum vapor 640b

amorque torret. intimīs saevus furit 641

penitus medullīs atque per vēnās meat 642

visceribus ignis mersus et vēnīs latens 643

ut agilis altās flamma percurrit trabēs. 644

HIPPOLYTUS   Amōre nempe Thēseī castō furis? 645

PHAEDRA   Hippolyte, sīc est: Thēseī vultūs amō 646

647 puer: not "boy," but "young man," as line 648 indicates.
648 signo, 1 -- to mark out, designate.
     gena -- cheek.
649 Gnosius -- of Cnossus, the royal palace of Crete.
     caecam...domum: cf. line 122.
650 curva...via: i.e., through the Labyrinth.
     filum -- thread. Ariadne, Phaedra's sister, helped Theseus find his
          way out of the Labyrinth by giving him a spool of thread which
          he unwound as he went into the Labyrinth.
651 quis = qualis.
     fulgeo, -ere, fulsi -- to flash, glisten, shine.
     vitta -- a head-band (often placed upon the heads of sacrificial vic-
          tims; Theseus was to be sacrificed to the Minotaur along with
          thirteen other Athenian boys and girls).
652 tinguo, -ere -- to wet, dye, color.
653 lacertus -- the upper arm.
     torus -- muscle.
654 Phoebe, -es, f. -- the moon-goddess, Diana, sister of Phoebus, the
          sun-god (Apollo). *Tuae Phoebes* -- because Hippolytus worshipped
          Diana as goddess of the hunt. *Phoebi mei* -- because Phaedra was
          descended from the sun-god.
     vultus (sc., *erat ei* possessive dative): "he had the face..."
656 hosti: i.e., Minos. Seneca seems to be following a version of the
          legend that made Theseus the minion of Minos. Or, *hosti* may
          refer to Ariadne.
     celsus -- raised high.
657 refulgeo, -ere -- to flash back, shine, glisten.
     incomptus -- unadorned, artless, rude.
     decor, -oris, m. -- grace, beauty.
658 genitor = pater.
     torvus -- wild, fierce, savage.
659 ex aequo -- equally. decus, -oris, n. -- grace, beauty, dignity.
660 Graius -- Greek.
     Scythicus: the Amazons lived in the area of the Scythians.
     rigor, -oris, m. -- hardness, firmness, severity.
661 fretum -- strait; sea.
662 neo, nere, nevi, netum -- to spin.
     soror: Ariadne, raised to the heavens as the constellation Corona
          after she was abandoned by Theseus.
663 sidereus -- of the stars.
     polus -- the north pole (as the axis of the heavens); the heavens.
664 invoco ad causam parem: an expression from the law courts. "I call
          for your support in a cause like your own." Ariadne's "cause"
          was her love for Theseus; Phaedra's is her love for Hippolytus.
     par, paris -- equal.
665 corripio, -ere, -ripui, -reptum -- to snatch up, seize upon; sweep
          away, carry away.
667 proles, -is, f. -- offspring, child. proles regiae domus: "child of
          a royal house."
668 respergo, -ere, -si, -sum -- to besprinkle, defile.
     labes, -is, f. -- a spot, stain, blot, disgrace, discredit.
     intactus -- untouched, undefiled, chaste (of virgins).

illōs priōrēs quōs tulit quondam puer,   647

cum prīma pūrās barba signāret genās   648

monstrīque caecam Gnosiī vīdit domum   649

et longa curvā fīla collēgit viā.   650

quis tum ille fulsit! presserant vittae comam   651

et ōra flammīs tenera tinguēbat pudor;   652

inerant lacertīs mollibus fortēs torī;   653

tuaeve Phoebēs vultus aut Phoebī meī,   654

tuusque potius -- tālis, ēn tālis fuit   655

cum placuit hostī, sīc tulit celsum caput: 656

in tē magis refulget incomptus decor;   657

est genitor in tē tōtus et torvae tamen   658

pars aliqua mātris miscet ex aequō decus: 659

in ōre Graiō Scythicus appāret rigor.   660

Sī cum parente Crēticum intrāssēs fretum,   661

tibi fīla potius nostra nēvisset soror.   662

tē tē, soror, quācumque sīdereī polī   663

in parte fulgēs, invocō ad causam parem: 664

domus sorōrēs ūna corripuit duās,   665

tē genitor, at mē nātus.   666a

falling at Hippolytus' knees in a gesture
of supplication

                                   Ēn supplex iacet   666b

adlapsa genibus rēgiae prōlēs domūs.   667

respersa nullā lābe et intacta, innocens   668

669   muto, 1 -- to change.
       certa; i.e., with my mind made up, determined.
671b deum = deorum.
672   lentus -- pliant; slow, sluggish, easy, calm, indifferent.
673   fulmen, -inis, n -- lightning.
674   serenum: i.e., the sky (supply *caelum*).
       impello, -ere, -puli, -pulsum -- to strike.
       ruo, -ere -- to fall down, tumble down, go to ruin.
675   condo, -ere -- to put together; to conceal, hide.
677a retortus -- twisted back.
678   radiatus -- having rays, radiant.
       Titan -- the sun-god.
       stirps, stirpis, f. -- stem, stalk, race, family.
679   speculor, 1 dep. -- to watch, observe. *Speculare* is an alternate
          form of *specularis*.
       tenebrae, -arum, f. pl. -- darkness.
681   trisulcus (tres-sulcus "furrow") -- three-pointed.
       mundus -- the heavens; the world; the earth.
683   transactus ignis: i.e., "a lightning bolt driven through (me)."
       transigo, -ere, -egi, -actum -- to drive or thrust through.
684b stuprum -- defilement, dishonor, disgrace, debauchery.

tibi mūtor ūnī. certa descendī ad precēs: 669

fīnem hic dolōrī faciet aut vītae diēs. 670

Miserēre amantis. 671a

HIPPOLYTUS *horrified; freeing himself from Phaedra's grasp and moving away from her; looking up to the heavens and addressing Jupiter and the sun*

                 Magne regnātor deum, 671b

tam lentus audīs scelera? tam lentus vidēs? 672

et quando saevā fulmen ēmittis manū, 673

sī nunc serēnum est? omnis impulsus ruat 674

aethēr et ātrīs nūbibus condat diem, 675

ac versa retrō sīdera oblīquōs agant 676

retorta cursūs. 677a

             Tūque, sīdereum caput, 677b

radiāte Tītan, tū nefās stirpis tuae 678

speculāre? lūcem merge et in tenebrās fuge. 679

Cūr dextra, dīvum rector atque hominum, vacat 680

tua, nec trisulcā mundus ardescit face? 681

in mē tonā, mē fīge, mē velox cremet 682

transactus ignis. sum nocens, meruī morī: 683

placuī novercae. 684a

addressing Phaedra

             Dignus ēn stuprīs ego? 684b

scelerīque tantō vīsus ego sōlus tibi 685

687   vincens -- surpassing.
690   tacitum diu: "kept silent or hidden for a long time."
691   crimen: i.e., her sinful mating with the bull.
      biformi...nota: referring to the Minotaur, half man, half bull, thus
          biformis.
      partus, -us, m. -- a giving birth, birth; the young or offspring.
          Subject of *exhibuit*.
      nota -- a mark or brand of disgrace ("with a two-formed mark of
          disgrace").
692   arguo, -ere, -ui, -utum -- to show, prove, make known.
      trux, -ucis -- wild, savage, fierce.
694   prosperus -- favorable, fortunate.
      fato: i.e., death.
695   haurio, -ire, hausi -- to draw (water); to tear up; to swallow,
          devour, consume.
      perimo, -ere, -emi, -emptum -- to take away, destroy.
697   Colchide noverca: Medea. See above, lines 563-564. Hippolytus is
          saying that Medea's attempt to poison Theseus (alluded to in
          696) was nowhere near so heinous a crime as Phaedra's attempt to
          seduce her step-son.
698   fata: i.e., the fatal curse on the descendants of the sun-god. See
          lines 113 and 124-128.
699   potens, -entis -- in control of + gen.
701   rupes, -is, f. -- a rock, cliff.
      torrens, -entis -- rushing, roaring.
702   gressus, -us, m. -- foot-step.
      agar: "I will be driven" (by my furious love for you).
703   advolvo, -ere -- to roll toward; (of suppliants) to throw oneself at
          the feet of. The passive voice makes the transitive verb
          intransitive.
704   procul -- far off. With *amove*.
705a tactus, -us, m. -- a touching, touch.

māteria facilis? hoc meus meruit rigor?   686

ō scelere vincens omne fēmineum genus,   687

ō maius ausa mātre monstriferā malum,   688

genetrīce pēior! illa sē tantum stuprō   689

contāmināvit, et tamen tacitum diū   690

crīmen biformī partus exhibuit notā,   691

scelusque mātris arguit vultū trucī   692

ambiguus infans -- ille tē venter tulit.   693

turning away from Phaedra

Ō ter quaterque prosperō fātō datī   694

quōs hausit et perēmit et lētō dedit   695

odium dolusque -- genitor, invideō tibi: 696

Colchide novercā maius haec, maius malum est.   697

PHAEDRA   *approaching Hippolytus and then falling again*
           at his knees in supplication

Et ipsa nostrae fāta cognoscō domūs: 698

fugienda petimus; sed meī nōn sum potens.   699

tē vel per ignēs, per mare insānum sequar   700

rupēsque et amnēs, unda quōs torrens rapit;   701

quācumque gressūs tuleris hāc amens agar.   702

iterum, superbe, genibus advolvor tuīs.   703

HIPPOLYTUS *attempting to push Phaedra away*

Procul impudīcōs corpore ā castō amovē   704

tactūs.   705a

706 stringo, -ere -- (of a sword) to draw.
     supplicium -- punishment.
     exigo, -ere -- to drive out; to demand, require, exact (payment of a
          debt or penalty). "Let my sword exact punishment."
707 contortus -- twisted.
708 laeva: supply *manu*.
     focus -- hearth.
709 arquitenens, -entis -- carrying a bow. I.e., Diana.
710 compos, -potis -- having mastery or power over, possessing, in
          possession of + gen.
711 maius hoc voto meo est: "this is a greater thing than what I was
          praying for."
712 salvo...pudore: "with my virtue intact." salvus -- safe, preserved,
          unharmed.
713 ne quid = ne aliquid.
     exoro, 1 -- to gain or obtain by entreaty; to obtain.
714 contactus -- touched, stained, polluted.
     desero, -ere -- to leave, desert.
715 eluo, -ere -- to wash off.
     Tanais...Maeotis. See line 401.
     Pontico...mari: the Black Sea.
     incumbo, -ere -- to lay one's self upon, recline upon. Here of Lake
          Maiotis which empties into the Black Sea.
718 tantum...sceleris: "so much of crime" = "so great a crime."
     expiarit = expiaverit = poterit expiare. expio -- to purge, purify.

as Phaedra thrusts herself into his arms

        Quid hoc est? etiam in amplexūs ruit? 705b

Hippolytus draws his sword, grasps Phaedra's
hair in his left hand and pulls her head back.
He is about to slay her as a sacrificial
victim after dragging her to the statue of
Diana, whom he addresses in the last lines
of this speech.

Stringātur ensis, merita supplicia exigat.   706

ēn impudīcum crīne contortō caput   707

laevā reflexī: iustior numquam focīs   708

datus tuīs est sanguis, arquitenens dea.   709

PHAEDRA   *taking hold of Hippolytus' sword in an effort*
             to help him slay her

Hippolyte, nunc mē compotem votī facis,   710

sanās furentem. maius hoc votō meō est,   711

salvō ut pudōre manibus immoriar tuīs.   712

Phaedra faints in Hippolytus' arms.

HIPPOLYTUS   *thrusting Phaedra away from himself, letting*
              her body fall to the ground, and throwing
              away his sword

Abscēde, vīve, nē quid exōrēs, et hic   713

contactus ensis dēserat castum latus.   714

quis ēluet mē Tanais aut quae barbarīs   715

Maeōtis undīs Ponticō incumbens marī? 716

nōn ipse totō magnus Oceanō pater   717

tantum expiārit sceleris. Ō silvae, ō ferae! 718

Exit Hippolytus, rushing off towards the woods.

719   deprehendo, -ere, -di, -sum -- to seize upon, catch.
      segnis, -e -- slow, tardy, lazy, inactive.
      stupeo, -ere -- to be stunned, benumbed, confounded.
720   regero, -ere -- to bring, throw, or cast back.
      ipsi: dat. = Hippolytus.
721   arguo, -ere -- to accuse, reprove, censure, charge with.
      velo, 1 -- to cover.
722   inferre...gradum: a military metaphor = "to attack."
723   priores -- first.
725   Athenae -- Athens.
726   Word order: Hippolytus, raptor nefandi stupri ("ravisher of unspeak-
           able lust" = "the unspeakably lustful ravisher").
727   insto, 1 -- to approach, threaten.
      intento, 1 -- to stretch out, extend towards; to threaten.
728   pudicam: i.e., Phaedra.
729   attonitus -- thunderstruck, terrified, amazed.
730a pignus, -oris, n. -- a pledge, security; token, assurance, proof.
730b prius: i.e., before we pursue Hippolytus or seek revenge.
731   recreo, 1 -- to remake, restore, revive.
      tractus -- pulled, torn.
      lacer, -era, -erum -- mangled, lacerated, torn to pieces.
732   notae -- indications, proofs.
733a perferte: (here) convey news, announce.
734   lacero, 1 -- to tear, rend, mutilate, lacerate.
      aspectus, -us, m. -- a seeing, sight, look; the sight, glance, look.

NUTRIX   *speaking to herself, but overheard and*
          observed by the chorus

Deprensa culpa est. anime, quid segnis stupes? 719

regeramus ipsi crimen atque ultro impiam   720

Venerem arguamus: scelere velandum est scelus; 721

tutissimum est inferre, cum timeas, gradum.   722

ausae priores simus an passae nefas,   723

secreta cum sit culpa, quis testis sciet?   724

summoning Phaedra's Athenian servants, and
charging Hippolytus with attempted rape as
the servants respond to her call

Adeste, Athenae! fida famulorum manus,   725

fer opem! nefandi raptor Hippolytus stupri   726

instat premitque, mortis intentat metum,   727

ferro pudicam terret; en praeceps abit   728

ensemque trepida liquit attonitus fuga.   729

pignus tenemus sceleris.   730a

                              Hanc maestam prius 730b

recreate. crinis tractus et lacerae comae   731

ut sunt remaneant, facinoris tanti notae.   732

perferte in urbem.   733a

Some of the servants depart to carry the news
to the city; others remain with Phaedra; the
nurse addresses Phaedra, as the latter regains
her senses.

                        Recipe iam sensus, era. 733b

quid te ipsa lacerans omnium aspectus fugis?   734

735   casus, -us, m. -- accident, chance, misfortune.

mens impudīcam facere, nōn cāsus, solet.   735

*The nurse helps Phaedra to her feet; exeunt
into the palace.*

736 fugit: subject is Hippolytus.
     procella -- a violent wind, hurricane.
737 ocior, -ius -- swifter.
     glomero, 1 -- to wind or form into a ball; to gather into a heap; to
         collect, crowd together.
     Corus -- the North-West Wind.
738f Comparison with the swiftness of a meteor.
     flamma: i.e., the fiery head of the meteor.
739 stella...ventis agitata: the ancients thought that meteors were
         stars pushed through the sky by winds.
740 porrigo, -ere -- to stretch or spread out, to put forth.
741 confero, -ferre -- to compare.
     decus, -oris, n. -- grace, splendor, beauty.
     priscus -- of former times, olden, ancient.
742 aevum -- time, age. senioris aevi: "of olden times."
744 mico, -are -- to sparkle, glitter, gleam. The subject is *Phoebe*
         (747), the moon.
745 suos ignes: the moon's fires. Object of *iunxit* (746): "has joined
         its fires as its horns come together." A description of the
         full moon.
746 pernox, -noctis -- that lasts all night. The moon is visible
         throughout the whole night only when it is full. Its chariot
         must hurry (*curru properante*), because it has its longest
         course to run.
747 exero, -ere -- to stretch out or forth, to put forth.
748 facies, -ei, f. -- figure; face, visage; look, sight. nec tenent...
         faciem = "they disappear."
749 qualis est: i.e., tua forma (743) talis est qualis est Hesperus (the
         evening star).
750 lotus -- washed, bathed.
751 pulsis iterum tenebris: i.e., in the morning.
752 Lucifer -- the morning star (*lux* + *fero*).
753 thyrsiger, -gera, -gerum -- bearing the thyrsis wand or Bacchic
         staff.
     Liber = Bacchus, god of wine. He conquered India and made its
         people worship him.
754 intonsus -- unshorn; with hair worn long.
     perpetuum: adverbial = perpetuo -- "always."
755 pampineus -- having tendrils of vine leaves.
     cuspis, -idis, f. -- a spear, javelin.
     territans: Bacchus rides in a chariot drawn by tigers, and he
         controls and guides them by frightening them (*territans*) with
         his spear that is wrapped in vine leaves.
756 mitra -- an oriental head-band or turban.
     cornigerum caput: Bacchus as a bull-god or a goat-god is represented
         with horns on his head.

The chorus sings its second song.

CHORUS   Fūgit insānae similis procellae,   736 sapphic strophe

               ōcior nubēs glomerante Cōrō,   737

               ōcior cursum rapiente flammā,   738

               stella cum ventīs agitāta longōs   739

                   porrigit ignēs.   740

               Conferat tēcum decus omne priscum   741

               fāma mīrātrix seniōris aevī: 742

               pulcrior tantō tua forma lūcet,   743

               clārior quantō micat orbe plēnō   744

               cum suōs ignēs coeunte cornū   745

               iunxit et currū properante pernox   746

               exerit vultūs rubicunda Phoebē   747

               nec tenent stellae faciem minōrēs;   748

               quālis est, prīmās referens tenebrās,   749

               nuntius noctis, modo lōtus undīs   750

               Hesperus, pulsīs iterum tenebrīs   751

                   Lūcifer īdem.   752

               Et tū, thyrsigerā Līber ab Indiā,   753 asclepiadean

               intōnsā iuvenis perpetuum comā,   754

               tigrēs pampineā cuspide territans   755

               ac mitrā cohibens cornigerum caput,   756

757 rigidas...comas: the adjective is intended as a compliment. Cf.
      Phaedra's descriptions of Hippolytus: *incomptus decor* (657)
      and *in ore Graio Scythicus apparet rigor* (660). Bacchus' hair
      was supple and undulating rather than "stiff."
758 nimium (adv.) -- too much.
      suspicio, -ere -- to look up at, to admire.
759 differo, differe, distuli, dilatum -- to carry different ways, to
      scatter, disperse, spread abroad, divulge.
760 Phaedrae...soror: i.e., Ariadne, who was carried off from Crete by
      Theseus, abandoned by him on the island of Dia, and rescued by
      Bacchus, who loved her and set her in the sky as a constellation
      (Corona). Since Ariadne first fell in love with Theseus and
      only loved Bacchus after being abandoned by Theseus, the chorus
      here claims that Ariadne "preferred" Theseus to Bacchus.
      quem: i.e., Theseus.
      Bromius: "the noisy one" = Bacchus.
761 anceps, -cipitis -- two-headed, two-fold; wavering, doubtful, uncer-
      tain; dangerous, perilous. Modifies *bonum*: "a good thing."
762 exiguus -- small, little, short.
763 labor, 3 dep. -- to slide, slip, glide down; to slip away.
764 non sic: "not so" (rapidly).
      pratum -- meadow.
      decens, -entis = decorus -- beautiful.
765 vapor, -oris, m. -- heat.
766 solstitio = in solstitio: "at the summer solstice" (about June 22);
        "in the heat of the summer."
      medius dies: "noon-time." With *saevit*: "when the noon-time (heat)
        rages."
767 praecipito, 1 -- to rush headlong.
      rota -- wheel; chariot. brevibus...rotis: not "on short wheels,"
        but "on short (courses over which) wheels (run)." I.e., in
        summer the path of the night through the sky is short because
        nights are short.
768 languesco, -ere -- to become faint, weak; to decline.
      folium -- leaf.
769 deficio, -ere -- to fail, cease, disappear.
770 radio, 1 -- to beam, shine.
773 fugax: modifies *res*.
      quis sapiens: "what wise (man)."
775 subruo, -ere -- to tear down, undermine, destroy.
776 praeterita (sc., hora): "worse than the hour that has just gone by."
777 deserta, -orum, n. pl. -- deserted places. I.e., the woods.
      petis: addressed to Hippolytus.
      tutus -- safe.
      avius -- pathless.
778 abditus -- hidden, concealed, secret. nemore abdito: abl. of place
        where.
779 Titan -- the sun-god.
      constituo, -ere, -ui, -utum -- to cause to stand.
780 turba licens: in apposition to *Naides* (water nymphs).
      licens, -entis -- free, unrestrained, licentious.

nōn vincēs rigidās Hippolytī comās.   757

nē vultūs nimium suspiciās tuōs: 758

omnēs per populōs fābula distulit,   759

Phaedrae quem Bromiō praetulerit soror.   760

Anceps forma bonum mortālibus,   761 dactylic

exiguī dōnum breve temporis,   762

ut vēlox celerī pede lāberis!   763

nōn sīc prāta novō vēre decentia   764 asclepidean

aestātis calidae despoliat vapor,   765

saevit solstitiō cum medius diēs   766

et noctēs brevibus praecipitant rotīs;   767

languescunt foliō ut līlia pallidō   768

et grātae capitī dēficiunt comae,   769

ut fulgor tenerīs quī radiat genīs   770

momentō rapitur nullaque nōn diēs   771

formōsī spolium corporis abstulit.   772

rēs est forma fugax: quis sapiens bonō   773

confīdat fragilī? dum licet, ūtere.   774

tempus tē tacitum subruit, hōraque   775

semper praeteritā dēterior subit.   776

Quid dēserta petis? tūtior avīis   777

nōn est forma locīs: tē nemore abditō,   778

cum Tītan medium constituit diem,   779

cingent turba licens Nāides improbae,   780

781 formonsus = formosus -- beautiful, handsome.
    claudo, -ere -- to shut, close; to enclose, surround, encompass.
    fons, -ntis, m. -- a spring (of water from the ground). There is an
         allusion here to the story of Hylas who went to fetch water from
         a spring and was caught and drowned by the nymphs of the spring
         who fell in love with him.
782 somnis...tuis: i.e., when you rest in the woods, exhausted from
         hunting.
783 lascivae...deae: subject of *facient insidias* (782).
784 Pan (acc. pl. *Panas*), m. -- Pan, god of woods and shepherds; (in pl.)
         minor woodland deities.
    quae Dryades: i.e., Dryades (tree-nymphs) quae Panas montivagos
         petunt. In apposition to *lascivae...deae* (783).
786 sidus post veteres Arcadas editum: the "heavenly body" (*sidus*) pro-
         duced or born after the Arcadians is the moon. The Arcadians
         boasted that they existed even before the moon.
787 currus...candidos: not the "white chariot," but the "white (horses
         that draw the) chariot."
    flecto, -ere -- to guide. Diana (the moon goddess) will fall in love
         with Hippolytus and not be able to guide her horse-drawn chariot.
788 nuper -- recently.
    rubesco, -ere, -ui -- to grow red, to blush.
789 sordidus -- dirty, foul, filthy. I.e., the ruddy color of the moon
         was not due to clouds covering it.
790 sollicitus -- troubled, disturbed.
    turbidus -- confused, disordered, troubled.
791 reor, reri, ratus -- to believe, think, suppose. "Thinking that it
         had been drawn down (*tractam*)..."
    Thessalicis carminibus: i.e., by magical incantations sung by
         Thessalian witches.
792 tinnitus, -us, m. -- a ringing, jingling, tingling. tinnitus dedimus:
         the reference is to magical noises made to counter the incanta-
         tions of the Thessalian witches.
    tu: i.e., Hippolytus.
    labor: i.e., the (cause of the moon's) suffering. The phrase *luna
         laborat* is used of eclipses.
793 causa morae: i.e., as if the moon had stopped in its course to
         admire Hippolytus' beauty, as explained in the remainder of the
         sentence. Cf. the moon and Endymion.
794 sustineo, -ere, -tinui, -tentum -- to hold up; to stay, check,
         restrain.
795 vexo, 1 -- to shake; to injure, damage. Subjunctive of wish.
    frigus, -oris, n. -- cold; the cold of winter, winter.
    parcius (comp. adv.) -- more sparingly; less.
798 torvus -- wild, fierce, savage.
799 tristis, -e -- (here) stern.
    supercilium -- the eye-brow.
800 licet...compares: "you may compare."
801 caesaries, -ei, f. -- a dark head of hair, the hair.
    nescia colligi: "that knows not to collect itself" = not used to
         being arranged or groomed.

formonsos solitae claudere fontibus,	781
et somnis facient insidias tuis	782
lascivae nemorum deae,	783 glyconic
Panas quae Dryades montivagos petunt.	784 asclepiadean

Aut te stellifero despiciens polo	785
sidus post veteres Arcadas editum	786
currus non poterit flectere candidos.	787
et nuper rubuit, nullaque lucidis	788
nubes sordidior vultibus obstitit;	789
at nos solliciti numine turbido,	790
tractam Thessalicis carminibus rati,	791
tinnitus dedimus: tu fueras labor	792
et tu causa morae, te dea noctium	793
dum spectat celeres sustinuit vias.	794

Vexent hanc faciem frigora parcius,	795
haec solem facies rarius appetat:	796
lucebit Pario marmore clarius.	797
quam grata est facies torva viriliter	798
et pondus veteris triste supercili!	799
Phoebo colla licet splendida compares:	800
illum caesaries nescia colligi	801

802 intego, -ere -- to cover.
803 hirtus -- rough, hairy, shaggy.
806 et: connects *viribus* (805) and *vasti spatio...corporis* (806). Word
        order (804-806): tu licet viribus et spatio vasti corporis
        asperos pugnacesque deos vincere audeas. licet...audeas: "you
        may dare."
     spatium -- (here) size, bulk, extent. viribus et spatio vasti
        corporis: "with the strength and bulk of your huge body."
807 aequo, 1 -- to equal, match.
     torus -- muscle.
808 latus -- wide, broad.
809 dorsum -- back.
     libeat (supply *tibi*): "should it please (you) to..."
     cornipes, -pedis, m. -- horn-hoofed; horse.
     vehi: "to be carried" = "to ride."
810 frena, -orum, n. pl. -- reins.
     Castoreus -- of or belonging to or like that of Castor. Castor, the
        brother of Pollux, was famed as a horseman.
     mobilis, -e -- easy to move; pliant, flexible; nimble, quick, active.
811 flecto, -ere -- to guide. Modified by *frenis*: "to guide with the
        reins."
     Cyllaros was Castor's horse, given to him by Juno. Cyllaron: Greek
        accusative. Castor and Pollux were Spartan heroes; hence
           Spartanum...Cyllaron.
812 ammentum -- a strap or thong on a javelin (used to help direct the
        throw).
     tendo, -ere -- to stretch.
813 dirigo, -ere -- to send in a straight line; to direct.
814 dociles spicula figere: "well taught in fixing (i.e., shooting)
        arrows or darts." *dociles* modifies *Cretes* (815).
815 harundo, -inis, f. -- arrow, dart.
816 modo...Parthico: "in the Parthian manner." The Parthians were
        a Scythian people famous for their skill in archery.
     spargo, -ere -- to scatter; (here, of arrows) to shoot.
817 ales, -itis, m. or f. -- bird.
818 viscus, -eris, n. -- the inner organs of the body.
     conditus -- thrust, plunged, hidden within.
820 perspicio, -ere -- to look into, look at, examine carefully.
821 impunitus -- unpunished.
822 tutum praetereat: "pass you by and leave you safe."
823 deformis, -e -- misshapen, ugly.
     822-823 I.e., may you escape the dangers associated with beauty
        (*forma*) and live to an old age (even though old age is neces-
        sarily ugly).
     senium -- the feebleness of age; an old man.

perfundens umerōs ornat et integit;   802

tē frons hirta decet, tē brevior coma   803

nullā lēge iacens; tū licet asperōs   804

pugnācēsque deōs vīribus audeās   805

et vastī spatiō vincere corporis: 806

aequās Herculeōs nam iuvenis torōs,   807

Martis belligerī pectore lātior.   808

sī dorsō libeat cornipedis vehī,   809

frēnīs Castoreā mōbilior manū   810

Spartānum poteris flectere Cyllaron.   811

ammentum digitīs tende priōribus   812

et tōtīs iaculum dīrige vīribus: 813

tam longē, docilēs spīcula fīgere,   814

nōn mittent gracilem Crētes harundinem.   815

aut sī tēla modō spargere Parthicō   816

in caelum placeat, nulla sine ālite   817

descendent, tepidō viscere condita   818

praedam dē mediīs nūbibus afferent.   819

Rārīs forma virīs (saecula perspice)   820

impūnīta fuit. tē melior deus   821

tūtum praetereat formaque nōbilis   822

dēformis seniī monstret imāginem.   823

824   sinat inausum: "leave undared."
825   insons, -ntis -- guiltless, innocent.
      apparat: the subject of this and the following verbs is the nurse,
          who is preparing the evidence to use against Hippolytus (cf.
          719-733a and especially 731-732).
826   lacero, 1 -- to tear, rend, mutilate.
827   umecto, 1 -- to moisten, wet.
828   instruo, -ere -- to build, erect, construct; to plan, devise.
      fraus, fraudis, f. -- deceit, fraud, treachery.
      dolus -- treachery, trick. Subject of *instruitur*.
830   alto vertice: "with the crown (of his head) high."
831   par, paris (pl., pares, paria) -- equal to, like + dat.
832   ni = nisi -- unless, except.
      languidus -- faint, weak, pale.
      pallor, -oris, m. -- pale color, pallor.
833   squalor, -oris, m. -- stiffness, roughness.
834   redditus -- given back.
835   plaga -- region, quarter.
836   manes, -ium, m. pl. -- the ghosts of the dead.
      carcer, -eris, m. -- a prison.
      umbro, 1 -- to shade, overshadow.
      polus -- a pole; the heavens; (here) the "sky" of the underworld.
837   vix -- scarcely. With *sufferunt*.
      suffero, -ferre -- to bear, endure.
838   Eleusin, -inis, f. -- Eleusis, city in Attica famous for the
          mysteries of Ceres; = Ceres (by metonymy).
      Triptolemus -- king of Eleusis, and the inventor of agriculture.
          dona Triptolemi = crops. Four harvests have passed since
          Theseus entered the underworld.
      seco, 1 -- to cut, reap.
839   libra -- balance, pair of scales; the constellation Libra, under
          which the days are of equal length with the nights (thus, *parem*
          composuit diem).
840   ut -- while. Word order: ut ambiguus labor sortis ignotae me
          detinuit.
      sors, -tis, f. -- fate.

*The chorus-leader comments in normal spoken
iambics on the plot which the nurse is
contriving and with which Phaedra, now
inside the palace with the nurse, is
cooperating.*

CHORUS-
LEADER   Quid sinat inausum fēminae praeceps furor?   824 iambic

          nefanda iuvenī crīmina insontī apparat.   825

          ēn scelera! quaerit crīne lacerātō fidem,   826

          decus omne turbat capitis, ūmectat genās: 827

          instruitur omnī fraude fēmineā dolus.   828

          Theseus approaches from off stage.

          Sed iste quisnam est, rēgium in vultū decus   829

          gerens et altō vertice attollens caput?   830

          ut ōra iuvenī paria Pīrithoō gerit,   831

          nī languidō pallōre candērent genae   832

          staretque rectā squālor incultus comā.   833

          ēn ipse Thēseus redditus terrīs adest.   834

THESEUS   *arriving on stage and addressing the audience*

          Tandem profugī noctis aeternae plagam   835

          vastōque mānēs carcere umbrantem polum,   836

          et vix cupītum sufferunt oculī diem.   837

          Iam quarta Eleusin dōna Triptolemī secat   838

          paremque totiens lībra composuit diem,   839

          ambiguus ut mē sortis ignōtae labor   840

842 extincto: not actually "dead" (the usual meaning of the perfect
         passive participle of *extinguo* -- to put out, extinguish,
         destroy, kill), but almost; Theseus retained only a *sensus*
         malorum while in the underworld.
843 finis: i.e., the person who ended my suffering in Hades.
     Alcides: Hercules, whose grandfather was Alceus.
844 revello, -ere, -velli, -vulsum -- to pull away.
     canem: Cerberus.
845 supernus -- that is above, upper.
     sedes, -is, f. -- a seat, chair, throne; a place where one stays, a
         place, spot, region.
846 robur, -oris, n. -- strength.
847 gressus, -us, m. -- step.
848 Phlegethon: a river of Hades.
849 Alciden sequi: Hercules' step was much longer than that of normal
         mortals.
850 fremitus, -us, m. -- a loud noise.
851 expromo, -ere -- to bring forth, show forth, utter, disclose, state.
     luctus, -us, m. -- sorrow, mourning.
852 limen, -inis, n. -- the threshold.
853 prorsus (adv.) -- certainly, truly.
     inferno hospite: abl. after *digna*: "worthy of a guest from the
         underworld."
854 nex, necis, f. -- death.
855 immineo, -ere -- to hang over, to border on; to be eager for, intent
         on.
856 reduce...viro: "now that her husband has returned."

dētinuit inter mortis et vītae mala.   841

pars ūna vītae mansit extinctō mihi: 842

sensus malōrum; fīnis Alcīdēs fuit,   843

quī cum revulsum Tartarō abstraheret canem,   844

mē quoque supernās pariter ad sēdēs tulit.   845

sed fessa virtūs robore antiquō caret   846

trepidantque gressūs. heu, labor quantus fuit   847

Phlegethōnte ab īmō petere longinquum aethera   848

pariterque mortem fugere et Alcīdēn sequī.   849

*The nurse and Phaedra have observed Theseus'
arrival from inside the palace. Phaedra has
decided to commit suicide, and this has
caused her handmaids to begin to weep and
wail loudly enough to be heard by Theseus
outside the palace.*

Quis fremitus aurēs flēbilis pepulit meās?   850

*Enter nurse from the palace. Theseus turns
to her for an answer to his next question.*

Exprōmat aliquis. luctus et lacrimae et dolor, 851

in līmine ipsō maesta lāmentātiō?   852

hospitia digna prorsus infernō hospite.   853

NUTRIX   Tenet obstinātum Phaedra consilium necis   854

flētūsque nostrōs spernit ac mortī imminet.   855

THESEUS Quae causa lētī? reduce cūr moritur virō?   856

857 maturus -- ripe; timely; early; speedy, with haste or hastened.
858 Word order: perplexa verba magnum nescio quid (= "something") tegunt.
859 effor, 1 dep. -- to speak out.
860 haut -- not at all.
     pando, -ere -- to spread out, open; to make known, explain.
861 statuo, -ere, -ui, -utum -- to decide, conclude, determine.
     ferre = auferre -- to take away (i.e., to Hades when she dies).
     quo moritur malum: "the evil thing on account of which she is
         dying."
862 pergo, -ere -- to go on, continue, proceed.
     properatus -- hurried, rapid, quick, speedy. properato est opus:
         "there is need for speed."
863 resero, 1 -- to unlock, unclose, open.
     postis, -is, m. -- a door-post; door.
     lar, -is, m. -- household god, Lar; the hearth; a dwelling, house.
864 sicine = sic + ne.
865 expetitus -- longed for.
866 quin -- why don't you...?
     viduo, 1 -- to deprive, bereave something (acc.) of something (abl.).
867 restituo, -ere -- to give back, return, restore.
     fugo, 1 -- to cause to flee, to drive or chase away.
868a expromo, -ere -- to bring forth, show forth, disclose, declare.
869 indoles, -is, f. -- inborn quality, nature; potential for growth.
870 reditus, -us, m. -- return.
     cinis, -eris, m. -- ashes.

NUTRIX   Haec ipsa lētum causa mātūrum attulit.   857

THESEUS   Perplexa magnum verba nescio quid tegunt.   858

          effāre apertē quis gravet mentem dolor.   859

NUTRIX   Haut pandit ullī; maesta sēcrētum occulit   860

          statuitque sēcum ferre quō moritur malum.   861

          iam perge, quaesō, perge: properatō est opus. 862

THESEUS   Reserāte clausōs regiī postēs laris.   863

          The double doors of the palace are thrown
          open to reveal Phaedra about to commit
          suicide with Hippolytus' sword.

          Ō socia thalamī, sīcine adventum virī   864

          et expetītī coniugis vultum excipis?   865

          quīn ense viduās dexteram atque animum mihi   866

          restituis et tē quidquid ē vītā fugat   867

          exprōmis?   868a

PHAEDRA   Ēheu, per tuī sceptrum imperī,   868b

          magnanime Thēseu, perque natōrum indolem   869

          tuōsque reditūs perque iam cinerēs meōs,   870

          permitte mortem.   871a

THESEUS   Causa quae cōgit morī?   871b

872 fructus, -us, m. -- fruit; the benefit to be derived from something.
874 pudica: i.e., a chaste woman.
875 arcanum -- a secret.
     occulo, -ere -- to cover, hide, conceal.
876 sileo, -ere -- to be silent; to keep silent.
877 facultas, -atis, f. -- capability, opportunity.
     contingo, -ere -- to touch, fall to one's lot, be available to one.
878 desum, desse -- to be away, absent from + dat. (*volenti*).
879 luo, -ere -- to release from debt; to atone for, expiate.
     delictum -- offense, crime.
881 lacrimandum suis: i.e., by one's family or friends.
882b verber, -eris, n. -- lash, whip. Slaves were forced to give
         testimony by being whipped and tortured.
     anus, -us, f. -- an old woman.
883 for, (*future*) fabor, 1 dep. -- to speak, say.
     abnuo, -ere -- to deny, refuse.

PHAEDRA   Sī causa lētī dīcitur, fructus perit.   872

THESEUS   Nēmō istud alius, mē quidem exceptō, audiet.   873

PHAEDRA   Aurēs pudīca coniugis sōlās timet.   874

THESEUS   Effāre: fīdō pectore arcāna occulam.   875

PHAEDRA   Alium silēre quod volēs, prīmus silē.   876

THESEUS   Lētī facultās nulla continget tibi.   877

PHAEDRA   Morī volentī dēsse mors numquam potest.   878

THESEUS   Quod sit luendum morte dēlictum indicā.   879

PHAEDRA   Quod vīvō.   880a

THESEUS   Lacrimae nōnne tē nostrae movent?   880b

PHAEDRA   Mors optima est perīre lacrimandum suīs.   881

THESEUS   Silēre pergit.   882a

                         Verbere ac vinclīs anus   882b

          altrixque prōdet quidquid haec fārī abnuit.   883

885b mane: "stop!"
886 gena -- (usually plural) cheeks, eyelids, eyes. *Genis* with *coortas*:
      "rising or coming forth from your eyes."
887 coorior, -iri, -ortus -- to come forth, rise, appear.
      praetendo, -ere, -di, -tum -- to stretch forth, extend; to spread
        before or in front.
      optego, -ere -- to cover over, cover up.
889 coruscus -- flashing, gleaming.
      aetherius -- heavenly, celestial.
      iubar, -aris, n. -- the radiance of the heavenly bodies, light,
        splendor, brightness, sunshine.
890 ortus, -us, m. -- a rising of the heavenly bodies; any rise, begin-
        ning, or origin.
891 tempto, 1 -- to handle, touch, attack.
      resisto, -ere, -stiti -- to stop; to oppose, resist.
      minae, -arum, f. pl. -- threats, menaces.
893 labes, -is, f. -- spot, stain, blemish.
      eluo, -ere -- to wash out, wash clean.
      cruor, -oris, m. -- blood.
894 edo, -ere -- to give out, put forth, utter, tell, declare.
      eversor, -oris, m. -- a subvertor, destroyer.
895a rere = reris (2nd sing. of *reor* -- to think).
895b expeto, -ere -- to long for, seek after, desire.

to slaves from the palace

Vincite ferrō. verberum vīs extrahat   884

sēcrēta mentis.   885a

*Phaedra speaks the following words and then
turns her face aside out of shame, weeps
profusely, and covers her face with the folds
of her tunic.*

PHAEDRA   Ipsa iam fābor, manē.   885b

THESEUS   Quidnam ōra maesta āvertis et lacrimās genīs   886

            subitō coortās veste praetentā optegis?   887

PHAEDRA   *unveiling her face and looking up at the sky*

            Tē tē, creātor caelitum, testem invocō,   888

            et tē, coruscum lūcis aetheriae iubar,   889

            ex cuius ortū nostra dēpendet domus: 890

            temptāta precibus restitī; ferrō ac minīs   891

            nōn cessit animus: vim tamen corpus tulit.   892

            Labem hanc pudōris ēluet noster cruor.   893

THESEUS   Quis, ēde, nostrī decoris ēversor fuit?   894

PHAEDRA   Quem rēre minimē.   895a

THESEUS   Quis sit audīre expetō.   895b

897 stuprator, -oris, m. -- a defiler, seducer.
     accursus, -us, m. -- a running together.
898 intuor, 3 dep. -- to look at.
899 asper, -era, -erum -- rough.
     signum -- a mark, token, sign; an image, picture, decoration.
     ebur, -oris, n. -- ivory (the hilt of the sword is of ivory).
900 capulus -- handle.
     Actaeus -- Attic. gentis Actaeae: i.e., of the Athenian royal
          family.
902 famulus -- a servant, attendant.
     concitus -- shaken up, excited, agitated, hastened.
903 pro -- introduces an oath. "By holy piety..."
904 secundum...regnum: the three kingdoms are the sky (Jupiter), the sea
          (Neptune), and the underworld (Pluto).
905 lues, -is, f. -- plague, pestilence. generis infandi lues: the
          reference is to Hippolytus' Amazon mother.
906 hunc: Hippolytus.
     alo, -ere, alui, altum -- to feed, nourish.
     Taurus (a singular where we would expect a plural) -- the Taurians, a
          Scythian (*Scythes* is an adjective) people living in what is now
          the Crimea.
907 Colchusque Phasis: the Colchian Phasis, a river at the foot of the
          Caucasus Mountains. The Taurians and Colchians are mentioned
          here as typically barbarian peoples; the former offered human
          sacrifices, and Medea was one of the latter.
     auctor, -oris, m. -- progenitor, father, ancestor.
908 stirps, -is, f. -- stem, stalk, stock (of a family or race).
     degener, -is -- that departs from its race or kind, degenerate.
          degener sanguis: his blood is unworthy of the family of
          Theseus. stirpem primam...refert: "it returns to its first
          stock" (i.e., the barbarian race of Amazons).
909 prorsus (adv.) -- certainly, truly.
     gentis armiferae: i.e., the Amazons.
910 foedus, -eris, n. -- covenant, agreement. Veneris foedera: any kind
          of sexual relations, including those sanctioned by marriage (as
          here).
911 vulgo, 1 -- to spread among the multitude, to prostitute. Amazons
          did not marry, and they thus remained chaste longer than usual
          (*castum diu*); in order to perpetuate their race they offered
          themselves to strangers who passed through their territory
          (*vulgare populis corpus*).
     taeter, -tra, -trum -- offensive, foul, hideous, abominable.
912 melioris soli: i.e., of a civilized country, namely, Greece. When
          Theseus addresses "the abominable race" (of the Amazons), he has
          Hippolytus in mind, and in line 912 he is thinking of how
          Hippolytus' inherited barbarism has not yielded to ("been over-
          come by") the laws and morals of civilized Greece.
913 fera -- wild beast.
     Veneris...nefas: i.e., incest.

PHAEDRA   *holding up the sword for Theseus to see*

            Hic dicet ensis quem tumultu territus   896

            liquit stuprator civium accursum timens.   897

THESEUS   Quod facinus, heu me, cerno?   quod monstrum intuor?   898

            regale parvis asperum signis ebur   899

            capulo refulget, gentis Actaeae decus.   900

            sed ipse quonam evasit?   901a

PHAEDRA   Hi trepidum fuga   901b

            videre famuli concitum celeri pede.   902

THESEUS   Pro sancta Pietas, pro gubernator poli   903

            et qui secundum fluctibus regnum moves,   904

            unde ista venit generis infandi lues?   905

            hunc Graia tellus aluit an Taurus Scythes   906

            Colchusque Phasis?   redit ad auctores genus   907

            stirpemque primam degener sanguis refert.   908

            est prorsus iste gentis armiferae furor,   909

            odisse Veneris foedera et castum diu   910

            vulgare populis corpus.   o taetrum genus   911

            nullaque victum lege melioris soli!   912

            ferae quoque ipsae Veneris evitant nefas,   913

            generisque leges inscius servat pudor.   914

915f Theseus mocks his son's austere life-style.
fictus -- feigned, fictitious, false.
maiestas, -atis, f. -- greatness, dignity.
916 habitus, -us, m. -- habit; appearance, dress; nature, character.
horrens, -entis -- bristly, shaggy, rough.
priscus -- ancient.
917 senium -- feebleness of age; an old man; peevishness, moroseness.
tristis, -e -- (here) severe. morum senium triste: "the stern
severity of your character."
affectus, -us, m. -- disposition.
918 abditos sensus: "hidden sentiments, feelings."
919 animis -- (here) instincts.
induo, -ere -- to clothe, put something on over something.
920 pudor: "this (appearance of) modesty."
celo, 1 -- to conceal.
audacem quies: i.e., quies audacem celat. "Your (appearance of)
tranquillity conceals (your true) audacious (self)."
921 probo, 1 -- to approve, to represent, to pass off. vera...probant:
"try to pass off as true" (that which is false). fallaces --
deceitful, hypocritical people (such as Theseus now believes
Hippolytus to be).
922 simulo, 1 -- to imitate, copy; to feign, pretend, counterfeit.
incola, m. -- inhabitant.
923 efferatus -- wild, savage.
924 torus -- bed.
925 ordior, 4 dep. -- to begin, set about, undertake. ordiri virum: "to
set about (proving yourself) a man."
927 Antiope: Hippolytus' mother.
929b profugus -- fugitive, (a) banished (person).
930 ultimo...mundo: abl. of place where. "At the farthest (part of the)
world."
931 summotus -- withdrawn, removed.
dirimo, -ere -- to take apart, separate, divide.
Oceani plagis: abl. of means with *dirimat*. The tracts of the Ocean
will separate Hippolytus in a land at the edge of the world far
from the known world of the Mediterranean basin.
plaga -- region, quarter, tract.
932 orbem nostris pedibus obversum: "the world turned towards our feet" =
the other side of the world.
colo, -ere -- inhabit.
933 recessus, -us, m. -- a distant, retired, or secret spot.
penitus (adv.) -- deeply, far within, into the inmost part.
abditus -- hidden, concealed.
934 celsi...poli: the north pole. celsus -- high, lofty.
935 "placed beyond (the reach of) winter and its white snows." I.e.,
among the Hyperboreans ("Beyond the North Wind"), a legendary
people dwelling at the fringes of the world.
936 "although you leave behind the roaring threats of chill Boreas..."
Boreas was the North Wind.
938 pertinax, -acis -- that holds fast, stubborn, persevering.
latebra -- a hiding-place.
premo, -ere -- to press; (here) to pursue.

Ubi vultus ille et ficta maiestas viri   915

atque habitus horrens, prisca et antiqua appetens, 916

morumque senium triste et affectus graves?   917

o vita fallax, abditos sensus geris   918

animisque pulcram turpibus faciem induis: 919

pudor impudentem celat, audacem quies,   920

pietas nefandum; vera fallaces probant   921

simulantque molles dura. silvarum incola   922

ille efferatus castus intactus rudis,   923

mihi te reservas? a meo primum toro   924

et scelere tanto placuit ordiri virum?   925

Iam iam superno numini grates ago,   926

quod icta nostra cecidit Antiope manu,   927

quod non ad antra Stygia descendens tibi   928

matrem reliqui.   929a

                    Profugus ignotas procul   929b

percurre gentes: te licet terra ultimo   930

summota mundo dirimat Oceani plagis   931

orbemque nostris pedibus obversum colas,   932

licet in recessu penitus extremo abditus   933

horrifera celsi regna transieris poli,   934

hiemesque supra positus et canas nives   935

gelidi frementes liqueris Boreae minas   936

post te furentes, sceleribus poenas dabis.   937

profugum per omnes pertinax latebras premam: 938

939 abstrusus -- hidden, concealed.
940 emetior, 4 dep. -- to measure out; to pass over, traverse.
941 unde redeam: i.e., from Hades.
     quo -- to which place, where.
942 vota: i.e., prayers or curses.
     genitor aequoreus: Neptune.
943 pronus -- turned forward; inclined to favor, favorable.
944 invocata...Styge: the gods invoked the river Styx when they swore
         oaths.
     munus hoc sanxit: "he confirmed this gift" (of the three prayers or
         curses).
     sancio, -ire, -xi, -ctum -- to establish, decree, confirm.
945 perago, -ere -- to carry through, accomplish, execute.
946 ultra (adv.) -- further, beyond (the present moment).
947 manes...iratos patri: the ghosts in the underworld are angry at
         Theseus for his expedition with Pirithous to carry off the queen
         of the underworld.
948 abominandus -- abominable, detestable.
     ops, opis, f. -- power, strength; aid, help, support.
949 supremum...munus: i.e., the last of the three prayers or curses.
950 ni = nisi -- unless.
952 imminens, -entis -- threatening.
953 parco, -ere, peperci -- to spare; not to use + dat. Theseus did not
         use the magic prayer to help him escape from Hades.
     pactus -- agreed upon, settled, stipulated.
956 subtexo, -ere -- to weave under or below; to cover, hide, darken,
         obscure.
957 vulgus aequoreum: "the multitude of marine animals." vulgus, -i,
         n. -- mass, people, multitude.
     cieo, -ere -- to put in motion, move, stir, rouse.
958 tumidus -- swollen.

longinqua clausa abstrūsa dīversa invia   939

ēmētiēmur, nullus obstābit locus: 940

scīs unde redeam.   941a

                         Tēla quō mittī haud queunt,   941b

hūc vōta mittam. genitor aequoreus dedit   942

ut vōta prōnō terna concipiam deō,   943

et invocātā mūnus hoc sanxit Styge.   944

ēn perage dōnum triste, regnātor fretī!   945

nōn cernat ultrā lūcidum Hippolytus diem   946

adeatque mānēs iuvenis īrātōs patrī.   947

fer abōminandam nunc opem gnātō, parens: 948

numquam suprēmum nūminis mūnus tuī   949

consūmerēmus, magna nī premerent mala;   950

inter profunda Tartara et Dītem horridum   951

et imminentēs rēgis infernī minās,   952

vōtō pepercī; redde nunc pactam fidem.   953

genitor, morāris? cūr adhūc undae silent?   954

nunc ātra ventīs nūbila impellentibus   955

subtexe noctem, sīdera et caelum ēripe,   956

effunde pontum, vulgus aequoreum ciē   957

fluctūsque ab ipsō tumidus Ōceanō vocā.   958

Exeunt into palace.

959 deum = deorum.
960 igniferi: the reference is to the thunderbolts wielded by Jupiter.
     Olympus: the mythological home of the gods on Mount Olympus.
961 cito...mundo: "the swift(ly) (whirling) heavens" (abl. of place
         where).
962 cursus vagos...astrorum: "the paths of the wandering stars" =
         planets as opposed to the fixed stars.
963 polus -- the end of an axis, a pole; the heavens.
     cardo, -inis, m. -- the pivot and socket on which a door swings; the
         point about which something turns, a pole.
964 perennis, -e -- that lasts or continues the year through; everlast-
         ing.
966 bruma -- winter.
967 arbustum -- a place where trees are planted, an orchard (used by the
         poets as a synonym of *arbor* for the sake of the meter).
968 aestivus -- of or pertaining to summer. The constellation Leo (969)
         returns in July and brings hot summer days.
970 Cererem = the crops (which Ceres as the goddess of agriculture
         oversees).
     coquo, -ere -- to cook, roast, parch; (here) to cause to ripen.
971 tempero, 1 -- to regulate, moderate. Autumn is being described.
974 libro, 1 -- to balance.
975 securus -- free from care for + gen.
976 sollicitus -- disturbed, troubled, solicitous.
     prosum, prodesse -- to be of use to, to benefit.
979 regit sparsitque: the present tense indicates a continuing state of
             affairs; the perfect indicates the repetition of a certain
             number of definite actions.
     manu: with *caeca* (980).
980 foveo, -ere -- to warm; to foster, favor, support, assist.
981 sanctos: i.e., homines -- men pure of faults. Allusion to
             Hippolytus.
     dira libido: allusion to Phaedra.

The chorus sings its third song.

CHORUS   Ō magna parens, Nātūra, deum,   959 anapestic

tūque igniferī rector Olympī,   960

quī sparsa citō sīdera mundō   961

cursūsque vagos rapis astrōrum   962

celerīque polōs cardine versās,   963

cūr tanta tibi cūra perennēs   964

agitāre viās aetheris altī,   965

ut nunc cānae frīgora brūmae   966

nūdent silvās, nunc arbustīs   967

redeant umbrae, nunc aestīvī   968

colla leōnis   969

Cererem magnō fervōre coquant   970

vīrēsque suās temperet annus?   971

sed cūr īdem quī tanta regis,   972

sub quō vastī pondera mundī   973

lībrāta suōs dūcunt orbēs,   974

hominum nimium secūrus abes,   975

nōn sollicitus prodesse bonīs,   976

nocuisse malīs?   977

Rēs hūmanās ordine nullō   978

Fortūna regit sparsitque manū   979

mūnera caecā, peiōra fovens;   980

vincit sanctōs dīra libīdo,   981

982 fraus, fraudis, f. -- deceit, fraud, crime. Allusion to the nurse's
          deceitful strategem which has been carried out by Phaedra.
     sublimis, -e -- uplifted, high, lofty, eminent.
     aula -- a palace, royal court.
983 tradere turpi: sc., homini: "to hand over to a base man." Allusion
          to Theseus.
     fascis, -is, m. -- a bundle of wood; in pl. a bundle consisting of
          rods and an ax with which criminals were scourged and beheaded;
          a symbol of high political office; political power.
985 tristis -- (here) severe, harsh, austere. An "austere virtue" does
          not appeal to the populace and so does not receive its just
          reward.
     perversa...praemia recti: "perverse or warped rewards of upright-
          ness."
987 vitio potens: modifies *adulter*. vitium -- crime.

fraus sublīmī regnat in aulā.   982

tradere turpī fascēs populus   983

gaudet, eōsdem colit atque ōdit.   984

tristis virtūs perversa tulit   985

praemia rectī: castōs sequitur   986

mala paupertās vitiōque potens   987

regnat adulter: ō vāne pudor   988

falsumque decus!   989

989   citatus -- hurried, speedy.
990   rigo, 1 -- to wet, moisten, water.
      lugubris, -e -- of or belonging to mourning, mournful.
      genae -- cheeks, eyes.
991   acerbus -- harsh, bitter.
      famulatus, -us, m. -- servitude, slavery.
992   word order: cur me ad nuntium nefandi casus vocas?
993   clades, -is, f. -- destruction, misfortune, disaster.
994   imparatus -- unprepared, unprovided, unfurnished.
      aerumna -- trouble, toil, hardship, calamity.
995   luctificus -- causing sorrow or lamentation, doleful, woeful.
996   aggravo, 1 -- to add to the weight of, to make heavier; to oppress,
           burden.
      quassus -- shaken, battered, shattered.
997   occubo, 1 -- to lie in a place; to rest, repose (in the grave); to
           be dead.
998   obeo, -ire, -ii, -itum (*pf. infin.* obisse) -- to go to or towards;
           to fall, perish, die. "(As a) father I know long since (that
           my) son has died."
999   raptor: i.e., the man who has ravished my honor.
1000 profugus: Hippolytus fled voluntarily to avoid further pollution
           from Phaedra (see line 713 and following); he does not appear
           to know that his father has returned and that Phaedra has
           falsely accused him.
      infestus -- made unsafe, disturbed; that makes unsafe, that acts in
           a hostile manner, hostile. Hippolytus' pace as he departs from
           Athens expresses his anger and hostility against the city and
           Phaedra.
1001 passus, -us, m. -- a step, pace.
      explico, 1 -- to unfold, stretch out.
1002 sonipes, -pedis -- with sounding feet; a horse.
      ocius (comparative adv.) -- very quickly.
      subigo, -ere (sub + ago) -- to bring under, put under.
1003 Word order: ora domita frenis substrictis ligat.
      substringo, -ere, -nxi, -ctum -- to bind beneath, to bind, tie, draw
           up.
      ligo, 1 -- to tie, bind.

The chorus-leader observes the approach of a
messenger. Theseus emerges from the palace.

CHORUS- LEADER	Sed quid citātō nuntius portat gradū	989 iambic
	rigatque maestīs lūgubrem vultum genīs?	990
NUNTIUS	Ō sors acerba et dūra, famulātus gravis,	991
	cūr mē ad nefandī nuntium cāsūs vocās?	992
THESEUS	Nē metue clādēs fortiter fārī asperās:	993
	nōn imparātum pectus aerumnīs ferō.	994
NUNTIUS	Vōcem dolōrī lingua luctificam negat.	995
THESEUS	Prōloquere quae sors aggravet quassam domum.	996
NUNTIUS	Hippolytus, heu mē, flēbilī lētō occubat.	997
THESEUS	Gnātum parens obisse iam prīdem sciō:	998
	nunc raptor obiit. mortis effāre ordinem.	999
NUNTIUS	Ut profugus urbem līquit infestō gradū	1000
	celerem citātīs passibus cursum explicans,	1001
	celsō sonipedēs ōcius subigit iugō	1002
	et ōra frēnīs domita substrictīs ligat.	1003
	Tum multa sēcum effātus et patrium solum	1004

1005 abominor, 1 dep. -- to curse.
     cieo, -ere -- to call upon by name, to call upon for help.
         Hippolytus does not know that his father has cursed him.
1006 habenis...permissis: "with the reins let loose."
     lorum -- a thong; reins; a lash, whip.
1007 tono, -are, -ui -- to thunder.
1008 cresco, -ere, crevi -- to grow, increase.
     in astra = in caelum.
     salum -- the sea.
1009 strepo, -ere -- to make a noise, to murmur, roar.
1010 pelagus, -i, n. -- the sea.
     proprius -- one's own, its own.
1011 Auster: the South Wind.
     Sicula...freta: the strait separating Italy from Sicily.
1012 furenti: with *sinu*. sinus, -us, m. -- bay, gulf, sea.
1013 Corus -- the North-West Wind.
     fluctus, -us, m. -- flow, flood; wave, billow, surge.
1014 spuma -- foam, froth.
     Leucaten: with *summum*: "the top of Leucates." Leucates was a
         promontory on the island of Leucadia in the Ionian Sea. The
         promontory is now known as Capo Ducato.
1015 agger, -eris, m. -- a dam, dike, pier, rampart, wall (anything made
         by piling up masses of rubbish, stone, earth, etc.; here of a
         wall of waves).
1016 tumidus -- swollen). Translate with *monstro*.
     ruo, -ere -- to rush.
1017 construo, -ere -- to heap up, pile up; to construct, make.
     lues, -is, f. -- a plague, pestilence.
1018 minor, 1 dep. -- to threaten.
1019 onerato sinu: "in its burdened bosom." sinus, -us, m. -- (here)
         bosom, lap.
1020 quae: with *tellus*.
1021 Cyclas...nova: i.e., a new Cycladic island. The Cyclades are a
         group of islands in the Aegean Sea.
1022 lateo, -ere, latui -- to be hidden or concealed. latuere =
         latuerunt.
     rupes: with *nobiles* "famous for" + abl. numine Epidauri dei:
         Asclepius, the god of medicine, who had a sanctuary at
         Epidaurus. rupes, -is, f. -- rock, cliff.
1023 petrae...Scironides: famous for the crimes of Sciron, a thief who
         forced his victims to wash his feet and then kicked them over
         the cliff and into the sea. He was slain by Theseus.
1024 et quae...terra = et terra quae...
     comprimo, -ere -- to press or squeeze together, to compress. The
         Isthmus of Corinth is meant.
     fretum -- sea.
1025 stupeo, -ere -- to be struck senseless, to be stunned, benumbed,
         amazed.
     queror, 3 dep. -- to complain, lament, bewail.
1026 immugio, 4 -- to bellow, roar, resound in or at.
     scopulus -- a rock, crag, cliff.
     adstrepo, -ere -- to make a noise at.

abōminātus saepe genitōrem ciet   1005

ācerque habēnīs lōra permissīs quatit: 1006

cum subito vastum tonuit ex altō mare   1007

crēvitque in astra. nullus inspīrat salō   1008

ventus, quiētī nulla pars caelī strepit   1009

placidumque pelagus propria tempestās agit.   1010

nōn tantus Auster Sicula disturbat freta   1011

nec tam furentī pontus exsurgit sinū   1012

regnante Cōrō, saxa cum fluctū tremunt   1013

et cāna summum spūma Leucātēn ferit.   1014

consurgit ingens pontus in vastum aggerem,   1015

tumidumque monstrō pelagus in terrās ruit.   1016

nec ista ratibus tanta construitur luēs: 1017

terrīs minātur; fluctus haud cursū levī   1018

prōvolvitur: nescio quid onerātō sinū   1019

gravis unda portat. quae novum tellūs caput   1020

ostendit astrīs? Cyclas exoritur nova?   1021

latuēre rūpes nūmine Epidaurī deī   1022

et scelere petrae nōbilēs Scīronidēs   1023

et quae duōbus terra comprimitur fretīs.   1024

Haec dum stupentēs querimur, ēn tōtum mare   1025

immūgit, omnēs undique scopulī adstrepunt;   1026

1027   cacumen, -inis, n. -- the top point of anything; (here) the top of
       the wave.
       roro, 1 -- to let fall, drop, trickle, distill; (here) to throw off
       spray.
       sal, salis, m. -- salt; salt water, brine.
1028   spumo, 1 -- to foam, froth.
       vicibus alternis: "in an alternating rhythm." vicis (gen. of a
       noun with no nom.), f. -- change, interchange, alternation.
1030   refundo, -ere -- to pour back.
       physeter, -eris, m. (Greek word) -- a blow-pipe; a whale.
1031   globus -- a ball, sphere, globe.
1034   quasso, 1 -- to shake violently. The messenger is terrified even
       now as he tells the story.
1035   quis = qualis.
       habitus, -us, m. -- condition, appearance.
1036   caeruleus -- dark blue.
1037   erigo, -ere, -rexi, -rectum -- to raise up.
       viridans, -antis -- green.
       iuba -- the mane of an animal.
1038   hispidus -- rough, shaggy, hairy, bristly.
       orbis, -is, m. -- circle; eye.
1039   quem (colorem).
       feri dominator...gregis: i.e., a bull.
1040   sub undis natus: i.e., some marine creature.
       hinc...hinc. I.e., the beast's eyes are alternately fiery like a
       bull's and bluish like those of a sea-monster.
1041   caerula insignes nota: "wondrous with a blue mark" (or "gleam").
1042   opimus -- fat, rich, plump, corpulent.
       arduus -- high, elevated, lofty, steep.
       torus -- (here) muscle, brawn. arduos...toros: "bulging muscles."
1043   hiulcus -- gaping, split, open.
       haustus, -us, m. -- a drawing (of water), a drinking, swallowing,
       drawing in; here of the beast's drawing in of air; his respira-
       tion, breathing.
       patulus -- standing open, open.
1044   muscus -- moss.
       tenax, -acis -- that clings or holds fast, tenacious.
       palear, -aris, n. -- the skin that hangs down from the neck of an
       ox; the dew-lap.
       vireo, -ere -- to be green.
1045   fucus -- rock-lichen (used to make a red dye), red color.
1046   pone (prep. + acc.) -- behind.
       tergus, -oris, n. -- back.
       in monstrum: i.e., it comes together (*coit*) so as to make a
       creature that is monstrous or contrary to nature. The subject
       of *coit* is *ultima...facies*.
1047   facies, -ei, f. -- form, figure, shape. With *ultima* (1046): "the
       farthest or last part of his shape."
       belua -- a beast, monster.
1048   squamosus -- covered with scales, scaly.
1049   pistrix, -icis, f. -- a sea-monster; whale, shark, sawfish.
       sorbeo, -ere -- to suck in, swallow.

summum cacumen rorat expulso sale,   1027

spumat vomitque vicibus alternis aquas   1028

qualis per alta vehitur Oceani freta   1029

fluctum refundens ore physeter capax.   1030

inhorruit concussus undarum globus   1031

solvitque sese et litori invexit malum   1032

maius timore, pontus in terras ruit   1033

suumque monstrum sequitur -- os quassat tremor. 1034

Quis habitus ille corporis vasti fuit!   1035

caerulea taurus colla sublimis gerens   1036

erexit altam fronte viridanti iubam;   1037

stant hispidae aures, orbibus varius color,   1038

et quem feri dominator habuisset gregis   1039

et quem sub undis natus: hinc flammam vomunt 1040

oculi, hinc relucent caerula insignes nota;   1041

opima cervix arduos tollit toros   1042

naresque hiulcis haustibus patulae fremunt;   1043

musco tenaci pectus ac palear viret,   1044

longum rubente spargitur fuco latus;   1045

tum pone tergus ultima in monstrum coit   1046

facies et ingens belua immensam trahit   1047

squamosa partem. talis extremo mari   1048

pistrix citatas sorbet aut frangit rates.   1049

1050   attonitus -- thunderstruck, terrified, amazed.
1051   passim -- in every direction, everywhere.
1052   saltus, -us, m. -- a forest-pasture.
1053   exsanguis, -e -- without blood.
1054   immunis, -e -- free from, without + abl.
1055   artus -- close, short, tight
1056   hortatus, -us, m. -- encouragement.
       cieo, -ere -- to call upon by name.
1057   collibus ruptis: i.e., through an opening in the hills.
1058   "touching upon the stretches (of land) that border on the sea
          below."
       suppositus -- placed, lying beneath.
1059   moles, -is, f. -- a huge shapeless mass or bulk; (here) the monster.
       acuo, -ere, -ui, -utum -- to make sharp or pointed; to whet.
1060   praetempto, 1 -- to feel, search out, or test beforehand.
1061   proludo, -ere, -si, -sum -- to play or practice for something (+
          dat.) beforehand.
       praepes, -etis -- swift, nimble, quick.
1062   summam...humum: "the surface of the ground."
1063   torva: supply *moles* (1059). torvus -- wild, fierce, savage.
       currus, -us, m. -- chariot; team of horses driving a chariot.
1064   contra (adv.) --opposite.
       feroci: with *vultu* (1065).
1065   intono, 1 -- to thunder; to cry out vehemently, to thunder forth.
1067   Word order: nam mihi paternus labor est vincere tauros: "for it
          was my father's task to conquer bulls." For example, the
          Minotaur (half-bull, half-man) and the bull of Marathon that
          Hercules had previously brought from Crete.
1068   inobsequens, -entis -- not yielding or complying, disobedient. With
          frenis.
       protinus (adv.) -- immediately.
1069   rapuere = rapuerunt.
       derro = deerro, 1 -- to wander away, stray.
1070   quacumque -- wherever.
1071   pergo, -ere -- to go on, continue, proceed.
       se...agunt: instead of the charioteer driving the horses, the
          horses drive themselves.
       scopulus -- a rock, cliff, crag.
1072   rector, -oris, m. -- a guider, leader, director; a helmsman.
1073   retento, 1 -- to hold back firmly, to hold fast.
       ne det obliquum latus: "lest (the ship) give its side slantways"
          (to the waves).

Tremuēre terrae, fūgit attonitum pecus   1050

passim per agrōs, nec suōs pastor sequī   1051

meminit iuvencōs; omnis ē saltū fera   1052

diffūgit, omnis frīgidō exsanguis metū   1053

vēnātor horret. sōlus immūnis metū   1054

Hippolytus artīs continet frēnīs equōs   1055

pavidōsque nōtae vōcis hortātū ciet.   1056

Est alta ad agrōs collibus ruptīs via,   1057

vīcīna tangens spatia suppositī maris;   1058

hīc sē illa mōlēs acuit atque īrās parat.   1059

ut cēpit animōs sēque praetemptans satis   1060

prōlūsit īrae, praepetī cursū ēvolat,   1061

summam citātō vix gradū tangens humum,   1062

et torva currūs ante trepidantēs stetit.   1063

contrā ferōcī gnātus insurgens minax   1064

vultū nec ōra mūtat et magnum intonat: 1065

'haud frangit animum vānus hic terror meum: 1066

nam mihi paternus vincere est taurōs labor.   1067

inobsequentēs prōtinus frēnīs equī   1068

rapuēre currum iamque dērrantēs viā,   1069

quācumque rabidōs pavidus ēvexit furor,   1070

hāc īre pergunt sēque per scopulōs agunt.   1071

At ille, quālis turbidō rector marī   1072

ratem retentat, nē det oblīquum latus,   1073

1074 fallo, -ere -- to deceive, trick, cheat, disappoint. The subject is
         the helmsman (*rector*).
1075 gubernat: the subject is Hippolytus.
      ora: the mouths of the horses.
1076 constringo, -ere, -strinxi, -strictum -- to draw together, tie up;
         to fetter, restrain, hold in check.
      tortus -- twisted.
      frequens, -entis -- (translate as adv.) -- frequently, repeatedly.
1077 verber, -eris, n. -- a lash, whip.
      coerceo, -ere -- to control, restrain.
      sequitur: subject is the bull, referred to as *adsiduus comes*.
      adsiduus -- constantly present, continual.
1078 carpo, -ere -- to pluck, snatch; to go, pass along, take one's way.
         aequa carpens spatia: i.e., keeping pace with the chariot.
      contra (adv.) -- on the contrary, on the other hand.
      obvius -- in the way, in front of.
1079 oberro, 1 -- to wander, hover in front.
1080 ultra (adv.) -- beyond, farther, more.
      toto...ore: with full face, full front, directly.
1081 corniger ponti: "the horned (monster) from the sea."
1082 sonipes, -pedis -- with sounding feet; a horse.
      excitus -- excited, frightened, terrified.
1083 luctor, 1 dep. -- to wrestle, struggle, strive.
1084 eripere: word order: luctantur se iugo eripere.
      onus, -eris, n. -- a load, burden. I.e., the chariot.
1085 fundo, -ere, fudi, fusum -- to pour out, to hurl forth.
      implico, 1 (*or* -ui, -itum) -- to enfold, entangle, entwine. The
         subject is Hippolytus.
1086 laqueus -- a noose, snare (consisting of the tangled reins).
1087 sequax, -acis -- following, pursuing; clinging.
      ligo, -are -- to tie, bind.
1088 sensere = senserunt.
      pecus, -udis, f. -- a beast, an animal; a horse.
      facinus, -oris, n. -- a deed, act, action; a bad deed, crime.
1090 suum...onus: their usual burden.
1091 indignor, 1 dep. -- to be angry or displeased at, to be indignant.
         "Indignant over the fact that the day had been entrusted to a
         false sun." The false sun is Phaethon, the son of Phoebus, who
         tried to drive his father's chariot through the sky. He was
         thrown from the chariot and fell to his death.
1092 devio...polo: "in an out of the way (part of the) heavens."
         Phaethon was not able to guide the chariot properly, and it
         wandered off course.
      devius -- lying off the high-road; out of the way.
1093 cruento, 1 -- to make bloody. The subject is Hippolytus.
      inlido, -ere, -si, -sum -- to strike or dash against.
1094 resulto, 1 -- to spring or leap back, to rebound.
      dumus -- a thorn-bush, bramble.
1095 populor, 1 dep. -- to lay waste, to ravage, devastate, spoil,
         plunder.

et arte fluctum fallit, haud aliter citōs   1074

currūs gubernat: ōra nunc pressīs trahit   1075

constricta frēnīs, terga nunc tortō frequens   1076

verbere coercet, sequitur adsiduus comes,   1077

nunc aequa carpens spatia, nunc contrā obvius   1078

oberrat, omnī parte terrōrem movens.   1079

nōn licuit ultrā fugere; nam tōtō obvius   1080

incurrit ōre corniger pontī horridus.   1081

Tum vērō pavidā sonipedēs mente excitī   1082

imperia solvunt sēque luctantur iugō   1083

ēripere rectīque in pedēs iactant onus.   1084

praeceps in ōra fūsus implicuit cadens   1085

laqueō tenācī corpus et quantō magis   1086

pugnat, sequācēs hōc magis nōdōs ligat.   1087

sensēre pecudēs facinus -- et currū levī,   1088

dominante nullō, quā timor iussit ruunt.   1089

Tālis per aurās nōn suum agnoscens onus   1090

Sōlīque falsō crēditum indignans diem   1091

Phaethonta currus dēviō excussit polō.   1092

Lātē cruentat arva et inlīsum caput   1093

scopulīs resultat; auferunt dūmī comās,   1094

et ōra dūrus pulcra populātur lapis   1095

peritque multō vulnere infēlix decor.   1096

1097   moribundus -- dying.
       pervolvo, 3 -- to roll or tumble about.
1098   truncus -- a trunk of a tree.
       ambustus -- burned.
       sudis, -is, f. -- a stake.   ambusta sude: abl. of description with
            truncus.
1099   inguen, -inis, n. -- the groin.
       stipes, -itis, m. -- the trunk of a tree.
1100   domino...affixo: i.e., while Hippolytus was caught on the burned
            stump of the tree trunk.   affigo, -ere, -ixi, -ixum -- to fix,
            fasten on.
1101   haesere = haeserunt.   haereo, -ere, -si, haesum -- to hang or hold
            fast, to hang, stick, cling, be fixed.
       biiugis, -e -- yoked two-together.   Supply *equi*.
       vulnere: abl. of cause; referring to Hippolytus stuck on the tree
            trunk.
       pariter -- at the same time.
1102   semanimem: sc., Hippolytum.   semanimis = semianimis, -e -- half-
            alive, half-dead.
1103   virgultum -- a bush, thicket, copse.
       vepres, -is, m. -- a thorn-bush, bramble-bush.
       rubus -- a bramble-bush, blackberry bush.   "Bushes rough with sharp
            brambles."
1104   omnis truncus: i.e., every tree-trunk in the field.
       tulit = abstulit.
1105   famuli: subject; *funebris...manus* ("a funereal band") is in apposi-
            tion to it.   famulus -- servant, attendant.
1106   Word order: per illa loca quae Hippolytus signat cruenta nota:
            "through those places which Hippolytus marked with spots of
            blood."
       distractus -- torn apart.
1107   longum...tramitem: accusative of extent: "throughout the long
            path" (over which he was dragged).   trames, -itis, m. -- a
            by-path, a foot-path; a path, road, course.
1108   vestigo, 1 -- to track, trace out, search after.
1109   doleo, -ere -- to feel pain; to grieve, lament.   Supply *famulorum*.
       sedulus -- busy, diligent, industrious.
1110b hocine = hoc + ne.   "Is this the glory of his beauty?"   "Has his
            beauty come to this?"
1111   paterni...imperii comes: "companion in his father's power or rule."
1112   heres, -edis, m. or f. -- an heir.
       siderum...modo: "in the manner of the stars."
1113   passim (adv.) -- everywhere.
       rogus -- a funeral pyre.
1115   quanto...vinclo: "with what a mighty bond."

moribunda celerēs membra pervolvunt rotae: 1097

tandemque raptum truncus ambustā sude   1098

medium per inguen stipite ērectō tenet,   1099

paulumque dominō currus affixō stetit.   1100

haesēre biiugēs vulnere -- et pariter moram   1101

dominumque rumpunt. inde sēmanimem secant   1102

virgulta, acūtīs asperī veprēs rubīs   1103

omnisque truncus corporis partem tulit.   1104

Errant per agrōs fūnebris famulī manus,   1105

per illa quae distractus Hippolytus loca   1106

longum cruentā trāmitem signat notā,   1107

maestaeque dominī membra vestīgant canēs.   1108

necdum dolentum sēdulus potuit labor   1109

explēre corpus.   1110a

*Hippolytus' companions begin to return to the
palace, each bringing a piece of his body.*

                    Hocine est formae decus?   1110b

quī modo paternī clārus imperiī comes   1111

et certus hērēs sīderum fulsit modō,   1112

passim ad suprēmōs ille colligitur rogōs   1113

et fūnerī confertur.   1114a

THESEUS   Ō nimium potens,   1114b

quantō parentēs sanguinis vinclō tenēs,   1115

nātūra, quam tē colimus invītī quoque: 1116

1117 noxius -- guilty.
      amissus -- lost.
1118 haud -- not at all. Word order: Haud quisque potest honeste flere
          quod voluit: "No one can honestly weep over what he (himself)
          wished for."
1119 cumulus -- a heap, pile; a heap added to a full measure, a surplus,
          addition; a summit, point, crown.
1120 Word order: si casus abominanda optanda efficit: "...makes abomin-
          able things (into) things to be desired."
1121 servo, 1 -- to keep, preserve.
      madeo, -ere -- to be wet or moist, to drip.
1122 interimo, -ere, -emi, -emptum -- to take away; to destroy, slay,
          kill. Word order: fleo non quod (eum) interemi, sed quod
          (eum) amisi.

occidere voluī noxium, āmissum fleō.   1117

NUNTIUS   Haud flēre honestē quisque quod voluit potest. 1118

THESEUS   Equidem malōrum maximum hunc cumulum reor,   1119

sī abōminanda cāsus optanda efficit.   1120

NUNTIUS   Et sī odia servās, cūr madent flētū genae?   1121

THESEUS   Quod interemī nōn, quod amīsī fleō.   1122

Theseus remains on stage as Hippolytus'
companions continue to bring parts of
his body.

1124   minor: translate as if *minus* (adverbial).
       parvis: neuter pl.
1125   levis, -e -- light; slight, trifling, small. levius: comparative
          adv.
       ferio, -ire -- to strike, smite.
1126   placidos: i.e., quiet, peaceful, unambitious people.
1127   praebeo, -ere -- to hold forth, give, grant, cause, make.
       casa -- a simple, humble hut or cottage (as opposed to a palace).
       securus -- free from care, untroubled, serene.
1128   admota aetheriis...sedibus: "moved close to the regions of the
          sky."
       culmen, -inis, n. = columen, -inis, n. -- a roof or gable of a
          building.
1129   Eurus -- the South-East Wind.
       Notus -- the South Wind.
1130   Boreas, -ae, m. -- the North Wind.
1131   Corus -- the North-West Wind.
1136   Cybele, -es, f. -- Cybele, the great-mother goddess, who lived in a
          forest on Mount Ida in Phrygia.
       metuens caelo: "fearful for (the safety of his dwelling place in)
          the sky."
1137   alto: with *caelo*.
       vicina: i.e., things such as mountains and skyscrapers which reach
          too *close* to the heavens.
       petit: i.e., with his thunderbolts.
1138   magnos motus: i.e., agitation, destruction, disaster.
1139   tectum -- roof; house. Modified by *humilis*.
       plebeius -- plebean; of or belonging to the common people.
1141   ambiguis...alis: i.e., wings that are now of good, now of bad omen;
          the flight of time (*mobilis hora*) is assimilated to the flight
          of birds of omen.
1143   hic qui clari: hic = Theseus. The relative pronoun *qui* lacks a
          verb, and it is assumed that a line has been lost from the text
          (the *lacuna* is marked by asterisks). We could supply something
          like *laetus videt* or *iterum videt*, and the references would be
          to Theseus' return from the underworld (*morte relicta* 1145).

The chorus sings its fourth song.

CHORUS   Quantī cāsūs hūmāna rotant!   1123 anapestic

Minor in parvīs Fortūna furit   1124

leviusque ferit leviōra deus;   1125

servat placidōs obscūra quiēs   1126

praebetque senēs casa sēcūrōs.   1127

admōta aetheriīs culmina sēdibus   1128 asclepiadean

Eurōs excipiunt, excipiunt Notōs,   1129

insānī Boreae minās   1130 glyconic

imbriferumque Corum.   1131 aristophanean

rārōs patitur fulminis ictūs   1132 anapestic

ūmida vallis: 1133

tremuit tēlō Iovis altisonī   1134

Caucasus ingens Phrygiumque nemus   1135

mātris Cybelēs: metuens caelō   1136

Iuppiter altō vīcīna petit;   1137

nōn capit umquam magnōs mōtūs   1138

humilis tectī plēbēia domus.   1139

circā regna tonat.   1140 pherecratean

Volat ambiguīs mōbilis ālīs   1141 anapestic

hōra, nec ullī praestat vēlox   1142

Fortūna fidem. hic quī clārī   1143

*   *   *

1145 lugeo, -ere -- to mourn, lament, bewail.
1146 tristis: in apposition to the subject of the sentence, Theseus.
1147 flebilis, -e -- to be wept over.
      Avernus -- without birds; a lake over which birds could not fly
            because of deadly exhalations that it gave off (the lake was
            thought of as near the entrance to the underworld); the under-
            world itself, Hades.
1148 hospitium: the hospitality of his ancestral home (*sedis patriae*).
      Modified by *magis flebile*.
1149 Pallas: i.e., Pallas Athena (in Latin: Minerva), the patron
            goddess of the Athenian people (*Actaeae...genti*).
1150 tuus...Theseus: as an Athenian hero, Theseus was protected by
            Athena (Minerva), thus *tuus*.
1151 palus, -udis, f. -- a swamp, marsh.
1152 casta: Athena (Minerva) was a virgin goddess.
      patruo rapaci: her "rapacious uncle" is Pluto, who snatches men at
            their death from this world.
1153 constat: "it remains fixed, undiminished." I.e., Hippolytus has
            taken Theseus' place in the underworld, so Pluto cannot com-
            plain, and Athena owes him nothing.
      numerus: sc., *mortuorum*.

sīdera mundī nitidumque diem   1144

morte relictā, lūget maestōs   1145

tristis reditūs ipsōque magis   1146

flēbile Avernō sēdis patriae   1147

videt hospitium.   1148

Pallas Actaeae veneranda gentī,   1149 sapphic

quod tuus caelum superōsque Thēseus   1150

spectat et fūgit Stygiās palūdēs,   1151

casta nīl dēbēs patruō rapācī: 1152

constat infernō numerus tyrannō.   1153

1155 stringo, -ere, -inxi, -ictum -- to draw tight, bind or press
      together; (of swords) to draw out from the scabbard.
      vecors, -cordis -- destitute of reason, senseless, mad, insane.
1156 percitus -- greatly moved, roused, stimulated, excited.
      instigo, 1 -- to urge, stir up, set on, incite.
1157 vociferatio, -onis, f. -- a loud wailing, clamor, outcry.
1158 planctus, -us, m. -- a beating of the breast, arms, and face in
      mourning; wailing, lamentation, lament.
      invisus -- hated.
1160 invado, -ere -- to enter in hostile fashion, assault, attack.
1161 quidquid: i.e., quidquid monstrorum: "whatever of monsters,"
      "whatever monster."
      Tethys...extrema -- Tethys was wife of Oceanus. The reference may
      be to the western Mediterranean Sea.
1162 gesto, 1 -- to bear, carry.
      vagis...undis: i.e., with his waves that wander around the whole
      circumference of the world. vagus -- wandering.
1163 complector, complecti, complexus -- to entwine around; to clasp,
      embrace. The perfect passive participle of deponent verbs is
      active in meaning and often has a present sense.
1164 ad tuos: i.e., to your family.
1165 tuto = tute (adv.) -- safely, in safety, without danger.
      gnatus: i.e., Hippolytus.
      genitor: i.e., Aegeus, who threw himself from a cliff when Theseus
      was approaching in his ship on his return from Crete. Theseus
      was supposed to have hoisted white sails symbolizing victory
      over the Minotaur instead of the black sails that the ship
      sailed with. He forgot, however, and his father, thinking him
      dead, threw himself into the sea in grief.
1166 luere = luerunt. luo, -ere, -ui -- to lose; to pay a debt; to
      atone for, expiate. reditus...luerunt: "they paid for your
      return with their lives" (*nece*). nex, necis, f. -- death.
      perverto, -ere -- to turn round; to overturn, overthrow, destroy,
      ruin.
1167 amore...coniugum aut odio: out of love for Phaedra Theseus cursed
      Hippolytus; he slew Antiope out of hatred.

*Phaedra, who has heard the news of Hippolytus'
death, wails within the palace. The doors
suddenly open and she appears with Hippolytus'
sword still in her hand.*

CHORUS-   Quae vox ab altīs flēbilis tectīs sonat   1154 iambic
LEADER
            strictōque vēcors Phaedra quid ferrō parat?   1155

THESEUS   *To Phaedra, lamenting over the body of Hippolytus*

            Quis tē dolōre percitam instīgat furor?   1156

            quid ensis iste quidve vōciferātiō   1157

            planctūsque suprā corpus invīsum volunt?   1158

PHAEDRA   *ignoring Theseus, and addressing Neptune*

            Mē mē, profundī saeve dominātor fretī,   1159

            invādē et in mē monstra caeruleī maris   1160

            ēmitte, quidquid intimō Tēthys sinū   1161

            extrēma gestat, quidquid Ōceanus vagīs   1162

            complexus undīs ultimō fluctū tegit.   1163

            to Theseus

            Ō dūre Thēseu semper, ō numquam ad tuōs   1164

            tutō reverse: gnātus et genitor nece   1165

            reditūs tuōs luēre; pervertis domum   1166

            amōre semper coniugum aut odiō nocens.   1167

            to Hippolytus

            Hippolyte, tālēs intuor vultūs tuōs   1168

1169 Sinis: also known as Pityocamptes (Pinebender), because he tied his
        victims' limbs to bent pine trees, which when released either
        tore his victims apart or hurled them high into the air.
        Theseus slew this brigand.
1170 Procrustes (Stretcher) invited travellers to spend the night with
        him, and if they did not fit his bed, he either stretched them
        out until they did or lopped off their limbs if they were too
        long. Theseus gave him a taste of his own medicine.
        Cresius -- Cretan. With *taurus biformis* (1172).
1171 Daedalea...claustra: the Labyrinth, built by Daedalus. claustra,
        -orum, n. pl. -- a lock, bar; a door; a place that is shut up.
        mugitus, -us, m. -- a lowing, bellowing.
1173 divello, -ere, -vulsi, -vulsum -- to rend asunder, tear to pieces.
1174 nostrum sidus: i.e., the star that determined my destiny; in appo-
        sition to *oculi*.
1175 ades: imperative of *adsum*.
        parumper (adv.) -- for a short time, for a moment.
1176 poenas tibi solvam: "I will pay the penalty (which I owe) to you."
        insero, -ere -- to plant in; to implant.
1178 pariter -- at the same time.
        exuo, -ere -- to draw out or off, to pull or strip off, to divest
        one's self of something (abl.).
1179 Tartareus -- of or belonging to Tartarus (= Hades).
1181a placo, 1 -- to reconcile, appease, soothe, pacify.
1181b exuviae, -arum, f. pl. -- that which is stripped off, spoils; here
        of a lock of hair torn from the head.
1182 lacer, -era, -erum -- mangled, lacerated, torn to pieces.
        abscido, -ere, -cidi, -cisum -- to cut off.
1184a iunxisse = iungere. The perfect infinitive is used *metri causa*.
1184b morere: imperative of *morior*.
1185 incesta: opposite of *casta*.
1186 impiatos: made impious by her crime (*facinore*) of lust for
        Hippolytus.
        derat = de-erat; "was lacking."
1187 vindico, 1 -- to lay claim to as one's own.
        sancta: i.e., considered as, or thought by Theseus to be "pure."
        fruor, 3 dep. (fruereris: imperfect subjunctive) -- to enjoy
        + abl. I.e., the last thing Phaedra could bring herself to do
        is to return to and enjoy sleeping with Theseus (a right which
        she could claim as hers), with him thinking her to be pure
        (*sancta*) while she would be conscience-ridden over her guilt.
1188 sedamen, -inis, n. -- a means of allaying, an allayment, sedative,
        remedy, cure.
1190 pando, -ere -- to open.

talēsque fēcī? membra quis saevus Sinis   1169

aut quis Procrustēs sparsit aut quis Crēsius,   1170

Daedalea vastō claustra mūgitū replens,   1171

taurus biformis ōre cornigerō ferox   1172

dīvulsit? heu mē, quō tuus fūgit decor   1173

oculīque nostrum sīdus? exanimis iacēs?   1174

ades parumper, verbaque exaudī mea.   1175

nīl turpe loquimur; hāc manū poenās tibi   1176

solvam et nefandō pectorī ferrum inseram,   1177

animāque Phaedram pariter ac scelere exuam,   1178

et tē per undās perque Tartareōs lacūs,   1179

per Styga, per amnēs igneōs amens sequar.   1180

placēmus umbrās.   1181a

cutting off a lock of her hair and placing
it on Hippolytus' remains.

                    capitis exuviās cape   1181b

laceraeque frontis accipe abscīsam comam.   1182

nōn licuit animōs iungere, at certē licet   1183

iunxisse fāta.   1184a

                    Morere, sī casta es, virō;   1184b

sī incesta, amōrī. coniugis thalamōs petam   1185

tantō impiātōs facinore? hoc dērat nefās,   1186

ut vindicātō sancta fruerēris torō.   1187

ō mors amōris ūna sēdamen malī,   1188

ō mors pudōris maximum laesī decus,   1189

confugimus ad tē: pande plācatōs sinūs.   1190

1191 funestus -- causing death, destruction, or calamity.
1192 memoro, 1 -- to bring to remembrance, to remind of; to mention,
         recount, relate, say, tell.
1193 haurio, -ire, hausi, haustum -- to draw up or out; to draw water.
         quod...pectore...hauseram: "which I drew forth from my
         heart."
1194 mentior, 4 dep. -- to lie. mentita = "lying."
      vana: "fictitious deeds."
1195 iacet: "lies" (dead).
1196a insons, -ntis -- guiltless, innocent.
1196b recipe iam mores tuos: "Receive back your (reputation for a) good
         character." I.e., Hippolytus is now vindicated, his honor
         restored.
1197 mucro, -onis, m. -- the point of a sword.
      pateo, -ere -- to lie open, to lie exposed to.
1198 inferiae, -arum, f. pl. -- sacrifices in honor of the dead.
         cruor...solvit inferias viro: "(my) blood pays its sacrifice
         to (this) man."
1200 condere: passive imperative with middle or reflexive sense: "hide
         yourself."
      Acheron, -ntis, m. -- a river in the underworld.
      plaga -- region.
1201 fauces, -ium, f. pl. -- the throat; an entrance, mouth.
      Averni: see on line 1147.
      Taenarei specus: the cave of Taenarus (a promontory in the south-
         eastern Peloponnesus) was thought to be one entrance to the
         underworld.
1202 word order: unda Lethes (quae est) grata miseris. Lethe, -es,
         f. -- the stream of forgetfulness in the underworld; all the
         dead drink from it, and the wretched thus forget their woes.
      torpeo, -ere -- to be stiff, numb, motionless, sluggish.
1203 impium: i.e., *me*.
1205 Proteus -- a sea god (able to change his form).
      abscondo, -ere -- to hide, conceal.

addressing the city and Theseus

Audīte, Athēnae, tūque, fūnestā pater	1191
pēior novercā: falsa memorāvī et nefās,	1192
quod ipsa dēmens pectore īnsānō hauseram,	1193
mentīta finxī, vāna pūnistī pater,	1194
iuvenisque castus crīmine incestō iacet,	1195
pudīcus, insons.	1196a

to Hippolytus

recipe iam mōrēs tuōs.	1196b
mucrōne pectus impium iustō patet	1197
cruorque sānctō solvit inferiās virō.	1198

*Phaedra plunges the sword into her breast and
falls, dying, on the remains of Hippolytus'
body.*

THESEUS Quid facere raptō dēbeās gnātō parens 1199

disce ā novercā: condere Acherontis plagīs. 1200

singing a lament

Pallidī faucēs Avernī, vōsque, Taenareī specus,	1201 trochaic
unda miserīs grāta Lēthēs, vōsque, torpentēs lacūs,	1202
impium rapite atque mersum premite perpetuīs malīs.	1203

Nunc adeste, saeva pontī monstra, nunc vastum mare,	1204
ultimō quodcumque Proteus aequorum abscondit sinū,	1205

1206 ovo, 1 -- to exult, rejoice.
      gurges, -itis, m. -- a raging abyss, whirlpool, gulf; waters,
            stream, sea.
1207 assensor, -oris, m. -- one who assents to or agrees with. I.e.,
            Neptune granted Theseus' prayer or curse too readily
            (*facilis*).
1208 nova...nece: "a (form of) death or punishment that is new" (in that
            it has never before been inflicted upon man).
1209 segrex, -egis -- apart, separate; far from the crowd; (here) far
            from oneself, i.e., torn to pieces that are scattered all
            about.
1210 vindex, -icis -- avenger, punisher.
      incido, -ere, incidi -- to fall into.
1211 Theseus has contaminated the whole world with his crimes.
      sidera: i.e., Ariadne, abandoned by Theseus and transformed by
            Bacchus into a constellation, attests to Theseus' crime in
            having abandoned her in the first place.
      manes: i.e., Theseus helped Pirithous in his attempt to carry off
            Proserpina.
      undas: i.e., Theseus brought about the death of his father Aegeus
            and made Neptune an accomplice in the killing of Hippolytus.
1212 amplius (adv.) -- further.
      sors nulla: "no lot." The reference is to the allotment of the
            three kingdoms of the sky, sea, and underworld to Jupiter,
            Neptune, and Pluto respectively. Theseus has filled each
            kingdom with his crimes, and so has no place left to flee.
      norunt = noverunt. nosco, -ere, novi, notum -- to come to know;
            (in pf. with present sense) to know.
1213 pateo, -ere, -ui -- to stand or lie open.
      ad caelum: i.e., the road back from Hades to this world with its
            sky above.
1215 caelebs, -libis -- unmarried.
      orbus -- bereaved, widowed.
      funebres: with *rogos* (1216).
1216 concremo, 1 -- to burn up. Here of kindling the funeral pyres with
            the torch (*fax*).
      proles, -is, f. -- offspring, child, son.
      thalamus -- bedroom; marriage-bed; marriage; wife.
1217 donator atrae lucis: "giver of light (that turned out to be) black
            (darkness)."
      Alcides, voc. Alcide: i.e., Hercules, who helped Theseus return
            from the underworld.
1218 Dis, -itis, m. -- the god of the underworld, Pluto.
      munus: Hercules' "gift" was Theseus himself.
1219a restituo, -ere -- to replace, restore, to give back, return.
1220 crudus -- cruel.
1221 exitium -- a going out; ruin, destruction. The reference is to
            Theseus' curse and destruction of Hippolytus and to his de-
            struction of brigands such as Sinis and Sciron.
      machinor, 1 dep. -- to contrive, devise, invent. The participle is
            active in sense.
      efferus -- very wild, savage.

mēque ovantem scelere tantō rapite in altōs gurgitēs   1206

tūque, semper, genitor, īrae facilis assensor meae.   1207

Morte facilī dignus haud sum quī novā natum nece   1208

sēgregem sparsī per agrōs quīque, dum falsum nefās   1209

exsequor vindex sevērus, incidī in vērum scelus.   1210

Sīdera et mānēs et undās scelere complēvī meō: 1211

amplius sors nulla restat; regna mē nōrunt tria.   1212

In hoc redīmus? patuit ad caelum via,   1213 iambic

bīna ut vidērem funera et geminam necem,   1214

caelebs et orbus fūnebrēs ūnā face   1215

ut concremārem prōlis ac thalamī rogōs?   1216

Dōnātor ātrae lūcis, Alcīdē, tuum   1217

Dītī remitte mūnus; ēreptōs mihi   1218

restitue mānēs.   1219a

                    Impius frustrā invocō   1219b

mortem relictam -- crūdus et lētī artifex,   1220

exitia machinātus insolita effera,   1221

1222 tibimet: *-met* is added for emphasis.
      supplicium -- punishment.
      irrogo, 1 -- to propose anything against one; to impose, appoint,
            ordain, inflict.
1223 pinus: cf. note to line 1169 *Sinis*.
1224 caelo remissum: "sent back to the sky."
      findo, -ere -- to split. Supply *me*.
      trabs, trabis, f. -- a timber, beam. in geminas trabes: a diffi-
            cult expression, but the idea seems to be that Theseus would be
            tied to two neighboring trees (*geminae trabes*). One of them
            would be bent to the ground (1223) and when released would
            split his body in two.
1225 saxa...Scironia. See above, line 1023.
1226 graviora: i.e., *supplicia* "punishments."
      Word order: graviora vidi, quae Phlegethon igneo vado cingens
            clausos nocentes pati iubet.
1227 Phlegethon: the fiery river of the underworld that surrounds
            (*cingens*) and shuts in (*clausos*) the wicked (*nocentes*).
      vadum -- stream.
1229 cedite: i.e., *mihi*: "make room for me!"
1230 degravo, 1 -- to weigh or press down.
1231 saxum: the stone which Sisyphus, son of Aeolus, labors eternally to
            push to the top of a hill, only to have it roll back down again.
1232 ludo, -ere -- to play; to delude, deceive.
      amnis: the river of water that flows near Tantalus but always dis-
            appears when he tries to drink from it to quench his thirst.
      alluo, -ere -- to wash against, flow near.
1233 Tityus was punished by having a vulture eat out his liver each day
            (it grew back each night).
      transvolo, 1 -- to fly across. Supply *ad me*.
1234 semper accrescat iecur: i.e., may it grow back each night to
            provide a further punishment the next day (*poenae* is dative of
            purpose).
1235 Pirithoi pater: Ixion, punished by being chained to a wheel that
            spins eternally.
1236 incitatus -- rapid, swift.
      turbo, -inis, m. -- that which spins or twirls around.
1237 resisto, -ere -- to stop.
1238 dehisco, -ere -- to part, divide, split open, gape, yawn.
      chaos, n. (Greek word) -- the emptiness of the underworld.
1239 iustior...via: i.e., the trip which he is now contemplating to
            Hades will be more justified and proper than his previous
            trip with Pirithous.
1240 qui manes regis: i.e., Pluto.
1241 casti: i.e., not to rape Proserpina, as on the previous trip.
1243 pronus -- turned forward; favorable.
      forent = essent.
1244 querela -- complaint, lament.
1245 iusta...solve: "pay the due rites."
      abscondo,-ere -- to put away, conceal, hide.

nunc tibimet ipse iusta supplicia irrogā.   1222

pīnus coāctō vertice attingens humum   1223

caelō remissum findat in geminās trabēs,   1224

mittarve praeceps saxa per Scīrōnia?   1225

graviōra vīdī, quae patī clausōs iubet   1226

Phlegethon nocentēs igneō cingens vadō: 1227

quae poena mēmet maneat et sēdēs, sciō.   1228

umbrae nocentēs, cēdite et cervīcibus   1229

hīs, hīs repositum dēgravet fessās manūs   1230

saxum, senī perennis Aeoliō labor;   1231

mē lūdat amnis ōra vīcīna alluens;   1232

vultur relictō transvolet Tityō ferus   1233

meumque poenae semper accrescat iecur;   1234

et tū meī requiesce Pīrithoī pater: 1235

haec incitātīs membra turbinibus ferat   1236

nusquam resistens orbe revolūtō rota.   1237

Dēhisce tellūs, recipe mē dīrum chaos,   1238

recipe, haec ad umbrās iustior nōbīs via est: 1239

gnātum sequor -- nē metue quī manēs regis: 1240

castī venīmus; recipe mē aeternā domō   1241

nōn exitūrum. nōn movent dīvōs precēs;   1242

at, sī rogārem scelera, quam prōnī forent!   1243

CHORUS-   Thēseu, querēlīs tempus aeternum manet;   1244
LEADER   nunc iusta nātō solve et absconde ōcius   1245

1246   foede (adv.) -- foully, cruelly, horribly.
       laniatus, -us, m. -- a tearing in pieces, a mangling, lacerating.
1248   pondus: i.e., the inert mass of the fragments of Hippolytus' body.
       artus, -us, m. -- limb.
       temere (adv.) -- at random.
1250   neu = neve -- and lest.
1251   audeo, -ere, ausus -- to dare.
1252   fruor, 1 dep. -- to enjoy + abl.
1253   fractis...annis: i.e., the years that await me in the future,
           broken by my grief over what I have done.
       orbitas, -tatis, f. -- the state of being *orbus*, bereaved.
1254   complectere: imperative; "embrace!"
       est super = superest -- is left over, remains.
1255   foveo, -ere -- to cherish.
1256   disicio, -ere, -ieci, -iectum -- to throw asunder, scatter, disperse.
       lacer, -era, -erum -- mangled, lacerated, torn to pieces.
1259   frenis docta moderandis: "taught to guide (or skilled in guiding)
           the reins."
1261   lacrimis...nostris: i.e., for me to weep over.
1262   lugubri officio: explains *trepidae*. lugubris, -e -- mournful,
           sorrowful.
1263   sisto, -ere -- to stop, check.
       areo, -ere -- to be dry, thirsty, parched, withered.
1265   fingit: i.e., reconstructs.

dispersa foedē membra laniātū efferō.   1246

THESEUS   *to Hippolytus' companions, who still*
          continue to bring in parts of his body.

Hūc, hūc, reliquiās vehite cārī corporis   1247

pondusque et artūs temere congestōs date.   1248

Hippolytus hīc est? crīmen agnoscō meum: 1249

ego tē peremī; neu nocens tantum semel   1250

solusve fierem, facinus ausūrus parens   1251

patrem advocāvī. munere ēn patriō fruor.   1252

Ō triste fractīs orbitās annīs malum!   1253

kneeling over the remains of his son,
embracing them and attempting to arrange
them into a human form

Complectere artūs, quodque dē nātō est super,   1254

miserande, maestō pectore incumbens, fovē.   1255

disiecta, genitor, membra lacerī corporis   1256

in ordinem dispōne et errantēs locō   1257

restitue partēs: fortis hīc dextrae locus,   1258

hīc laeva frēnīs docta moderandīs manus   1259

pōnenda: laevī lateris agnoscō notās.   1260

quam magna lacrimīs pars adhūc nostrīs abest!   1261

dūrāte trepidae lūgubrī officiō manūs,   1262

flētūsque largōs sistite, arentēs genae,   1263

dum membra nātō genitor adnumerat suō   1264

corpusque fingit. hoc quid est formā carens   1265

et turpe, multō vulnere abruptum undique?   1266

1267   dubito, 1 -- to be uncertain.
1270   inimica flectens lumina: i.e., capable of turning even the eyes of
             his enemies (with an allusion to Phaedra, who, as his step-
             mother, could be expected to be hostile to him).
1272   ex voto: "in accordance with the prayer" (expressed by his father).
1273   suprema dona: i.e., the last rites.
1274   effero, -ferre -- to carry out for burial.
             interim: i.e., we must cremate the parts of the body that we have
             now, and then later we can search for the remaining parts.
1275   patefacio, -ere -- to open, throw open.
             caede funesta: abl. explaining *acerbam*: "sad with mournful death."
1276   Mopsopia: Athens: see line 121.
1277   apparo, 1 -- to prepare.
1279a anquiro, -ere -- to look about for on all sides.
1279b defodio, -ere, -fodi, -fossum -- to dig up; to bury in the earth.

quae pars tuī sit dubito; sed pars est tuī: 1267

hīc, hīc repōne, nōn suō, at vacuō locō. 1268

Haecne illa faciēs igne sīdereō nitens, 1269

inimīca flectens lūmina? hūc cecidit decor? 1270

ō dīra fāta, nūminum ō saevus favor! 1271

sīc ad parentem nātus ex votō redit? 1272

en haec suprēma dōna genitōris cape, 1273

saepe efferendus; interim haec ignēs ferant. 1274

to attendants and companions of Hippolytus

Patefacite acerbam caede fūnestā domum; 1275

Mopsopia clārīs tōta lamentīs sonet. 1276

vōs apparāte rēgiī flammam rogī; 1277

at vōs per agrōs corporis partēs vagās 1278

anquīrite. 1279a

removing Phaedra's body from Hippolytus'
remains, and thrusting it aside

Istam terra dēfossam premat, 1279b

gravisque tellūs impiō capitī incubet. 1280

Curtain.

Hippolytus
Apulian Krater by Darius Painter, ca. 330 B.C.
Photo: R. Schoder, S.J. Courtesy of Museo Iatta, Ruvo.

PART II

METRICS

1. The metrical patterns in Latin poetry are based on alternations of long and short syllables. Long syllables will be marked -, and short syllables ∪ .

2. A syllable is long by nature if it contains a long vowel or a diphthong (ae, au, ei, eu, oe, ui):

Īte, umbrōsās cīngite silvās.

semper cānōs nive Rīphaea.

3. A syllable is long by position if its vowel, although short by nature, is followed by two or more consonants or a double consonant (*x, z*):

Ite, ūmbrosas cīngite sīlvas.

sēmpēr canos nive Riphaea.

tēxitur ālno, qua prata iacēnt.

4. But, if the first of the two consonants is *b, p, d, t, g,* or *c* and the second is *l* or *r*, the syllable may be either long or short, depending on the requirements of the meter:

hic versatur, metus āgricolis.

tendant Cretes fortiă̆ trito.

5. A vowel or dipthong at the end of a word is suppressed when the next word begins with a vowel or with *h*. This is called elision. Thus, *ite, umbrosas* would be pronounced *itumbrosas*, and *mittite habenas* would be *mittitabenas*. Or, the suppressed syllable may be sounded lightly and quickly.

6. A final *m*, with the preceding vowel, is suppressed when the next word begins with a vowel or *h*. Thus, *obsidem invisos* would be pronounced *obsidinvisos*. Or, the suppressed syllable may be sounded lightly and quickly.

7. The favorite lyric or choral meter is based on the anapest (∪ ∪ -). A spondee (- -) or dactyl (- ∪ ∪) may be substituted for an anapest. A trochee (- ∪) or tribrach (∪ ∪ ∪) may be substituted for the final anapest. A line may contain either four feet (= a dimeter) or two feet (= a monometer). The following table shows which feet may occur in each place:

1	2	3	4
∪ ∪ _	∪ ∪ _	∪ ∪_	∪ ∪ _
- -	- -	- -	- -
_ ∪ ∪		_ ∪ ∪	
	(- ∪)		(- ∪)
	(∪ ∪ ∪)		(∪ ∪ ∪)

The play opens with an anapestic song sung by Hippolytus. The opening lines may be scanned as follows:

Īte, um- / brōsās / cīngite / sīlvās

summaque / mōntis / iuga, Cec- / ropiī.

celerī / plāntā / lūstrā- / te vagī

quae sāx- / ōsō / loca Pār- / nēthī

8. The usual meter for dramatic dialogue is based on the iamb (∪ -).
It is arranged in pairs or dipodies (∪ - ∪ -), with three dipodies
in a line. The iamb may be replaced by the tribrach (∪ ∪ ∪), the
spondee (- -), the anapest (∪ ∪ -), the dactyl (- ∪ ∪), or the
proceleusmatic (∪ ∪ ∪ ∪). The following table shows which feet may
occur in each place:

1	2	3	4	5	6
∪ _	∪ _	∪ _	∪ _	∪ _	∪ _
∪ ∪ ∪	∪ ∪ ∪	∪ ∪ ∪	∪ ∪ ∪		
- -		- -		- -	
∪ ∪ _		∪ ∪ _		∪ ∪ _	
_ ∪ ∪		_ ∪ ∪		_ ∪ ∪	
∪ ∪ ∪ ∪					

The opening lines of Phaedra's first speech may be scanned as follows:

Ō mag- / na vās- / tī Crē- / ta domi- / nātrīx / fretī,

cuius / per om- / ne lī- / tus īn- / numerāe / ratēs

tenue- / re pon- / tum, quid- / quid Ās- / syriā / tenus

tellū- / re Ne- / reus per- / vius / rostrīs / secat.

9. The first choral ode opens with a meter called sapphic after the
    famous Greek poetess, Sappho of Lesbos. Its scheme is as follows:

$$- \cup / - - / - \, \mathbf{,} \, \cup \cup / - \cup / - -$$

The symbol **,** marks an obligatory caesura (i.e., word division within
a foot). The opening lines of the ode may be scanned as follows:

    Dīvā / nōn mī- / tī   genĕ- / rātă / pontō,

    quăm vō- / căt māt- / rēm   gemĭ- / nūs Cup- / īdō.

10. With line 325 the meter switches to anapests, which are scanned in
    the same way as Hippolytus' opening song. See paragraph 7 above.
    The first two lines of this section of the ode are scanned as
    follows:

    Vīdĭt / Persīs / dītī- / quĕ fĕrāx

    Lȳdĭă / rēgnō / deiēc- / tă fĕrī

11. The second choral ode (736f.) opens with two sapphic strophes, which
    consist of sapphic lines (see above, paragraph 9), closed by short
    adonics (- $\cup$ $\cup$ / - -). Thus, lines 736 and 740 are scanned as
    follows:

    Fŭgĭt / īnsā- / nae simĭ- / lĭs prō- / cellāe

    porrĭgĭt / īgnēs.

12. With line 753 Seneca switches to asclepiadeans, named after another
    famous Greek poet, Asclepiades. Their invariable metrical pattern is
    as follows:

$$- - / - \cup \cup / - / - \cup \cup / - \cup / \breve{\cup}$$

Lines 753 and 754 are scanned as follows:

    Ēt tū, / thyrsĭgĕ- / rā / Lībĕr ăb / Īndĭ- / ā,

    īntōn- / să iuvĕ- / nīs / pērpetŭ- / ūm cŏ- / mā.

13. Lines 761-763 are dactylic. A spondee (- -) may be substituted for
    a dactyl (- $\cup$ $\cup$).

    Āncēps / fōrmă bŏ- / nūm mōr- / tālĭbŭs,

    exĭgŭ- / ī dō- / nŭm brĕvĕ / tēmpŏrĭs,

    ŭt vē- / lōx cĕlĕ- / rī pĕdĕ / lābĕrĭs!

14. Lines 764-823 are asclepiadean (see paragraph 12 above), except for line 783 which is glyconic (- - / - ◡ ◡ / - ◡ / ◡̱).

15. The next ode (959-989) is entirely anapestic. See paragraph 7 above.

16. Most of the meters in the next ode (1123-1153) have already been illustrated. The aristophanean (1131) is as follows:
- ◡ ◡ / - ◡ / - - . The pherecratean (1140) is as follows:
- - / - ◡ ◡ / - .

17. Theseus' lament (1201-1212) is in a lugubrious trochaic rhythm, consisting of four trochaic dipodies (- ◡ - ◡) in each line. This is the trochaic tetrameter catalectic (i.e., it lacks the final short syllable of the final foot = ∧), called the trochaic septenarius. The first member of a dipody may be a tribrach (◡ ◡ ◡); the second member may be a spondee (- -), anapest (◡ ◡ -), or dactyl (- ◡ ◡). The following table shows which feet may occur in each place:

	1	2	3	4	5	6	7	8
	- ◡	- ◡	- ◡	- ◡	- ◡	- ◡	- ◡	- ∧
	◡ ◡ ◡		◡ ◡ ◡		◡ ◡ ◡		◡ ◡ ◡	
	- -		- -		- -			
	◡ ◡ -		◡ ◡ -		◡ ◡ -			
	- ◡ ◡		- ◡ ◡		- ◡ ◡			

The first two lines of the lament are scanned as follows:

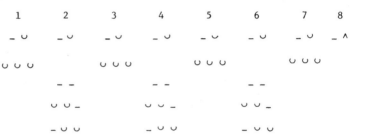

Palli- / dī fau- / cēs A- / vernī, / vōsque, / Taenare- / ī spe- / cūs,

unda / miserīs / grāta / Lethēs, / vōsque, / torpen- / tēs la- / cūs.

STUDY QUESTIONS AND COMMENTS

ON SENECA'S PHAEDRA

1-84   What do we learn about Hippolytus in this scene? In what ways
          does he reveal his character? Point to specific lines that tell
          us something about his personality. Is he an individual figure
          or merely a typical hunter? What impression do the repeated
          commands to his companions convey? Is Hippolytus confident,
          aggressive, domineering? Is he comfortable within the vast
          domain of untamed nature, or does he seek to control it?

          Study closely Hippolytus' feeling for nature. Does he regard
          nature as merely a reserve for plunder, or does he have any
          deeper, emotional sympathy for the world of nature and its ani-
          mals? If so, how does he reveal it? What lines are especially
          expressive of nature's beauty? of nature's charm? of nature's
          majesty? In what ways does Hippolytus express an awareness of
          nature's infinite variety?

          Consider carefully the geographical references throughout the
          passage. Is Hippolytus a credible character from the primitive
          and geographically restricted heroic age of Greece, or does he
          have an awareness of the world more representative of men living
          in the far-flung Roman empire of Seneca's own age? If Seneca has
          modernized his hero by giving him a Roman and imperial sense of
          the vast dimensions of the world, is this detrimental? How would
          a Roman reader or audience respond to Hippolytus? What charac-
          teristics of Hippolytus would a Roman audience find especially
          sympathetic or admirable? In what ways is Hippolytus the hunter
          similar to the ideal of an imperial Roman general?

31-53   Trace the progress of the hunt from beginning to end through
          these lines. Note in particular vocabulary expressive of energy
          and violence on the one hand and restraint and control on the
          other; point to specific words. How is success in the hunt
          dependent on control? control of what? Note also vocabulary
          expressive of deception, treachery, and fear. With what are the
          hunters armed, and how will they deploy their weapons in order to
          capture the quarry? What action takes place at the climax of the
          hunt? Note the military metaphor of the hunter as *victor* (52).

54-82a   What kind of a goddess is Diana? Exactly what does she repre-
          sent? Why does Hippolytus devote himself to this particular
          goddess? What is his relationship to her? How does he appeal to
          her? How does he flatter her? What does he expect from her in
          return? What kind of religion is this? emotional? personal?
          mystic? formal? business-like?

Diana as a global huntress: note the geographical references to peoples and places throughout the Roman empire. Study carefully Diana's relationship to the beasts of this world over which she rules. What does she do to the beasts? Note the theme of pursuit. What feelings do the beasts have toward her? How would a Roman reader or audience respond to this kind of goddess and the way she wields her power?

73-80 Triumph of the hunter who has Diana's favor: over what is Hippolytus victorious? Is the victory his own or Diana's? Note the inescapable nets and snares in which the animals are caught and the rustic triumphal procession. Compare this with the triumphal processions in which Roman generals celebrated their victories over the nations and peoples of the Empire. How does the implied parallel between the hunter and the general help us to understand Hippolytus' role as a hunter? How are both the imperial general and the triumphant hunter symbols of man extending his control, power, and dominion over himself, his destiny, and his world?

1-84   Consider carefully how you would dramatize this entire scene. Would it be an effective opening for the play? How could the energy, movement, and vitality implied in the words (note particularly the commands and the lively adjectives in the opening sections) be dramatized in the delivery of the monologue?

Do you have any sense of how this opening scene might be related to the theme or imagery of the drama to follow? What would be the purpose of impressing upon the audience's minds the image of Hippolytus as a hunter? Consider carefully the implications of the hunter figure, of the theme of pursuit, and of the images of snaring and entrapment, along with the related theme of man's control over himself, his environment, and his life. Observe how Seneca plays on these themes in the course of the drama. As you read on in the play, return periodically and re-read this opening scene and consider how it foreshadows the movement, themes, and imagery in the play as a whole.

*   *   *

85-128   Dramatic technique: in the preceding scene Hippolytus presented
          himself to the audience in a monologue addressed partly to his
          companions and partly to his patron goddess Diana; here Phaedra
          presents herself in a soliloquy addressed not so much to the
          nurse who accompanies her as to the audience in an exposition of
          her present situation, its background, and her feelings and at-
          titudes toward herself in the extraordinary predicament in which
          she is caught. Her soliloquy touches upon her Cretan home
          (85-88), her marriage to Theseus (89-91a), Theseus' infidelity
          (91b-98), her passion for Hippolytus and how it has transformed
          her (99-111), and her passion as inherited from her mother
          (112-123) and as the fulfillment of a curse upon her entire
          family (124-128). Note the fatalism in her address to Crete and
          her feeling of helplessness in her life situation and in her
          present emotional state. Note her desire to gain control by
          becoming a hunter rather than remaining a victimized woman.

85-88   What is it about Phaedra's Cretan homeland that especially
          impresses her? What feelings or attitude does she appear to
          have toward Crete?

89-91a   What does Phaedra think of her new Athenian home, her marriage
          to Theseus, and her present life?

91b-98   How does Phaedra portray Theseus and what feelings does she have
          toward him? Does she believe Theseus will return? How does she
          characterize the expedition and its purpose? What qualities of
          mind or character should have restrained Theseus?

99-111   What specific words, images, and metaphors does Phaedra use to
          describe her passionate desire for Hippolytus? What do the
          images reveal about Phaedra's conception of and attitude toward
          her passion?

          How, specifically, has her passion transformed her? Why does
          she no longer take part in the Eleusinian mysteries or worship
          of Athena? What is it about her passionate love for Hippolytus
          that keeps her away from these religious rites?

          Why does Phaedra want to go hunting? to kill wild beasts? to be
          with Hippolytus? or to "hunt down" and "capture" him? Does she
          really know why? Is she trying to exchange a dissatisfying
          feminine role for a masculine one? to what end?

112-123   What makes Phaedra think of her mother? To what does Phaedra
          attribute her own mad passion? What feelings does she have
          toward her mother? How does she view her mother's love for the
          bull? Is Phaedra excusing her own passion by attributing it to
          heredity, or is she simply recognizing the fact of an inherited
          lust for the forbidden? In what specific ways is Phaedra's love
          for Hippolytus like that of Pasiphae for the bull? Note the way
          the bull is described; is there any similarity between the bull

and Hippolytus? (Note particularly *torvus, impatiens iugi...
ductor indomiti gregis* 117-118).

Why is it that not even Daedalus or a god could help Phaedra in
her love with Hippolytus? How did Daedalus help Pasiphae in her
love with the bull?

124-128   Is Phaedra merely trying to find excuses for her illicit love,
           or is she expressing a deep feeling of fatalism and human help-
           lessness? What attitude does she take toward her passion? Is
           she attracted or repulsed by it? What words express her moral
           shock and outrage over the illicit love affairs of her entire
           family? Is Phaedra most unhappy because of the unspeakable
           taboo she violates, or is she disturbed because she fears her
           passions will not be happily fulfilled? or both?

 85-128   Review the entire soliloquy (85-128) and observe how Phaedra
           uses the following key moral terms as she conveys her own deeply
           divided feelings about herself, her husband, her love for
           Hippolytus, and her family history: *fides, furor, timor, pudor,
           stupra, illicitus, castus, pius, fatale, misera, peccare,
           infandus, nefas*. Phaedra feels *pudor* and *timor* which restrain
           her from pursuing Hippolytus although they did not restrain
           Theseus from pursuing Persephone in the underworld; yet she is
           "caught up in an unspeakable evil" (*infando malo / correpta*),
           just as was her mother, and is drawn toward "unspeakable acts of
           shame" (*probra...nefanda*) although simultaneously repulsed by
           the "sin" (*nefas*) with which all the women in her family have
           been fatally cursed. Is infidelity to Theseus the problem?
           or forbidden love? or both?

129-135   How does the nurse's opening line attempt to recall Phaedra to
           her senses? Is there any irony in her use of the phrase *Thesea
           coniunx* just after Phaedra has expressed her hatred of her mar-
           riage (89-91a)? Does the nurse think of Phaedra as basically a
           good or an evil woman? (Consider *casto pectore* 130.) Generally
           does the nurse pass moral judgment, or is her attitude toward
           Phaedra more one of a helpful counselor? What imagery does she
           use to describe Phaedra's love? What recourse does she recom-
           mend that Phaedra take? Does the nurse believe in fatalism or
           in free will? in the responsibility of human beings for control-
           ling their own fate? How does the nurse's philosophy of life
           differ from Phaedra's?

136-139   What are the nurse's real feelings about Phaedra? What charac-
           ter does the nurse attribute to Phaedra? Are you drawn toward
           the nurse as a decent human being and a sure judge of other
           people's moral character? Is the nurse right in her rationalis-
           tic approach, or is she oversimplifying in ignorance of the
           depth of Phaedra's predicament? Consider lines 132b-135; has
           the nurse rightly assessed the situation? How do these lines
           foreshadow what is to come?

140-177a Consider carefully the nurse's strategy in appealing to Phaedra
and attempting to restrain her.

140-141 How effective is this abstract moralizing likely to be?
Note the use of the word *pudor* here and throughout this scene;
how has Phaedra already used the word?

142-144 How does the nurse begin to play on areas of sensitiv-
ity that Phaedra has already revealed? her Cretan home? her
mother? Is the nurse improving her psychological tactics? How
does she argue against Phaedra's fatalistic view?

145-164 The nurse now appeals to Phaedra's fear, her sense of
shame or honor, and her natural desire to maintain a good reputation, by pointing out that her evil actions would surely be
observed. The nurse is evidently playing on Phaedra's horror
at the widely known disgrace of her mother. Note the careful
structure of this passage, with a progression toward a climax:
Theseus (147-148), Minos (149-152), Phoebus (154-155a), Jupiter
(155b-157a), and most important of all, her own conscience
(162-163). What one line neatly sums up the thought of the
entire passage?

165-177a What aspect of Phaedra's love for Hippolytus is the
nurse emphasizing here for the first time in her speech? What
strategies does she use to try to shock Phaedra? Does Phaedra
need to be lectured and shocked, or does she already feel just
as great a horror at her incestuous love as the nurse expresses
here? How does the Minotaur symbolize the unnaturalness of
Phaedra's love just as surely as it did Pasiphae's? What does
the nurse mean by *natura*? What is a *monstrum* or a *prodigium*,
and how are these related to the concept of *natura*?

177b-183 Is Phaedra's analysis of her situation here consistent with the
fatalistic view that she expressed in lines 112-128 above? If
so, how? And, in what ways is her analysis now different?

177b-179a Compare Medea's words in Ovid (*Metamorphoses*
7.19-21a), as she yields to her love for Jason:

> sed gravat invitam nova vis, aliudque cupido,
> mens aliud suadet: video meliora proboque,
> deteriora sequor.

> But some strange power holds me down against my
> will. Desire persuades me one way, reason another.
> I see the better and approve it, but I follow the worse.

                    -- tr. F. J. Miller

179b-183 Compare the simile of the boat with the following
passage from Vergil's *Georgics* (1.199-203):

> sic omnia fatis
> in peius ruere ac retro sublapsa referri,
> non aliter, quam qui adverso vix flumine lembum
> remigiis subigit, si bracchia forte remisit,
> atque illum in praeceps prono rapit alveus amni.

> Thus by law of fate all things speed towards
> the worst, and slipping away fall back; even
> as if one, whose oars can scarce force his
> skiff against the stream, should by chance
> slacken his arms, and lo! headlong down the
> current the boat sweeps him away.

> -- tr. H. R. Fairclough

What changes has Seneca made in adapting the simile from Vergil?
What light do the changes throw on Phaedra's conception of her
situation? How does Seneca's simile express an entirely different philosophy of life from Vergil's? Analyze your attitude
toward Phaedra as she portrays herself here. Does she really
attempt to take control of her emotions? her life?

184-194 What key word links this passage with the one above (178-183)?
Analyze the simile of the sailor and the boat in terms of *ratio*
and *furor*. To what extent is Phaedra's life controlled by her
ratio? to what extent by her *furor*? How can the entire confrontation between the nurse and Phaedra be seen as a dramatic
materialization of the struggle within Phaedra herself between
the dictates of her *ratio* and the force of her *furor*?

Analyze the elements of irony in the examples of gods overcome
by love; how is each example incongruous, paradoxical, or
ironic? How does the irony add to the rhetorical force of
Phaedra's argument? Do you find her argument convincing? Is
she merely trying to find excuses for herself by rationalizing
her inability to control her *furor*, or is she seriously trying
to analyze the nature of the force of love which has overcome
her?

195-203 What strategies does the nurse use to deflate Phaedra's rhe-
toric? Note especially the bitter sarcasm of lines 198-201.
How does the nurse stress the absurdity of Phaedra's arguments?
On what does she place the blame?

204-214 How has the nurse's aside in lines 136-139 prepared for the line
of argument she now takes up? To what exactly does she now attribute Phaedra's trouble? Is her view convincing? In what
ways is it oversimplified? How is it at variance with Phaedra's

own analysis of her trouble (lines 112-128, 177b-185)? Is
Seneca here making a statement about social decadence in his
day, or is he making a more universal statement about avarice
and resultant loss of self-control?

215   Is this *sententia* (i.e., a "terse, pointed, epigrammatic expression of a striking thought...which often is of general
application" *OCD*) an effective summation of the nurse's argument? Is it adequate as an explanation of the source of
Phaedra's trouble, or does the nurse's sententious moralizing
miss the mark?

216-217 Is the exhortation of *noblesse oblige* likely to carry weight
with Phaedra? What indications have there been that she has a
high ideal of queenly propriety or that she could be held back
by fear (*timor*), a sense of shame or honor (*pudor*), or a desire
to protect her reputation (*fama*)? Note that the nurse has
implied (204-214) that the nobility, far from setting good
examples for others, are themselves the trend-setters of moral
decay.

218-245 Note the quickening of the dramatic exchanges now that both
parties have set forth their positions in lengthy speeches. Is
there any middle ground between their respective positions? Is
there any room for compromise or a reasonable solution? Is
Phaedra really listening to the nurse's arguments? And, con-
versely, does the nurse really understand Phaedra? Does Phaedra
become more or less determined as she progresses? Is her determination based on a realistic assessment of the situation or on
fantasies and wish fulfillment? How do you react to Phaedra as
she presents herself in these lines?

218-227 How much credence does Phaedra give to the possibility
of Theseus' return? How realistic is her belief that he would
pardon her love for his son?

228-235 Compare lines 119-123 where Phaedra expressed her
realization that neither Daedalus nor a god could help her
attain the intractable object of her desires, as Daedalus had
helped Pasiphae. Also, compare lines 110-111 where Phaedra
expressed her desire to go hunting. That desire is now expressed as a fantasy of Phaedra pursuing Hippolytus through the
wild landscapes that Hippolytus described in the opening scene
of the play. Note the paradox of the hunter being hunted.

236-239 Note the nurse's conjecture (*forsitan*) as to why
Hippolytus has come to be a misogynist.

240-245b The exchange quickens as Phaedra fantasizes over the
possibility of love with Hippolytus and argues away all re-
straints. 240 Hippolytus is overcome with love (*amore...
vinci*); 242b Pasiphae's mating with the bull is a model for

Phaedra's mating with Hippolytus; 243 Phaedra's affair with
Hippolytus will be free of rivals; 244 Phaedra will not fear her
husband, because he is in Hades, and he has abandoned her in
favor of his friendship with the rapist, Pirithous, anyway;
245 even Minos, her father, will not be harsh with her when he
learns of her affair with Hippolytus, but will be as gentle as
he was with Ariadne (in her affair with Theseus).

The heightened dramatic tension of rapid-fire exchanges
(stichomythia) goes hand in hand with the heightening of
Phaedra's determination and the overt expression of her fantasies. She mentally removes all the barriers that stand in the
way of her lust and thus appears to make reality harmonize with
her sexual fantasies. Through her fantasies she tries to seize
mental control in an attempt to overcome fate, and she expresses
optimism over the possibility of union with Hippolytus. The
nurse can offer no further arguments. Phaedra's *furor* is
untouched by the nurse's practical *ratio*. The dialogue thus
ceases abruptly and the nurse tries one final strategy -- an
emotional appeal through supplication. Phaedra's fragile and
falsely conceived fantasy will founder, and she will plunge to
talk of *pudor* and suicide.

246-249   Note the vocabulary of madness and restraint. 249 another
           sententia (see on line 215). Pick out other examples of
           sententious utterances in the nurse's speeches. Does Phaedra
           here use *sententiae*? Why are they more congenial to the role
           being played by the nurse in this dialogue? Phaedra will begin
           to use *sententiae* later.

250-254   This is one of the key passages in the play for interpretation
           of Phaedra's character and assessment of her tragic predicament.
           Look back at this passage frequently as you read on in the play.

           250 *pudor*: locate other occurrences of this word earlier in
           the scene. How has Phaedra expressed her sense of *pudor*
           earlier? How has the nurse played on it in her attempts to
           restrain Phaedra?

           animo...ingenuo: compare Phaedra's sense of her nobility
           earlier in the scene.

           250-251 *pudor...amor*: note the placement of these key words
           which define Phaedra's tragic dilemma.

           251 *qui regi non vult amor*: how has Phaedra earlier expressed
           her inability to cope with her love? (Compare especially 181-
           183.)

           252 *haud te, fama, maculari sinam*: how has Phaedra earlier
           expressed concern for the reputation (*fama*) of herself and
           other members of her family? How has the nurse played on this
           concern of Phaedra's? Do Phaedra's words ring true now?

253 *ratio*: compare 184 where Phaedra recognizes the impotence of *ratio* in the face of her *furor* or *amor*; now a newly found *ratio* will provide the only escape from her ills (*unicum effugium mali*). Why is death the only solution to Phaedra's tragic dilemma?

254 *virum sequamur, morte praevertam nefas*: instead of "following" Hippolytus as in her fantasized pursuit (235), Phaedra will "follow" her husband to the underworld by committing suicide. Note that Phaedra's speech ends on the same word (*nefas*) with which her first speech ended (128). Study the last lines of her first speech: *nulla Minois levi/ defuncta amore est, iungitur semper nefas* (127-128). Note that suicide provides an escape from the fatal curse upon her family as well as an escape from the tragic dilemma of *pudor* and *amor*.

250-254 Comment on Phaedra's final yielding or obeying (*paremus* 251). Why was she not able to yield or obey earlier? How does the new solution she has found for her dilemma permit her now to yield to the nurse? Phaedra can neither control her love (her *amor/furor*) nor fulfill it (cf. the vain fantasy of lines 240-245); her determination upon suicide is the only answer to the nurse's sententious injunction, *pars sanitatis velle sanari fuit* (249); it is the only way to save her reputation (*fama*), to avoid sin (*nefas*), and to obey the dictates of the *pudor* which has not completely deserted her noble mind (250).

255-256a Note the nurse's desire to see restraint exercised -- now applied to Phaedra's wish for death as it was before applied to her lust for Hippolytus.

256b-257 Analyze the logic of the nurse's statement here. What exactly is she saying? How has Phaedra revealed her true worth or nobility? Does the comment of the nurse express the feelings of the audience?

258-261 How has the last comment of the nurse merely served to harden Phaedra's determination to commit suicide? What image of herself does Phaedra wish to create and to preserve? Note the conception of *castitas*; compare lines 130 and 169.

263b Note the vocabulary of restraint/unrestraint here and in 255-256a above; compare 248. Is Phaedra's new determination just as insane as her lust for Hippolytus, or is it the only rational solution (*sola ratio* 253) to her dilemma? Should the nurse be restraining Phaedra now or encouraging her? Does the nurse really understand the depth of Phaedra's tragic dilemma?

264 How does this line undermine one of the main arguments the nurse had used earlier in her attempt to restrain Phaedra?

265-266   Note that Phaedra now speaks in *sententiae*. How is this appro-
           priate to her present determination? Note that *periturum* is
           masculine because Phaedra is uttering a generalizing *sententia*
           rather than making a statement applicable to herself alone.
           Perhaps also she is visualizing herself in a conventional mascu-
           line role of a "noble Roman," normally inapplicable to women.
           How would this further show her determination to gain control of
           her life?

267   Note the similarity between the appeal the nurse makes now and
           the appeal she made in lines 246-248. What is it that the nurse
           wants most of all? Note that she is now willing to compromise
           her moral principles (*contemne famam*) in order to save Phaedra's
           life. Is the nurse inconsistent or merely pragmatic? How will
           the audience respond to her role?

269-270   How does the nurse's advice derive from her genuine pragmatism
           and love of life? Is the conception of *fama* as an unreliable
           indication of men's true worth borne out by the often cited
           example of Phaedra's mother, Pasiphae? Is the nurse now trying
           to delude herself (as well as Phaedra), or do you see her in a
           more positive role of trying to help Phaedra to master her fate,
           even while attempting the impossible?

271-273   How is Hippolytus now portrayed? How is the nurse's description
           of him here different from the picture of him provided by the
           opening scene of the play? Note again the paradoxical theme of
           the hunter hunted. What words of the nurse suggest that
           Hippolytus is being thought of as a wild animal (cf. 117-118 and
           239-240)? Is the nurse likely to have any more success in
           "taming" Hippolytus than she had in taming Phaedra? Line 272
           echoes line 240; the nurse will now play out a tragic role
           alongside Phaedra in the latter's fantasy world.

           Note that the nurse has the last word and that Phaedra apparent-
           ly abandons her suicide plans and yields to the proposal of the
           nurse without any further comment.

           Review lines 246-273. In lines 246-249 the nurse begs Phaedra
           to cease her mad desire for Hippolytus. Phaedra knows she can-
           not do that and proposes suicide as a way out of her dilemma
           with honor. The nurse rejects this for her own personal rea-
           sons, but the situation has obviously become desperate, and the
           nurse makes her final proposal -- forget your honor, and let's
           see if we can get Hippolytus for you. And, note that in lines
           269b-270 the nurse suggests that it may be possible to save
           Phaedra's honor, too, because sometimes less deserving men have
           higher reputations than more deserving. This will allay Phaedra's
           qualms, and while there is any hope at all of getting
           Hippolytus, she will continue to live. The nurse is, however,
           deceiving both herself and Phaedra on two counts: Hippolytus
           cannot be tamed, and honor cannot be preserved through

dishonorable actions. The nurse knows all of this full well;
compare lines 228-232, 236-239, and 145-158.

How do you expect the action of the play to develop from this
point? What do you expect in the next dramatic scene?

*   *   *

274-357   What are the dramatic advantages of having an interlude at this
           point in the play? Consider the relationship between this ode
           and the previous scene. Does the chorus' view of love seem
           closer to that of the nurse or of Phaedra? What specific rela-
           tionships can you see between this ode and particular passages
           in the previous scene? Is this ode simply an interlude, or does
           it contribute anything important to our understanding of or our
           perspective upon what is happening in the dramatic action of the
           play?

           With the themes of lovers being transformed by their passions
           one may compare episodes from Ovid's *Metamorphoses* such as the
           stories of Apollo and Daphne (I. 452-552) and Jupiter and Europa
           (II. 833-875).

274-282   Venus as a goddess born from the sea (274) recalls Phaedra's
           homeland, Crete, described as mistress of the sea (85-88). What
           other words or images in this passage recall Phaedra's speeches?
           Compare especially lines 186-194. What is the dominant image
           Seneca is using to describe the power of Venus and Cupid? Is
           this image merely conventional, or is it chosen and developed to
           express the particular nature of the power of love which the
           chorus is celebrating here?

283-290a   Note the references to the East, West, South, and North. Com-
           pare the universality of Diana's powers as praised by Hippolytus
           (55-72). Note the parallel between the weapons of Diana and
           those of Cupid. What new dimension does this parallel between
           two all-powerful deities add to the dramatic action of the play?

           287-290a These lines are reminiscent of two famous passages of
           Augustan poetry on the power of love:

                  non illum [Amorem] nostri possunt mutare labores,
                  nec si frigoribus mediis Hebrumque bibamus
                  Sithoniasque nives hiemis subeamus aquosae,
                  nec si, cum moriens alta liber aret in ulmo,
                  Aethiopum versemus ovis sub sidere Cancri.
                  omnia vincit Amor: et nos cedamus Amori.

                  No toils of ours can change that god, not though in the
                  heart of winter we drink the Hebrus and brave the Thracian
                  snows and their wintry sleet, not though, when the bark
                  dies and withers on the lofty elm, we drive to and fro the
                  Aethiopians' sheep beneath the star of Cancer! Love
                  conquers all; let us, too, yield to love!

                                        Vergil, *Eclogue* X.64-69, tr. H.R. Fairclough

pone me pigris ubi nulla campis
arbor aestiva recreatur aura,
quod latus mundi nebulae malusque
   Iuppiter urget;

pone sub curru nimium propinqui
solis in terra domibus negata:
dulce ridentem Lalagen amabo,
   dulce loquentem.

Place me on the lifeless plains where no tree revives under
the summer breeze, a region of the world o'er which brood
mists and a gloomy sky;

set me beneath the chariot of the sun where it draws too
near the earth, in a land denied for dwellings! I will
love my sweetly laughing, sweetly prattling Lalage.

                        Horace, *Odes* I. 22. 17-24, tr. C. E. Bennett

290b-329   Draw up a list of the victims of Cupid's power. Is there any
           particular order discernible in the list? What does love do to
           each group of people and to each of the individual gods and the
           demi-god, Hercules? with what results? Be very specific in your
           analysis of this passage. What lines of Phaedra does this pas-
           sage recall? How has Phaedra been affected in the same way as
           the gods and Hercules? Are the transformations that the gods
           and Hercules experience ironic, humorous, comic, pathetic, or
           tragic? Why is Phaedra's case different? Does this part of the
           ode tend to reinforce our understanding of and sympathy for
           Phaedra? or does it confirm the skeptical and critical views of
           the nurse (195-215)?

330-351   What does this section of the ode add that has not already been
           said? (Note the personal reference of the chorus to their own
           experience of love in lines 330-331a.) How does this part of
           the ode reinforce the idea of the universality of love's power?
           (Again, compare Diana's power described in 54-72.) What is the
           major image or metaphor used of the sex life of animals? What
           is the tone of this passage, and how does the effect of the sex
           drive on animals differ from the effect of the sex drive on the
           gods and the demi-god Hercules?

           Compare the following passages from the third book of Vergil's
           Georgics, which Seneca surely had in mind while composing this
           part of the ode:

               Therefore men banish the bull to lonely pastures afar, be-
               yond a mountain barrier and across broad rivers, or keep
               him well mewed beside full mangers. For the sight of the
               female slowly inflames and wastes his strength, nor, look
               you, does she, with her soft enchantments, suffer him to

remember woods or pastures; nay, oft she drives her proud
lovers to settle their mutual contest with clash of horns.
She is grazing in Sila's great forest, a lovely heifer:
the bulls in alternate onset join battle with mighty force;
many a wound they deal, black gore bathes their frames,
amid mighty bellowing the levelled horns are driven against
the butting foe; the woods and the sky, from end to end,
re-echo. (212-223)

Yea, every single race on earth, man and beast, the tribes
of the sea, cattle and birds brilliant of hue, rush into
fires of passion: all feel the same Love (*amor omnibus idem* =
Seneca's *vindicat omnes natura sibi* 352). At no other
season doth the lioness forget her cubs, or prowl over the
plains more fierce; never doth the shapeless bear spread
death and havoc so widely through the forest; then savage
is the boar, then most fell the tigress. Ah! it is ill
faring then in Libya's lonely fields! (242-249)

What of the battles fought by peaceful stags? But surely
the madness of mares surpasses all. Venus herself inspired
their frenzy....Love leads them over Gargarus and over the
roaring Ascanius; they scale mountains, they swim rivers.
(265-270)

-- tr. H. R. Fairclough

Returning to Seneca's ode, how do the geographical references
and the references to wild animals recall Hippolytus' prayer to
Diana? Does the picture or conception of nature here harmonize
with or conflict with that offered in Hippolytus' prayer to
Diana? Are the powers of Diana and those of Cupid in opposition
to one another, or are they complementary aspects of a single
world of nature's violence, savagery, and unending vitality,
embracing the life cycle from procreation to death? Are questions of morality and justice raised by Hippolytus' prayer to
Diana and by the chorus' description of the power of the sex
drive? Or, do both Hippolytus and the chorus accept the forces
of nature as amoral powers?

Compare Phaedra's attitude to the passion she feels within her.
What are her feelings about its moral implications? In what
ways do the human characters of the play differ from the gods
and demi-gods (294-329) on the one hand and the animals (331-
351) on the other? Study carefully the similarities and the
differences in how these three groups, which constitute a cosmic
hierarchy of animals, humans, and gods, respond to the compul-
sions of nature that are laid upon them. What is it that is
unique to the human situation, and why is it alone truly tragic?

352-357   The chorus finally relates its message specifically to Phaedra's
           situation. As a *noverca*, Phaedra could be expected to be *saeva*
           toward her step-son Hippolytus, and to be full of *odium* and *ira*
           toward him. But, she, too, has been transformed from a spiteful
           noverca into a desperate *amator*. The "natural" order of things
           is paradoxically overturned by a force of nature (352); compare
           lines 175-177.

           Review Hippolytus' speech, the Phaedra-nurse scene, and the
           choral ode, noting the movement of the drama and the reinforce-
           ment of themes. How is the movement of the Phaedra-nurse scene
           with the nurse finally giving in, accepting the fatalistic
           forces that control us all, and becoming Phaedra's accomplice
           (for the sake of the latter's survival) echoed in the choral ode
           with its celebration of the triumph of love over all? If every-
           thing is held in love's sway, there can be hope; if even harsh
           stepmothers can be overcome, there may be grounds for optimism,
           thus keeping the nurse, Phaedra, and the audience hoping for the
           best.

                            *   *   *

358-359   What sequel to the events of the Phaedra-nurse scene were we led
           to expect? Seneca is delaying that sequel by having the chorus-
           leader, who knows about Phaedra's love for Hippolytus, question
           the nurse about her. What dramatic purpose is served by this
           delay? The chorus has just sung of the effects of the sex drive
           on men, gods, demi-gods, and animals; it is appropriate that the
           chorus-leader now questions the nurse about its effects on
           Phaedra.

360-383   Study this description of Phaedra carefully alongside of the
           descriptions of gods, Hercules, and animals in the choral ode.
           Phaedra, too, has been transformed by love, but how and why are
           its effects on Phaedra different from its effects on the gods,
           Hercules, and animals?

           How is the picture that the nurse gives of Phaedra here differ-
           ent from the conception of Phaedra that emerges in the previous
           Phaedra-nurse scene? Comment on the graphic quality of this
           passage. Compare the essentially external description of
           Phaedra here with the inner, psychological self-portrayal that
           emerges from Phaedra's soliloquy and dramatic dialogue with the
           nurse in the previous scene. Are the two presentations of
           Phaedra compatible? complimentary? What does the external por-
           trait here add that was not already clear from the dialogue?
           Does it help us to understand Phaedra better?

           What is the nurse's attitude toward or feeling about Phaedra
           now? Would she have given this same description of Phaedra
           before the previous dialogue? or would she have given a more
           critical and less sympathetic portrayal? How does the descrip-
           tion express the nurse's new attitude toward Phaedra's passion
           that she was forced to accept at the end of the previous scene?
           Does it express a new awareness of the inevitability of
           Phaedra's passion and of Phaedra's helplessness? Examine again
           its relationship to the themes of the choral ode.

           The nurse is here describing Phaedra as a victim of irrational
           and uncontrollable emotions; her external appearance is a clear
           and unambiguous index of her inner feelings. Keep this in mind
           as you read on to later scenes, where appearances become prob-
           lematical and ambiguous.

387-403   Why does Seneca give us this second glimpse of Phaedra? Is it
           solely for the sake of the chorus? In changing her dress from
           that of a stately queen to that of an Amazon, how is she playing
           out one of the major themes of the choral ode?

           Compare lines 110-111 and the study questions. In the present
           passage Phaedra not only removes the vestments of her queenly
           status but also strips off all traces of her soft, elegant, and
           luxurious life in the palace in favor of a simple, more
           "natural," manly, and aggressive role as an Amazonian warrior-

hunter. How does this express a desire to take control of her
life rather than allowing herself to remain a weak, vacillating,
tearful victim of forces beyond her control (as the nurse has
just described her in lines 360-383)? Compare lines 233-235
where Phaedra expresses her determination to pursue Hippolytus
over the hills, rocks, woods, and mountains. How is her present transformation into an Amazonian warrior-hunter related to
this theme? Compare also the nurse's decision at the end of the
previous scene to join Phaedra in an "attack" upon the wild
Hippolytus. The glimpse of Phaedra transforming herself into a
hunter thus foreshadows the themes of the hunting, stalking, and
snaring of Hippolytus, which are developed in the following
scenes. The hunter's aggressive role in nature again becomes a
prime consideration, but it is now Phaedra and the nurse rather
than Hippolytus who play out this role.

406-423   Why did the chorus-leader suggest that the nurse pray to Diana
(404-405)? Is the nurse's prayer what the chorus-leader
expected, or does it move in a different direction? How does
her prayer develop the plot set forth by the nurse in 271-273?
Compare the nurse's prayer with Hippolytus' prayer to Diana
(54-82a). What aspects of the triple-formed Diana does the
nurse appeal to? Compare lines 309-316 and the theme of
Diana's love for Endymion. Why is it appropriate for Diana as
the moon-goddess who had fallen in love with Endymion to aid
Phaedra in her love for Hippolytus? Observe the irony of the
nurse's appeal to the huntsman's own goddess as an ally in an
attack upon him. How does the language the nurse uses to describe Hippolytus suggest the image of a wild beast? What verbs
suggest the activities of a hunter? How is Hippolytus to be
snared?

424   Consider the dramatic effect of having Hippolytus enter immedi-
ately after the nurse concludes her prayer to Diana for help in
subduing him.

425-430   How do these lines continue to develop insight into the character and moral development of the nurse? Is she a credible
character? a continuous character? How does she waver between
confidence and hesitancy? between assertiveness and restraint
(*pudor*)? Was her prayer to Diana a sign of confidence or an
expression of a feeling that a miracle is needed? How does she
urge herself into action here (427-430)? Note that she tries to
justify her attempt to approach and seduce Hippolytus on the
basis that she is carrying out the orders of the queen (*mandatum
scelus; iussa...regis; regii imperii*). Yet, whose idea was it
to "attack" Hippolytus in the first place? (See lines 271-273.)
Has Phaedra given any overt approval of the nurse's plan? What
has happened to the moral stance of the nurse who uttered the
brave words of lines 136-139?

435-482   Study the strategy that the nurse uses in appealing to Hippoly-
          tus. Is her appeal moral, immoral, or a subtle blend of the
          two? Is it in character for the nurse? Does she show restraint?
          Does she propound a recognizable philosophy of life? Is it more
          Epicurean or Stoic? Is it an extremist or a moderate philo-
          sophy? outrageous or reasonable? What points could you readily
          accept? What would you reject? Do any of her arguments contra-
          dict the views she expressed when trying to restrain Phaedra?
          (Compare the advocacy of permissiveness in lines 455-460 with
          the exhortation to self-discipline in lines 130-135.) Note the
          nurse's attempt to portray Hippolytus' life in the woods as
          negatively as possible and her demonstration that his celibacy
          is contrary to nature. (Compare the celebration of sex as
          natural and universal in the choral ode.) How does the nurse
          use the rhetorical device of *reductio ad absurdum*? Is she
          convincing?

          481 Nature as the proper guide of life (a commonplace of both
          Epicurean and Stoic philosophy): for the full perversity of the
          nurse's argumentation, compare 165-177a, where she described
          incest such as Phaedra's mating with Hippolytus as an unnatural
          nefas (166-168) and a perversion of nature (*nefandis verte
          naturam ignibus* 173) destined to produce *monstra* (174) and
          prodigia (175).

483-557   Hippolytus' speech may be read as a powerful although general-
          ized invective against the evils of society in a "civilized"
          age, but it is also a deeply personal statement on the part of
          Hippolytus. What is he seeking in life, and what is he trying
          to avoid? Is his ideal attainable, or is he seeking an impos-
          sible fantasy? Is his ideal form of life expressed more in
          positive or negative terms? What positive values does his ideal
          life embody? Does he express a real love for nature? Does his
          speech here harmonize with his first speech in the play? Is
          Hippolytus' ideal life or the life recommended by the nurse more
          a life "according to nature" (see line 481)? Is Hippolytus'
          refusal to participate in "real life" and his horror at the
          evils of the "real world" a virtue or a kind of cowardice? Is
          the "real world" necessarily all as evil and wicked as he de-
          scribes it? Is there no middle ground between total flight to
          the woods on the one hand and a total embracing of the evils of
          civilized life on the other?

          With Hippolytus' rejection of the glittering luxury of the pal-
          ace and desire for a simple life close to nature, compare the
          following passage from Lucretius (2.20-36):

              Therefore we see that few things altogether are necessary
              for the bodily nature, only such in each case as take pain
              away. Granting also that you may lay a man on a bed of
              luxury to his greater contentment at times—yet nature her-
              self feels no lack if there be no golden images of youths

about the house upholding fiery torches in their right
hands that light may be provided for nightly revellings, if
the hall shine not with silver and glitter not with gold,
if no cross-beams panelled and gilded echo the lyre; when
all the same stretched forth in groups upon the soft grass
beside a rill of water under the branches of a tall tree
men merrily refresh themselves at no great cost, especially
when the weather smiles, and the season of the year be-
sprinkles the green herbage with flowers:--yet no quicker
do hot fevers fly away from your body, if you have pictured
tapestry and blushing purple to toss upon, than if you must
lie sick under the poor man's blanket.

-- tr., W. H. D. Rouse

For the contrast between the Golden Age of the past and the
morally debased Iron Age of the present, compare the following
passage from Catullus (64.384-404):

For in bodily presence of old, before religion was de-
spised, the heavenly ones were wont to visit pious homes of
heroes, and show themselves to mortal company....But when
the earth was dyed with hideous crime, and all men banished
justice from their greedy souls, and brothers sprinkled
their hands with brothers' blood, the son left off to mourn
his parents' death, the father wished for the death of his
young son, that he might without hindrance enjoy the flower
of a young bride, the unnatural mother impiously coupling
with her unconscious son did not fear to sin against
parental gods...

-- tr., F. W. Cornish

588   Compare lines 356-357 for the step-mother theme, and lines
238-239 for Hippolytus' hatred of Phaedra. Has Hippolytus
generalized his hatred of Phaedra as his step-mother into an
uncompromising hatred of all women?

559-564   Note how consistent Hippolytus' misogyny is with his philosophy
of life in general.

559 *scelerum artifex*: with this characterization of women,
compare the nurse's self-exhortation, *utendum artibus* (426).

The nurse's advice was to get into the swing of things and move
with the crowd. Hippolytus, on the other hand, is determined to
shape his life as he sees fit and in accordance with his own
preferences, with no interference from the pressures of society,
the city, and the royal palace, untainted by the moral degenera-
tion of the Iron Age world around him, and especially with no
interference from what he regards as the source of all evils --
woman.

What indications are there of heightened emotion in this last part of Hippolytus' speech?

566-568a   What new depths of Hippolytus' personality do these lines reveal? With his recognition of the possibility of an irrational force driving him to hate women, compare his earlier image of rational self-control. Will the audience's response to Hippolytus shift as he speaks these lines?

Note the rhetorical device of asyndeton.

568b-573   Study closely these *adynata* (Greek for "impossibilities"), a common rhetorical device in which it is stated that X will not happen before Y, and in which Y consists of one or more impossible inversions of natural order.

574-575a   Compare line 240 spoken by Phaedra and lines 353-355 of the choral ode.

578-579   Theseus' murder of Antiope, Hippolytus' mother, made way for him to marry Phaedra, whom Hippolytus hates as his step-mother (cf. 238-239 and 558). He has generalized that hatred to include all women (238-239), and he finds in this hatred a consolation for the loss of his real mother (578).

580   *intractabilis*: just as she had predicted (see line 229); for the impossibility of dealing with Hippolytus, see also 119-123.

582   *verba sic spernit mea*: just as Phaedra had previously rejected her words. The nurse is not able to cope with either Phaedra or Hippolytus; neither of them can be turned aside from the drives of love and hatred that dominate their existences.

585-586   How has the nurse's description of Phaedra in lines 360-383 as love-sick, haggard, and distraught prepared the audience for seeing her faint now? Note how line 586 continues the same kind of physical description given in lines 360-383. What does Phaedra's fainting reveal about what is going on inside her? Remember that it was the nurse who suggested that Hippolytus be approached (Phaedra acquiesced tacitly). On the basis of the Phaedra-nurse scene, how do you think Phaedra feels about this tactic? Remember that Phaedra was ready to kill herself rather than suffer disgrace. How is she going to feel about approaching Hippolytus now? Note that she rushes impetuously onto the stage (*praeceps graditur, impatiens morae* 583), and then suddenly collapses. Has Phaedra's attempt to take on the active role of the hunter failed? Has it ended in emotional exhaustion?

With Seneca's dramatic representation of the painful inner life of a woman desperately in love with a forbidden beloved, one should compare Ovid's presentation of women such as Medea,

Scylla, Byblis, and Myrrha in the *Metamorphoses* (7.1-99, 8.11-151, 9.447-665, 10.298-502).

588   Note the alliteration of *t*'s; how does it reinforce the dramatic tension of the action?

589-590   What do these lines tell us about Phaedra's state of mind? With her fainting and momentary unconsciousness as relief from her emotional torment, compare her earlier conviction that death was the only way of escape from her troubles (253b).

592-599a Compare the nurse's self-exhortation in lines 425-430. What does Phaedra's self-exhortation here reveal about her feelings? How comfortable is she with the role she is playing? If it is her *pudor* which is holding her back (595; cf. 250), it is her *furor* (584) and a realization that she has in fact already sinned (594-596) that are driving her on. Note that just as the nurse hinted that Phaedra might be able to have Hippolytus without damaging her *fama* (269-270), so here Phaedra hopes to be able to conceal her crime and even make it respectable through marriage. How realistic is this? Note Phaedra's simultaneous realization of her sinful, criminal state and her grasping after a superficial appearance of respectability. With what is Phaedra more concerned, external appearances or the state of her inner being? Is she still caught in a tragic dilemma from which death (250-254) is the only way out?

600-601   The chorus and nurse remain on stage; neither would be regarded as an *arbitrium*.

602-605   Note the conflicting pulls of *amor/furor* (*vis magna*) and *pudor/ timor* (*vis maior*), and the paradox of Phaedra's not wanting what she wants (*hoc quod volo / me nolle*). The force of this conflict was expressed dramatically and physiologically by Phaedra's rushing impetuously onto the stage, impatient of delay, and abruptly fainting. Phaedra alternately tries to take control of her life and relinquishes control, as may be seen throughout the present scene.

605 *me nolle*: an unusual, incomplete line.

607   Is it because Phaedra's *curae* are *ingentes* that she cannot utter them, or because they are shameful?

608   *mater*: recall the nurse's shock over Phaedra's violation of the incest taboo in falling in love with her step-son (165-170). Phaedra's desire in the next passage to redefine the relationship between herself and Hippolytus by naming her his slave (611, 612, 617, 622), and her description of herself as widowed (623a) can be seen as attempts to remove the incest taboo (at least in her own mind) and to fantasize that marriage with

Hippolytus might be legally possible and morally acceptable (cf. line 597).

With Phaedra's desire to be called slave rather than mother by Hippolytus, compare Byblis' naming of Caunus as "lord" rather than "brother" in Ovid's telling of their story of incestuous love (*Metamorphoses* 9.466-467):

> iam dominum appellat, iam nomina sanguinis odit,
> Byblida iam mavult, quam se vocet ille sororem.

> Now she called him her lord, now hated the name of brother,
> and wished him to call her Byblis, rather than sister.

-- tr. F. J. Miller

613-616   Phaedra's willingness to undertake any feats or undergo any dangers imposed upon her by Hippolytus might suggest the devotion of a lover rather than a slave, but Hippolytus does not yet have any reason to interpret it this way.

623b-635 Note how Hippolytus rejects the thought that Theseus is dead and is convinced that he will soon return. This can only undercut Phaedra's hopes for a legitimate marriage with Hippolytus, and she protests that return will not be granted to Theseus (625-627), while at the same time emphasizing as she had earlier (91b-98) that she regards Theseus' adventure in the underworld as an infidelity to herself (627-628). Hippolytus "reassures" her that Theseus will return (629), and by promising to take the place of his father in the latter's absence (633) unwittingly sets Phaedra's hopes ablaze again.

637a   Compare 603-605.

638   *in novercam*: compare lines 558 and 356-357.

640b-644 Note the concentration of images of heat and fire (cf. 101-103 and 279-282).

646-666a Note Phaedra's brilliant transition from Hippolytus' question about her love for Theseus to her very indirect approach to a revelation of her infatuation with Hippolytus. How does she flatter Hippolytus in the meantime? What does she reveal about herself in her description of the youthful Theseus? Notice how her description of Hippolytus underscores the physical side of her infatuation -- first apparently with Theseus as a young man, now with Hippolytus.

          Previously Phaedra had seen a parallel between herself and her mother (112-123); she now recognizes a parallel with her sister, too.

668-669   Note Phaedra's re-making of reality in her fantasy of being
           transformed into a virgin for Hippolytus. Note that this would
           remove the incest taboo (cf. above on line 608) and make pos-
           sible a legitimate marriage with Hippolytus.

670   Note the alternatives: an end to her grief (through consumma-
           tion of her love) or death.

671a   Note the echo of lines 636 and 623a.

671b-684a Note that in appealing to Jupiter and Phoebus (the sun-god),
           Hippolytus is appealing to Phaedra's paternal and maternal
           grandfathers respectively (cf. lines 154-158).

           Compare the theme of the disruption of the order of nature in
           lines 175-177. Hippolytus expects some kind of cosmic sympa-
           thy; when things are so out of joint and monstrous on this
           earth, the heavens themselves should reverse their movements
           in shock and horror, and the sun should go into eclipse.

           678-679 Compare lines 124-128 and Phaedra's realization that
           her trouble stems from Venus' curse on the descendants of
           Phoebus.

           Note that in lines 672-673 Hippolytus has in mind that Jupiter
           should punish Phaedra's wickedness (*scelera*) by smiting her
           with a thunderbolt. In lines 682-684a, on the other hand, he
           sees himself as deserving punishment for having attracted
           Phaedra's love. Here we see the seeds of his own destruction
           in his inadvertent crime. Compare Hippolytus' feelings of
           guilt here (*sum nocens...placui novercae*) with Phaedra's feel-
           ings of guilt over having fallen in love with Hippolytus
           (*amavimus nefanda* 596).

           Is Hippolytus' reaction rational or irrational and emotional?
           Is it in keeping with the character, thinking, and feelings
           that he expressed in his two great speeches (483-564 and
           566-573)? Is his reaction in his entire speech here that of a
           sane, sensitive, humane person, or that of a madman? Is his
           inability to show the least bit of understanding or sympathy
           for the obviously distraught Phaedra one of the negative
           aspects of his life lived in remote isolation from the real
           problems of real people? How might one have better coped with
           Phaedra's passion? Is there any better way? Is there anything
           more that could have been done than what the nurse tried to do
           in the first Phaedra-nurse scene (i.e., try to persuade her out
           of it -- a tactic that got her nowhere)? Yet, even if the
           answer to these questions is negative, surely Hippolytus'
           "moral" reaction is of no help whatsoever, nor is it intended
           to be. To what extent do you blame Hippolytus?

684b-686   To what extent are the severity of Hippolytus' character and
            life style and his famed rejection of womankind in themselves
            incentives to Phaedra's aggression? Compare her mother's bold
            (*audax* 117) love for the fierce, untamed bull (117-118) and the
            pleasure that Phaedra takes in her fantasy of pursuing
            Hippolytus (233-241).

684b-693   The climax of Hippolytus' indignation; the lines are to be de-
            livered with the maximum of fury, hatred, and contempt.
            Hippolytus finally expresses his horror of Phaedra and of her
            mother which is at the heart of his hatred of women in general
            (cf. lines 238-239).

     697   Note the hammering on the *noverca* theme here and in 684a. For
            Medea, see lines 563-564. Both Theseus and Hippolytus have
            been threatened by women, and in both cases by stepmothers.
            One may recall other symmetries in the legendary material: the
            two daughters of Pasiphae, Ariadne and Phaedra, have been
            ruined respectively by Theseus and Hippolytus (663-666).

698-699   Compare lines 112-114 for Phaedra's recognition of the curse on
            her family and lines 178-185 for her inability to control her-
            self.

700-702   The pursuit theme again; compare lines 233-241.

     703   *superbe*: is Phaedra justified in this accusation of Hippoly-
            tus?

704-705a   The nurse was right: cf. 236-237.

708-709   Recall the prayer made by the nurse to Diana just before
            Hippolytus entered (406-423). Her prayer seemed to be answered
            by the appearance of Hippolytus, but it is now no longer Hippo-
            lytus who is being hunted down but Phaedra who is about to be
            sacrificed as a monster (captured by the hunter Hippolytus) on
            the altar of the goddess of the hunt -- a dramatic and ironic
            reversal of expectations and a brilliant piece of theatrics.

710-712   *sanas furentem*: compare line 249 *pars sanitatis velle sanari
            fuit* (spoken by the nurse). Phaedra wishes to be cured (*nunc
            me compotem voti facis* 710) just as strongly as the nurse
            wishes to see her cured, but except for her threat of suicide,
            Phaedra has so far seen no way to cure herself. Now a remedy
            will come with the blow of Hippolytus' sword. Her *furor* or
            amor will be extinguished, her honor (at least in one sense)
            saved (*salvo...pudore*). And, the slaying itself as the sword
            is thrust into her body would be more than she could wish for
            (*maius hoc voto meo est*); it would be a desired submission to
            male domination (compare her wish to be Hippolytus' slave:
            611-622) and a vicarious consummation of her sexual desires
            (*nunc me compotem voti facis* -- understood in a different sense

from the one which Phaedra consciously intends). Phaedra has long been prepared to die, and she eagerly seeks a final, quick, and emotionally satisfying solution to her tragic dilemma.

713-714   Hippolytus' throwing away of his contaminated sword is an insult to Phaedra and womankind, and it turns out to have been a fatal gesture for Hippolytus, because the nurse and Phaedra will use the sword as evidence in bringing a false charge of rape against Hippolytus. Hippolytus has lost his self-control momentarily because of his over-reaction to Phaedra, suggesting real *timor* on his part. His life in the woods has not prepared him for real life.

719-724   Note that it is the nurse and not Phaedra who concocts the stratagem of charging Hippolytus with rape. By what is she motivated? Will the audience admire her pragmatism or despise her immoral opportunism? To what extent does the nurse serve poetic justice upon Hippolytus for his callous rejection of Phaedra?

725-733a   Comment on the nurse as *scelerum artifex* (the phrase used of womankind by Hippolytus in line 559; and compare *utendum artibus* in line 426). But, note that it is Hippolytus' own actions (his pitiless rejection of Phaedra) and Phaedra's inaction that force the nurse to take matters into her own hands.

735   Comment on the irony of this line. What meaning does the nurse intend to convey to the onlookers? How else could the line be understood by Phaedra?

*   *   *

763-823   Study the relationship between the thematic structure of this
            ode and the shifts in meter.

736-740   Study the similes; what exactly is being compared with what in
            each simile? Are the similes themselves of any particular
            importance or relevance? How do the clouds and the comet com-
            ment on the dramatic situation and the impending tragedy?

741-752   What special importance does the moon have for Hippolytus?
            Compare line 654.

753-760   Note the way Seneca ties the comparison with Bacchus closely to
            the story of Phaedra's sister, Ariadne (developed at length by
            Phaedra in lines 646-666).

741-760   Of what relevance to the drama are these praises of Hippolytus'
            beauty? Are they purely gratuitous? Are they intended to make
            Phaedra's desire for him more understandable? Is Seneca trying
            to arouse our sympathy for Phaedra by praising the irresistible
            beauty of Hippolytus? And, at the same time, is he beginning to
            emphasize positive qualities of Hippolytus in order to prepare
            our emotions for his death? Are there any suggestions of ambi-
            valence in the chorus' attitude toward beauty?

761-776   Is the theme of these lines of any relevance to the dramatic
            action of the play up to this point? Is Hippolytus concerned
            with the fact that his beauty will soon wither? Would the
            statements in lines 773-774 be of any interest to Hippolytus?
            Does the introduction of the theme of beauty's brevity look for-
            ward to the denouement of the tragedy and the death of
            Hippolytus?

            764-776 Analyze the diction with which the theme of these lines
            is developed. Do the lines merely illustrate the proposition
            that *forma* is an *anceps bonum*? What is it in each instance that
            destroys *forma*? Note vocabulary that emphasizes the violence
            and suddenness of the forces of nature and of the passage of
            time. This passage provides a framework within which the audi-
            ence can view the sudden withering and violent destruction of
            Hippolytus' beauty that is soon to take place. Is what happens
            to him, then, just as natural and inevitable as the withering of
            the beauties of nature described in this passage?

777-784   How does this passage expose Hippolytus' idealization of country
            life (483-564) as an illusion? Note particularly how line 782
            refutes lines 520-521 and comments ironically on lines 510-514.
            Hippolytus' idealization is asexual and childlike; sexuality, in
            his eyes, is the property of evil stepmothers like Phaedra.
            Here and in the following passage (785-794) the chorus confronts
            Hippolytus with the sexuality that inevitably accompanies his
            beauty and with nature's pressure to put it to use.

785-794   Compare Diana and Endymion, introduced in lines 309-316 as an
           example of love's dominion over the gods. Now who is "hunting"
           whom? Instead of sacrificing Phaedra on the altar of Diana and
           thus freeing himself from the threat of attack by women,
           Hippolytus is being watched and will perhaps ultimately be
           seduced by Diana herself, who is already so enamoured of his
           beauty that she slows the course of her chariot. The goddess to
           whom Hippolytus prays for successful hunting in turn lingers
           over him. As a human being, and an extremely handsome one at
           that, Hippolytus is exposed to the same dangers as all other
           people; there is no escape, even in the depths of the woods.
           How does this passage comment on the confident optimism of
           Hippolytus in his opening address to his hunting companions and
           his prayer to Diana?

795-819   How does this praise of Hippolytus as a man endowed with special
           gifts of body, strength, and skill modify our attitude toward
           him? Note the emphasis on his potential superiority in all the
           skills needed by a hunter (804-819).

820-823   What is the chorus' attitude toward Hippolytus? How has this
           choral ode crystallized our perception of Hippolytus' dilemma?
           How do the final lines increase the tension that Seneca wishes
           the audience to experience at this point in the drama?

                              *   *   *

824-828   These lines presumably describe a continuation of the actions of
           the nurse at the end of the previous scene. There the nurse
           urged that Phaedra's hair remain torn and disheveled as evidence
           of Hippolytus' alleged attempt to rape her (731-732). Here
           additional efforts are mentioned to make Phaedra's appearance
           convincing. The nurse is playing out her role as *scelerum
           artifex* (Hippolytus' description of women; cf. 559-564).

829-849   What impression does Theseus make as he arrives on stage? What
           mental and physical state is he in? How well prepared is he to
           cope with the crisis in his palace?

           Emphasis on the difficulty of Theseus' escape from Hades pre-
           pares for the reversal at the end of the play when Theseus will
           wish that he could return to Hades to escape from the horror
           that he will have created in this world.

850   The plot to charge Hippolytus with rape was designed simply as a
           measure to cover Phaedra's improper advances to Hippolytus (see
           721). It was not intended explicitly as a punishment of
           Hippolytus nor as an act of revenge. Phaedra was not intending
           to kill herself nor was she even threatening suicide as part of
           the plot (see 824-828). Theseus' return changes everything
           (consider 856-857). Instead of using the sword as evidence
           against Hippolytus (730a), Phaedra apparently decides to use it
           against herself and to do now what she had threatened to do be-
           fore but did not carry through -- commit suicide. Yet she does
           not kill herself now. Why doesn't she? Does she have any clear
           plan in mind now that Theseus has suddenly and unexpectedly
           returned? Or is she reacting impulsively and out of panic?
           Theseus hears wailing from the palace; the nurse apparently
           tries to dissuade Phaedra from her threatened suicide (854-855)
           and then emerges from the palace to solicit Theseus' help (862).
           As always, the nurse wishes above all to preserve Phaedra's
           life (cf. 246-247 and 267).

857   What apprehensions will this answer raise in Theseus' mind?

860-861   A lie, but the nurse can hardly launch into a full account of
           why Phaedra is threatening suicide, and Phaedra's motivation at
           this moment may not be clear to the nurse or even to Phaedra
           herself. Note that the nurse does not charge Hippolytus with
           rape -- something she could have done quickly and easily if she
           were so minded. The plot to charge Hippolytus with rape has
           apparently been forgotten momentarily because of the crisis pro-
           duced by Theseus' return and Phaedra's sudden threat to commit
           suicide.

866-868   Ironically, the two requests (*animum mihi / restituis* and *te
           quidquid e vita fugat / expromis*) are mutually exclusive. If
           Phaedra tells why she is about to commit suicide, she will be

separating herself from Theseus by revealing her lust for
Hippolytus, not restoring herself to him.

872   Phaedra means that if she tells the truth as to why she is
        threatening suicide, she will lose her honor in the telling,
        but that she will preserve it if she dies in silence (cf. *haud
        te, fama, maculari sinam* 252).

874   Note Phaedra's expression of her reluctance to tell in terms of
        pudicitia. Compare the role of her *pudor* in her earlier threat
        of suicide (*non omnis animo cessit ingenuo pudor* 250).

876   An effective *sententia*.

878   Note the echo of lines 265-266 and the accompanying recall of
        Phaedra's former decision to commit suicide as the only way out
        of her tragic dilemma. Yet, she does not kill herself. She
        weakens again and ultimately exposes Hippolytus. Again, she
        exhibits a lack of resolve. Perhaps realizing this in self-
        disgust, she utters the famous *Quod vivo* (880a).

880a   *Quod vivo*: the most striking utterance in the entire play. The
        answer makes no sense to Theseus, who ignores it in his follow-
        ing question.

        In the older legends virtuous women killed themselves rather
        than bear sexual dishonor. Compare the story of Lucretia as
        told by Livy in Book 1.58.6-12:

            Lucretia they found sitting sadly in her chamber. The
            entrance of her friends brought the tears to her eyes, and
            to her husband's question, "Is all well?" she replied, "Far
            from it; for what can be well with a woman when she has lost
            her honour (*pudicitia*)? The print of a strange man,
            Collatinus, is in your bed. Yet my body only has been vio-
            lated; my heart is guiltless, as death shall be my witness.
            But pledge your right hands and your words that the
            adulterer shall not go unpunished. Sextus Tarquinius is he
            that last night returned hostility for hospitality, and
            armed with force brought ruin on me, and on himself no
            less -- if you are men -- when he worked his pleasure with
            me." They give their pledges, every man in turn. They
            seek to comfort her, sick at heart as she is, by diverting
            the blame from her who was forced to the doer of the wrong.
            They tell her it is the mind that sins, not the body
            (*mentem peccare, non corpus*: cf. line 735 *mens impudicam
            facere, non casus, solet*); and that where purpose has been
            wanting there is no guilt. "It is for you to determine,"
            she answers, "what is due to him; for my own part, though I
            acquit myself of the sin, I do not absolve myself from
            punishment; not in time to come shall ever unchaste women

live through the example of Lucretia." Taking a knife
which she had concealed beneath her dress, she plunged it
into her heart, and sinking forward upon the wound, died as
she fell. The wail for the dead was raised by her husband
and her father.

Phaedra's *quod vivo* gives lip service to this tradition. Yet,
the phrase has a deeper meaning in the play. What do you see in
these words?

The audience will recall Phaedra's earlier suicide threat (see
note to line 878 above). Now that the nurse's plan to seduce
Hippolytus has failed, Phaedra will feel that her very existence
is a crime, because she should have committed suicide earlier
rather than acquiescing in the nurse's ill-fated plan. At a
deeper level, the real crime for which she must die is simply
the fact that she is alive (*quod vivo*). Her guilt is tantamount
to her existence; it is part of her heritage (113-128). For
Phaedra, life, illicit love, and guilt form an inseparable and
tragic complex (cf. *magna pars sceleris mei / olim peracta est
...amavimus nefanda* 594-596), from which the only escape is
through death (*unicum effugium mali* 253). Her enigmatic *quod
vivo* gives expression to all of this. Just before Phaedra is
forced to accuse Hippolytus, bring about the death of an innocent person, and create the circumstances in which she will
finally commit suicide, Seneca reminds the audience of the full
depth of her tragic predicament and makes it clear that she must
be judged as a truly tragic character and not in simplistic
moral terms.

881   How does this statement emphasize Phaedra's desire to maintain
external appearances, a noble reputation, and her *fama*? How
does her speaking in *sententiae* reveal a desperate attempt to
cover her real sentiments and her fear of the pressure that
Theseus is exerting on her?

885b   Why must Phaedra not let Theseus interrogate the nurse under
torture? Out of humanity to the nurse, or out of fear that the
truth would come out? If the truth were revealed, what would
happen to Phaedra's reputation (*fama*)?

886-887 Phaedra, under tremendous pressure from Theseus and terrified
that the truth will be revealed, breaks down and impulsively
yields to the nurse's plot to cover crime with crime (721).
There is no other way to assure the preservation of herself, her
nurse, and her external image as an honorable woman. Even suicide is no longer practicable, since the nurse might reveal all
under torture afterwards.

With Phaedra's real tears here, compare the faked tears described at the beginning of this section of the play (827).

888-889   Phaedra here calls upon her paternal and maternal grandfathers
           respectively (Jupiter and Phoebus), the same gods upon whom
           Hippolytus called in lines 671b-683a.

890   The line recalls the curse upon Phaedra's family (cf. lines
           124-128) at the very moment when she is about to accuse Hippoly-
           tus. How does this add tragic depth to the action she is about
           to take?

891-892   *temptata precibus restiti*: an ironic inversion of what actually
           happened; it was Hippolytus who stood firm although tempted by
           prayers. Earlier Phaedra had stood firm while tempted by the
           prayers of her nurse.

           ferro ac minis / non cessit animus: a true statement in that
           Phaedra did not yield to Hippolytus' sword and threats (706-712)
           but rather welcomed death at his hands.

           vim tamen corpus tulit: again, a true statement; Phaedra did
           suffer violence at the hands of Hippolytus (see lines 707-708a).
           Phaedra is thus not fabricating a charge of rape out of whole
           cloth, but is alluding to the scene in which she was threatened
           by Hippolytus when she attempted to seduce him. Why does she do
           this instead of making a straightforward accusation? Why does
           she not openly charge Hippolytus with rape? Is she trying to
           protect Hippolytus? Or is she trying desperately to preserve a
           sense of honesty and self-respect?

893   In the light of the clear allusions to the scene of Phaedra's
           attempted seduction of Hippolytus, her words here must be taken
           in two senses. Theseus will understand her to mean that her
           suicide would wash away the stain of the alleged rape (cf.
           Lucretia); Phaedra herself can mean that her suicide would wash
           away the stain of her attempt to seduce Hippolytus, of her sin-
           ful lust that led to that attempt, and of the blot upon her
           pudor caused by her not committing suicide when she first
           proposed it (250).

895a   *Quem vere minime*: further ambiguity: Phaedra could be refer-
           ring either to Hippolytus or to herself.

896-897   Further ambiguity: Theseus will take the sword as proof that
           Hippolytus raped Phaedra, yet if the sword were to speak the
           truth it would tell a very different story.

898   *monstrum*: compare the uses and associations of this word
           earlier in the play; Theseus knows not what *monstrum* he is
           looking upon.

901b-902   Again, Phaedra does not take the blame for the lie (as in 896
           hic dicet ensis), but merely quotes what the slaves say, and
           the slaves have been deceived by the nurse (see lines 725-730).

903f   Compare Hippolytus's reaction at lines 671b and following. How
           do father and son share the same tendency to overreact and
           bring about their own destruction?

905-914   Much of what Theseus says about Hippolytus really applies to
           Phaedra: hers is the *generis infandi lues* (905), hers the
           untamed barbarian background (906-907a), hers the degenerate
           blood that recalls her family stock (allusion to Pasiphae)
           (907b-908), and so forth. The irony runs deep here as Theseus
           in mocking Hippolytus is unwittingly describing the real
           culprit, Phaedra.

915-925   All of the positive values that Hippolytus spoke of in his great
           speech (483-564) are here mocked as hollow pretentions. The
           audience which has seen Hippolytus' principles put into action
           in his uncompromising rejection of Phaedra will feel the irony
           of Theseus' misplaced accusations.

           In describing what he thinks is Hippolytus' deceitful hypocrisy
           (918-922a), Theseus is describing Phaedra exactly.

926-929a   Compare lines 578-579 for the effect that Theseus' slaying of
           Antiope has had on Hippolytus.

929-941a   The themes of flight, pursuit, and hunting down the victim reap-
           pear, with Hippolytus the hunter again being pursued, this time
           by his father. Hippolytus will have no place to hide: compare
           the previous choral ode (especially lines 777-784) and note the
           repetition of the adjectives *abditus* (778, 933) and *avius*
           (777) = *invius* (939). Line 938 implies that Theseus thinks of
           his son as a wild beast whom he should track down as he flees
           per omnes latebras (so also line 941b).

941b-942   Note the effective transition from the theme of pursuit to that
           of the curse.

954-958   Compare lines 671b-677a. What kind of a world is it in which
           the "just" prayer of Hippolytus is ignored by the gods, while
           the errant prayer of Theseus is answered? This is the question
           raised by the following choral ode, which makes a moral commen-
           tary upon fate's blind justice and the social decadence of life
           in the palace.

                              *   *   *

959-989   Locate other references to the order of nature and the workings of natural forces in the play. Consider especially lines 54-72, 171-177, 184-194, 274-357, 406-423, 451-482, 525-557, and 761-776. Consider the dichotomy between nature as order and permanence (= *Natura*) on the one hand and nature as disruption, transformation, and violence (especially Diana, Venus-Cupid, and Neptune) on the other. What is man's life likely to be like in a world ruled by these two sets of divinities or natural powers? *Natura* is apparently oblivious to moral issues (976-977), while Diana, Venus, Cupid, and Neptune are either capricious or amoral. The chorus invites the audience to conclude pessimistically and despairingly that there is no order in human affairs, but only a blind chance (Fortune), which appears to dispense its gifts at random (*manu...caeca* 979-980) while actually favoring the morally wicked and perverse (980b-988).

Note the allusions to various characters in the play in lines 981 and following. *Pudor* and *decus* (988-989) will refer to Hippolytus. The chorus' tragic view of the world thus comes to center on the fate of Hippolytus, whose *pudor* and *decus* have not received their proper reward, while Phaedra's *dira libido* has triumphed. Note the avoidance of any suggestion that Hippolytus' character might be flawed and that his words and actions might be in any way the cause of his own downfall. Also note the absence of any note of sympathy for Phaedra's tragic predicament. Compare the previous ode. To what extent is Hippolytus' doom seen as part of the natural order of things? To what extent, if any, is it seen as something for which he is personally responsible? What kind of tragic denouement is the play moving toward?

989-999   Consider the messenger's feelings about Hippolytus and his
            death.   Compare the attitude of the chorus in the last two
            odes.

1000   *profugus*:   note the echo of Theseus' words in lines 929 and
            938.   Theseus there was thinking of Hippolytus as fleeing in
            guilt after his alleged rape of Phaedra; here Theseus will
            find confirmation of Phaedra's charge of rape in Hippolytus'
            flight.   Hippolytus knows nothing of his father's return,
            Phaedra's accusation, or his father's curse.   What, then, is
            he fleeing from?   Phaedra's contamination? personal guilt?

1002-1003   Note Hippolytus' careful control of his horses, and compare
            lines 31-43 with his advice on careful control of the dogs and
            his whole ideal of a controlled life in his great speech,
            lines 483-564.   Hippolytus regains control over fear, now that
            he is in his own element, nature, and will be undone by his
            horses' *timor* (1089) rather than his own.

1004   *multa secum effatus*:   Hippolytus would have been mulling over
            the frightening confrontation with Phaedra, as he now, in com-
            pensation for his loss of emotional control, reins in his
            horses tightly.   Note that he does not reveal Phaedra's lust
            to his companions, and so the messenger cannot report the
            truth to Theseus now.

1004-1005   *patrium solum / abominatus*:   Hippolytus curses Athens rather
            than the real object of his hatred, Phaedra.   Theseus can in-
            terpret Hippolytus' cursing of Athens as a natural action
            after his alleged rape of Phaedra and during his supposed
            flight from the scene of his crime.

1005   *saepe genitorem ciet:*   Hippolytus would in fact have been
            calling upon Theseus for very different reasons from those
            which Theseus, believing Hippolytus to have raped Phaedra,
            would imagine.

1007-1024   How does Seneca emphasize the uncanny nature of the disturb-
            ance in the sea?   One should compare Ovid's version of the
            story of Hippolytus and the bull from the sea in *Metamorphoses*
            15.497-546.

            1015-1020 What vocabulary suggests that the sea is thought of
            as pregnant?   Is there any allusion to Pasiphae and the
            Minotaur here?   Where else in the play has the word *monstrum*
            been used?   The sea is often thought of in ancient myth and
            literature as both procreative (cf. Venus as born from the
            sea: line 274) and destructive.

1026   *immugit*:   does this word suggest the sea or a bull?

1030   How does the reference to the *physeter capax* contribute to the uncanny atmosphere?

1035-1049   Carefully distinguish the details appropriate to a bull from those appropriate to a sea-monster. What other two-formed monster has been mentioned in the play, and how can this present monster be seen as a "re-appearance" of the earlier one? Who is ultimately responsible for the coming of this monster? How does it fulfill the fears voiced by the nurse in lines 174-177? How does this new monster, in essence the progeny of Phaedra's lust, complete the cycle of the inherited curse?

1039 *feri dominator...gregis*: compare Phaedra's description of the bull with which Pasiphae mated: *ductor indomiti gregis* (118).

1050-1054a   Note that the monster first disrupts Hippolytus' beloved world of the field and woods; compare Hippolytus' first speech in the play.

1054b-1056   Note the vocabulary of restraint.

1062   A remarkable line. Note the interplay of rhythm and sound in the description of the monster running so fast that its feet scarcely touch the ground.

1064-1067   Compare the chorus' description of Hippolytus in lines 797-819; he is a very capable young man. His physical and manly potential is put to the test, and his courage will hold until his death. His confidence is based in part on his father's success against the Minotaur. But, just as the one house of Theseus ruined two sisters (665-666), so this bull which re-enacts the Minotaur and which Phaedra's lust has brought to life, will ruin both Hippolytus and Theseus.

Hippolytus lost control of himself in his confrontation with Phaedra and fled to his beloved woods and wild beasts (718), where he reestablished control, only to be attacked by the ineluctable menace of the bull from the sea. Contrast Hippolytus' handling of this threat from raw nature with his handling of the "civilized" threat of Phaedra's lust.

1067 Ironic, in that it was his father who sent this bull against him. Note that Hippolytus never learns why he is being pursued by the bull from the sea.

1068-1071   Note the vocabulary of restraint and that expressing violence and fury. How effectual is restraint? How effectual have attempts at restraint proven to be earlier in the play?

1072-1081   Continue to study the vocabulary and imagery expressive of re-
             straint and control, especially in the simile of the helmsman.

1082-1089   What vocabulary here is reminiscent of the prologue and
             Hippolytus' instructions for the hunt? The hunter is now
             caught in his own devices (compare lines 44-47b, 74-76, and
             502-503).

1090-1092   How are Hippolytus' horses like those of the chariot of the
             sun? In what ways is Hippolytus like Phaethon? How does this
             simile recall and suggest the final fulfillment of the curse
             that Venus has put upon the descendants of Phoebus?

1093-1104   The chorus' worse fears (820-823) are now fulfilled. How does
             Hippolytus receive "poetic justice" for his rejection of sex?

1105-1110a   How is this scene a macabre parody of the end of a hunting ex-
             pedition? Compare lines 76-80. With the tale of Hippolytus
             the hunter hunted down by the monster and killed by the
             actions of his own horses, compare the story as told by Ovid
             (*Metamorphoses* 3.155-252) of Actaeon the hunter destroyed by
             his own hunting dogs.

1110b-1114a Compare the choral ode in lines 736-823, especially lines
             820-823. To what climax is the tragedy now coming? Audience
             sympathy for Hippolytus had been heightened in preparation for
             his fall as recounted now by the messenger. Hippolytus has
             lost his beauty and his partnership in his father's throne.
             Compare your feeling for Hippolytus here at the end of the
             messenger's speech with your reaction to him when he rejected
             Phaedra's advances in lines 671a-718. Note that here at the
             end of the messenger's speech attention is focused narrowly on
             the single theme of Hippolytus' fall from beauty and power to
             a horrible and ugly death. Note the very graphic description
             of his demise, stylistically akin to the physical descriptions
             of the love-sick Phaedra. Contrast the psychological afflic-
             tion of Phaedra to the purely physical suffering of Hippoly-
             tus. Nothing is said about the reasons for Hippolytus' fall;
             neither Phaedra's advances nor Theseus' curses are mentioned
             or apparently even known by the messenger. The focus is on
             Hippolytus' catastrophe alone (compare the following choral
             ode).

1114b-1122   Analyze Theseus' reaction to the messenger's speech. Are you
             able to sympathize with his reaction?

                              *   *   *

1123   Compare lines 1110b-1114a and notes.

1124-1140   Study the world-view expressed by the chorus here alongside of
            the view expounded in the previous choral ode.

            Is the chorus thinking of Hippolytus or of Theseus or of all
            the royal characters in the play? How are its thoughts here
            relevant to what has taken place in the play? Are they con-
            sistent with the chorus' earlier pronouncements (777-794) on
            the dangers even of a life in the woods? Compare the nurse's
            contrast between the luxury and lust of the rich and powerful
            and the virtue and moderation of simple folk (204-215). Note
            that the chorus avoids the overt moralizing of the nurse and
            focuses attention on the bare proposition that Fortune rages
            less against the little people (1124) while it thunders around
            palaces (1140).

1143b-1148 The chorus now sees its general lesson about the instability
            of human fortune as exemplified in the recent experience of
            Theseus and his reversal from joy (reading *laetus videt* in the
            lacuna after line 1143) to sorrow. Compare this passage with
            the messenger's description of the reversal or catastrophe
            suffered by Hippolytus (1110b-1114a). In neither passage is
            there any analysis of the causes or attempt to assign blame
            for the catastrophe but rather a narrow focus on the fact of
            the ironic and catastrophic reversal itself. We are meant to
            contemplate first Hippolytus and then Theseus as exemplifica-
            tions of the abstract, universal truths about life in a world
            governed by Fortune expressed in lines 1123, 1124-1125, and
            1141-1143a.

1149-1153   A further ironic pattern is discovered by the chorus in the
            workings of Fortune; not only has Theseus been plunged from
            joy to sorrow, but a certain equilibrium has been reestab-
            lished with Hippolytus replacing Theseus in the underworld
            (*constat inferno numerus tyranno* 1153). A kind of cosmic
            order has been restored, but only at the expense of humanity.

                        *   *   *

1154-1155   Note the similarity to the way the previous scene involving
             Phaedra and Theseus began (lines 850f.).

1159-1163   Note the echo of Phaedra's first line in the play (85). Com-
             pare the description of the sea in lines 1015-1020. Consider
             the sexual implications of Phaedra's prayer to the sea (*me me
             ...saeve dominator...invade*) as an appeal to be entered by the
             ruler of the deep and/or his *monstra*, thereby completing the
             curse of unnatural sexual union, Phaedra's heritage from her
             mother Pasiphae. Compare this desire for destruction to her
             appeal to Hippolytus to slay her with his sword (710-712).

1164-1167   Compare Phaedra's earlier statements about Theseus (91b-92).
             Although her lust has brought about the tragic situation, she
             nonetheless names Theseus as the destroyer of his home. *amore
             aut odio nocens*: love and hate have equivalent power. Both
             are equally noxious -- but in Theseus' hands, not her own.
             Then, after abdicating moral responsibility, Phaedra proceeds
             to assert a final control over her life, her guilt, and her
             death in the following lines.

1168-1181a   What is the tone of Phaedra's address to Hippolytus? Does she
             see herself as a kind of Sinis, Procustes, or Minotaur? Note
             that these are all creatures slain by her husband. Note
             themes of flight and pursuit throughout the passage.

             1176 *nil turpe loquimur*: as opposed to her speech in her
             earlier encounter with Hippolytus. Note how different things
             are now. Phaedra speaks openly now in front of witnesses,
             even her husband. Neither *pudor* nor *timor* restrains her
             speech. By committing suicide she will make amends to Hippo-
             lytus (1176b-1177), and at the same time she will strip
             herself of both life (*anima*) and sin (*scelere* 1178). Her
             shade will then be free to follow Hippolytus through the
             regions of the underworld (1179-1180).

1183-1184a   For the theme of lovers who were not allowed union in life
             seeking union in death as Phaedra does here, compare the story
             of Pyramus and Thisbe as told by Ovid (*Metamorphoses* 4.55-
             166).

1184b-1185a Are these two conditions (*si casta es...si incesta*) mutually
             exclusive? Or has Phaedra been both *casta* and *incesta* at the
             same time? To what extent has this been her dilemma all
             along?

1185b-1187   What do these lines tell us about Phaedra's integrity and
             honesty with herself?

1188-1189   Note the verbal play on the words *mors*, *amor*, and *pudor*. How does the verbal play here sum up Phaedra's tragic situation? Note that line 1188 speaks of death as the only cure for her evil love (i.e., as a cure of her inner trouble), while line 1189 speaks of death as restoring honor to her tarnished reputation (i.e., as having an external effect). With line 1189 compare her determination in line 252 not to allow her *fama* to be stained.

1190   Note the theme of flight. What do the words *pande placatos sinus* (addressed to death) imply that Phaedra is longing for in death? an opportunity to continue her pursuit of Hippolytus (as in lines 1179-1180)? or oblivion? Compare lines 589-590 for Phaedra's welcoming of oblivion.

1191-1198   Note Phaedra's final judgment of herself. Upon what does she place the blame for what she did? How does she view herself? Note the deliberate balance of diction in her final lines: *mucrone...iusto; pectus impium; sancto...viro*. What are your final feelings about Phaedra? Is she mad (*demens* 1193), or does she gain nobility at the moment of her death?

1199-1200   Theseus apparently accepts Phaedra's judgment of him (1191b-1192a) and condemns himself to the punishment that Phaedra has just inflicted upon herself. Some manuscripts, however, attribute these lines to Phaedra. Which attribution makes more dramatic sense?

1201-1207   Note the echoes of Phaedra's final speech: *impium* (1203 of Theseus, 1197 of Phaedra) and *monstra* (1160 of the monsters which Phaedra summons to punish her, 1204 of the monsters Theseus summons to punish him). Whom does Theseus blame? Why does he not blame Phaedra? Does Theseus gain stature in your eyes by taking full responsibility for his actions?

1213-1216   See lines 1141-1148 above for a similar statement of the reversal of Theseus' fortunes.

1217   *donator atrae lucis*: how does the oxymoron here express the essence of the tragic situation of Theseus who has been unable to distinguish appearance from reality?

1220b-1225   Comment on the irony of Theseus, the just punisher of legendary criminals such as Sinis and Procrustes, here calling down a just punishment upon himself for his unjust punishment of his son. The paradoxical reversal with the legendary punisher being himself punished is parallel to the larger paradox in the play of Hippolytus the hunter being himself hunted down and destroyed.

1226-1243   Punishment in Hades is denied to Theseus, who is condemned to
              live, but he has made his life into a worse hell than that
              below the earth. Compare lines 162-163 for the mental horrors
              one may create for oneself.

              1242b-1243 Note Theseus' bitterness toward the gods who once
              granted him favors and power. He now demands punishment for
              inadvertent misuse of his power. Theseus, the powerful male
              hero, is also a victim of fate -- no better than the helpless
              figures of Phaedra and Hippolytus, who now lie dead on the
              stage.

1244-1246   How does the chorus exhort Theseus to deal with his life and
              feelings, now so out of control?

    1249   *crimen agnosco meum*: compare Phaedra's line *fatale miserae
              matris agnosco malum* (113).

1256-1268   What is the dramatic purpose of this gruesome reassembling of
              Hippolytus' corpse? Does it symbolize an attempt to piece to-
              gether a shattered world? Can Theseus recreate the past,
              annul his crimes, and expiate his guilt? Can order be re-
              established? Or is the attempt vain and the world left perma-
              nently out of joint by the actions that have taken place in
              the course of the tragedy? (Compare lines 1149-1153 and
              notes.)

1269-1270   Theseus echoes Phaedra in lines 1173-1174. Locate other pas-
              sages in the play where Hippolytus' beauty is compared to that
              of heavenly bodies. Note that the verb *cecidit* (1270) can
              mean simply "has fallen" but is also used frequently of the
              setting of heavenly bodies. What meaning could be elicited
              here from an allusion to the orderly, cyclical movements of
              the cosmos? Is Hippolytus' "fall" merely one illustration of
              an eternal, fixed pattern of events played out in a world gov-
              erned by Nature and Fortune (cf. 959-989)?

1278-1279a   *per agros...vagas / anquirite*: The search through the fields
              and the adjective *vagus* recall Hippolytus' first speech in the
              play. The play has moved full circle from the hunter prepar-
              ing to hunt to the search for the hunter who has been trapped
              and slain and is now the object of the hunt.

1279b-1280   Theseus and the fate of Hippolytus dominante the final scene.
              Theseus' only reference to Phaedra is contained in these
              lines. What is its effect? Why has Theseus not referred to
              her earlier? What kind of a final comment on Phaedra does
              Seneca's handling of this final scene make? How does the
              guilt and the fate of Theseus reflect upon that of Phaedra?
              Are their guilts in any way equivalent? Note that this final
              scene is the only one in the play in which all three of the

major characters are on stage together. What are your final
feelings toward them? Does the final scene add a new dimen-
sion to the audience's perception of the tragic nature of the
world within which the events of the play have taken place?
Analyze your final emotional response to the fictional world
created by the play.

THE HIPPOLYTUS OF EURIPIDES

Translated by Gilbert and Sarah Lawall

DRAMATIS PERSONAE

APHRODITE (APH), goddess of love.

HIPPOLYTUS (HIP), bastard son of Theseus and the queen of the Amazons.

COMPANIONS (COMP) of Hippolytus.

SERVANT (SERV) of Hippolytus.

CHORUS (CH) of married women of Trozen.

NURSE (NUR) of Phaedra.

PHAEDRA (PH), wife of Theseus.

THESEUS (TH), king of Athens and Trozen, son of Poseidon or Aegeus.

CITIZENS of Trozen.

COMPANION (COMP) of Hippolytus.

ARTEMIS (ART), goddess of virginity.

*The Scene for the whole play is the open space before the
double-doors of the royal palace of Trozen. Directly beside
the doors is a statue of Aphrodite. Also on stage is a
statue of Artemis; possibly it should be to one side of the
stage, in a wooded setting suggested by scene painting.
Aphrodite, the goddess of love, enters, mounted on a mechanical contrivance that indicates her superior status as an
immortal.*

APH   Powerful among mortals and not without a name,
I am the goddess called Cypris -- and in heaven as well.

Of all the men who live between the Pontic Sea
and the boundaries of Atlas and see the light of the sun,
I give first place to those who reverence my power   5
but trip and throw down those who think big toward me.
For one thing holds true of gods as well as men:
they like people to honor them.

I will soon show how true this is.

Hippolytus, the son of Theseus and offspring of the   10
Amazon, was raised by chaste Pittheus.
Now he alone of all the citizens of this land of Trozen
says that I am by nature the worst of gods.
He refuses to make love and won't touch marriage;
instead, he honors Artemis, the sister of Phoebus and maiden   15
daughter of Zeus. He believes her the greatest of gods
and is always consorting with that virgin throughout the green woods,
while he and his swift dogs rid the land of wild beasts.
He's fallen in with a companionship above his mortal birth.

Now, I'm not jealous of them. Why should I be?   20
But for his sins against me I will exact vengeance
from Hippolytus this very day. Most of my preparations are
long since finished, and not much remains to be done.

He once went from Pittheus' palace
to see the stately mysteries performed   25
in Pandion's land. Then Phaedra, his father's noble wife,
saw him, and her heart was seized
with terrible love -- just as I planned!
And before coming to this Trozenian land,
she set up a temple to Cypris by the rock   30
of Pallas that overlooks this land, since her love
was a love away from home. For the rest of time
men will call this the goddess set up for Hippolytus.

But now Theseus has left the Cecropian soil,
fleeing the pollution of Pallantid blood.   35
He has sailed with his wife to this soil,
and consented to a year's exile away from home.

Now, groaning and struck out of her wits
by the goads of love, the poor woman is perishing
in silence, and no one in the household understands her illness.   40

But her love must not end in this way.
I will reveal the situation to Theseus, and it will be clear to all.
He will kill that young enemy of mine
with curses which the king of the sea,
Poseidon, once gave him as a gift of honor,   45
granting that he could call upon the god three times, and not in vain.
Phaedra will die with her good name, but she will die nonetheless.
For I will not honor her misfortune more
than paying back my own personal enemies
with just such punishment as pleases me.   50

But I see the son of Theseus
approaching here, coming back from the hunt.
It's Hippolytus. I'll be leaving now.
A large band of servants follows his footsteps and shouts
along with him, honoring the goddess Artemis   55
with hymns.

            For he does not know that the gates of
Hades stand open, and that this day's light is the last that he will see.

Exit.

Hippolytus enters, followed by his companions. They arrive
directly from the hunt and proceed toward the statue of Artemis.
Hippolytus sings as he exhorts his companions.

HIP   Follow me, follow me,
        singing of Zeus' heavenly daughter,
        Artemis, for we are in her care.   60

HIP   *singing a traditional cult song as they approach the statue*
and
COMP   Mistress, most holy mistress,
        offspring of Zeus,
        hail, hail, Artemis, most beautiful of
        maidens, virgin daughter   65
        of Leto and Zeus.
        You dwell
        in the great heaven, in your noble father's
            halls, the richly golden house of Zeus.
        Hail, O most beautiful, most   70
            beautiful of those on Olympus.

The song over, Hippolytus stands in front of the statue of
Artemis and addresses the goddess.

HIP   I have arranged this woven garland for you,

mistress, and I bring it from an untouched
meadow, where no shepherd dares pasture his flock   75
and iron has not yet come; only the bee in springtime
passes through the untouched meadow.
Aidos, goddess of self-restraint, tends it with streams of clear water,
for those whose virtues are not learned but in whose very nature
goodness has been assigned a place in all things forever.   80
These may pluck flowers there, but it is not right for the wicked.

placing a wreath on the gilded hair of the statue of Artemis

I alone of mortals have this privilege:
I consort with you, and we exchange words.   85
I can hear your voice, but not see your face.

May I round the goal of my life just as I began it.

*His offering and prayer made, Hippolytus turns away from the
statue of Artemis. As he moves toward the palace doors, an
older serving man steps forward from among Hippolytus'
companions and addresses him.*

SERV Prince -- for only the gods should be called masters --
      would you take some well-meant advice from me?

HIP   Of course -- otherwise I would not appear wise.   90

SERV Do you know what the custom is among mortals?

HIP   No, I don't. What are you getting at?

SERV They hate pride and not being friendly to all.

HIP   Rightly so. What proud man is not tiresome?

SERV Do you think courtesy gets you any thanks?   95

HIP   Yes, many thanks, and profit, too, gained with little effort.

SERV Don't you expect the same is true among the gods?

HIP   Yes, since we mortals observe their customs.

SERV *with a gesture toward the statue of Aphrodite*

      Why then don't you address a proud goddess?

HIP   *pretending not to notice his gesture*

      Which one? Watch out that your tongue doesn't trip you up.   100

SERV   *pointing*

       This one, standing right beside your door: Cypris.

HIP   *turning away*

       From afar I greet her, pure as I am.

SERV   Nonetheless, she is proud and widely known among mortals.

HIP   Each has his own likes and dislikes in gods as well as men.

SERV   I wish you luck, with all the good sense you need.   105

HIP   No god who is worshipped at night suits me.

SERV   My child, the gods must have their honors.

       Hippolytus turns abruptly away from the old servant and
       addresses his other companions.

HIP   Get along, men. Enter the house
       and see to the food. There's no pleasure after the hunt
       like a full table. And you'll have to rub down   110
       the horses, so that I may yoke them to my chariot
       when I've eaten my fill, and exercise them properly.

       to the servant, with a glance toward the statue of Aphrodite

       But as for your Cypris -- I bid her a fond farewell!

       Exit into the palace.

SERV   *pausing before the statue of Aphrodite on his way into the*
       house

       But I -- for young people should not be imitated   115
       when they think like that -- will speak as a slave should
       and pray to your image,
       mistress Cypris. One must understand and forgive.
       If someone is young and high-strung
       and talks nonsense, pretend not to hear him.
       Gods ought to be wiser than mortals.   120

       Exit into the palace.

*As the old servant exits, the chorus of fifteen Trozenian women
enters from the wings. They are young married women from
respectable families, who, having heard the gossip that something is wrong with Phaedra, have come now to find out what
the trouble is.*

CH   *singing as it enters the circular dance floor in front of
the palace doors*

STROPHE 1

They say it is Ocean's water that drips from the rock   121
whose steep sides send forth a flowing stream, to be dipped up in
                                        our pitchers.
There a friend of mine
was washing purple robes
in the stream's clear water
and was laying them out on the back of a rock
warm from the sun. From her I
first heard the news about the queen.   130

ANTISTROPHE 1

Worn out with illness she lies there, staying inside
the house, light robes shading her blond head.
By taking no food to her mouth   135
for three days, so I hear,
she now keeps her body
pure of Demeter's grain.
Suffering in secret she wishes
to beach her ship on the wretched shore of death.

STROPHE 2

Are you possessed, my daughter
by Pan or Hecate
or the sacred Corybantes or the Mountain Mother,
    that your mind is wandering?
Or have you offended Dictynna,
    great goddess of wild animals   145
by neglecting her rites and offerings, and now waste away unhallowed?
For she wanders even through this lagoon
    and over the sandbar along the sea
in wet swirls of brine.   150

ANTISTROPHE 2

Or is your husband, the Erechthids'
nobly born ruler,
tended by someone else in the house? Does he lie secretly
    with another, away from your bed?

Or has some sailor   155
    setting out from Crete sailed into the
harbor friendliest to seamen,
bringing news to the queen,
    so that in grief over her misfortunes
her soul is bound fast to her bed?   160

EPODE

Along with the dissonant harmony
of being a woman
    there dwells a wretched helplessness
coming from birth pangs and their unreasoning dread.
Through my womb this breath of pain once   165
    darted. I called on the heavenly easier of childbirth,
the mistress of the arrows,
Artemis, and (heaven willing) she always
comes to me greatly envied.

*The double doors of the palace open, and Phaedra is brought
out. She is lying on her sick-bed which is carried out and
set down by her servants in full view of the audience. Her
hair is arranged on top of her head, and folds of her light
robe are drawn up over her head to shade her face. Her old
nurse accompanies her and removes the folds of her robe as
she brings her out of doors.*

CH   *declaiming in a manner half way between singing and ordinary
         speech*

But here is her old nurse in front of the doors   170
bringing her out of the house.
My very soul desires to learn what the trouble is --
what has harmed
    the queen's body and changed her color.   175

*The chorus retires to the sides of the orchestra as the
nurse and Phaedra hold the center of the stage. This scene
is declaimed in the same way as the chorus' lines above.*

NUR   *to herself*

O troubles of mortal men, and hated illnesses!

turning to Phaedra

What should I do with you? What should I not do?
Here is your sunlight; here is the bright open air.
Your sick-bed is now

outside the house.   180
But the gloomy cloud on your brow grows larger.
All you could talk about was coming out here;
soon you'll be rushing back to your bedroom.
You're quickly upset and don't enjoy anything.
Nothing at hand pleases you, and you think
anything far off is better.   185

to herself again

I would rather be sick than tend the sick;
one is a simple matter, but along with the other
comes grief in the mind and work for the hands.

Man's whole life is painful,
    and there's no rest from labor.   190
But if there's anything better than life,
it's covered with clouds and concealed in darkness.
We seem to be madly in love
with what glitters here on earth,
through our ignorance of any other life,   195
and because we've never been shown what's beneath the earth.
    Mere tales carry us aimlessly about.

PH   *to her servants*

Lift up my body; hold up my head.
My limbs feel weak in the joints.
Take hold of my hands and my pretty arms, servants.   200
This thing on my head is heavy --
take it off, and let my hair curl down over my shoulders.

NUR *to Phaedra as she loosens her hair*

Steady, child, and don't shift your body about
so violently.
You'll bear your illness more easily   205
with a calm and noble spirit.
    Besides, suffering is forced on mortals.

PH   *delirious*

Ah!
If only I could take a drink
from a clear spring of pure water,
lie in the tall grass   210
under black poplars, and find rest.

NUR *shocked*

Child, what are you saying?

Won't you stop talking this way in front of everybody,
shouting words that ride forth on madness?

PH   *still delirious*

Take me to the mountains; I'll go to the woods   215
among the pines, where hunting
dogs run
in pursuit of spotted deer.
O gods, hear my prayer! I long to shout to the dogs,
throw a Thessalian javelin   220
from beside my blond hair, and hold a barbed
lance in my hand.

NUR   Why these troubled thoughts, child?
What do you care about hunting?
Why do you long for flowing springs?   225
There's clear water right here on the slope
next to the city walls. You could drink there.

PH   *still delirious*

Artemis, mistress of the lagoon by the sea
and of the courses resounding to horses' hooves,
I wish I were on your sacred grounds,
taming Venetian colts.   230

NUR   Now what nonsense are you shouting?
A minute ago you were in the mountains, setting out
on the hunting you longed for; but now you desire colts
on the sands beside the waves.   235
This needs a prophet's insight, and lots of it,
to tell what god draws you back by the reins
    and strikes your wits astray, child.

PH   *suddenly coming to her senses*

Oh misery! What have I done?
Where have I strayed from my right mind?   240
I went mad. A god clouded my mind, and I fell.

groans

Oh -- Oh -- miserable me!
Nurse, cover up my head again.
I'm horrified at what I have said.
Cover me! Tears fall from my eyes;   245
shame has come to my face.

Keeping my mind straight is painful,
but this madness is evil. It would be best of all
    to die with no awareness of either.

NUR   *replacing the robe over Phaedra's head*

       I am covering you. But when will death   250
       cover my body?

       to herself

       A long life has taught me many things.
       We mortals should mix our friendships
       with one another moderately,
       and not to the inner marrow of the soul.   255
       Our hearts' affections ought to be free and easy,
       whether we're pushing them aside or drawing them tight.
       It's a heavy burden when one soul suffers
       for two, as I'm
       agonizing over this woman.   260

       A rigid way of life, they say,
       trips and throws us instead of bringing pleasure,
       and wars against health.
       I admire excess less
       than moderation,   265
          and wise men agree with me.

       The chorus-leader steps forward and addresses the nurse. The
       lines of this scene are spoken in ordinary, conversational
       tones.

CH-L   Old woman, our queen's trusted nurse,
       we see Phaedra's miserable condition,
       but it is unclear to us what her illness is.
       We want to learn about it from you.   270

NUR   I don't know. I've tried to find out, but she won't tell.

CH-L   Not even what started her troubles?

NUR   It's the same thing. She keeps quiet about everything.

CH-L   How feeble and wasted her body is!

NUR   And why not? She hasn't eaten for three days.   275

CH-L   Because she's lost her mind? Or is she trying to die?

NUR   I don't know. But this fasting will soon end her life.

CH-L   It's amazing if what you say satisfies her husband.

NUR   She hides her pain and doesn't admit she's ill.

CH-L   Can't he tell by looking at her face?   280

NUR   As it happens, he's out of the country.

CH-L   Can't you force her to tell you
       about her illness and wandering mind?

NUR   I've tried everything and gotten nowhere.
       But even now I won't slacken my efforts,
       so that you who are here may see   285
       what kind of person I am toward masters in trouble.

       to Phaedra

       Come, dear child, let's both forget
       what has been said, and you be more pleasant.
       Relax your gloomy frown and way of thinking,   290
       and I will abandon my former, clumsy approach
       and pass to other and better words.
       If your illness is one we don't talk about,
       these people here are women to help cure your trouble.
       If your condition may be revealed to men,   295
       speak, so that doctors may be told of the case.

       pause

       Well then, why are you quiet? You musn't be silent, child,
       but either correct me if I say something wrong,
       or agree if what I have said is right.

       pause

       Say something!   Look at me!

       to chorus

       Oh, I'm miserable,   300
       women, for all my work is wasted,
       and I'm right back where I was before. She wasn't
       softened by my words then, nor is she won over now.

       to Phaedra

       But know this at least, and then be more stubborn
       than the sea itself. If you die, you will betray your   305
       children, who will not share in their father's estate:
       I swear by that horse-riding Amazon queen,
       who gave birth to a master for your children,
       a bastard who thinks high-born thoughts. You know very well whom I mean:
       Hippolytus...

PH   Oh!

NUR   Does this touch you?   310

PH   You've destroyed me, nurse! By the gods I beg you
      not to mention that man again.

NUR   You see? You can think clearly, but still you don't want
      to help your children and save your own life.

PH   I love my children. But I am tossed by a different storm of fate.   315

NUR   I assume your hands, child, are clean of blood?

PH   My hands are clean, but my mind is polluted.

NUR   From harmful spells cast by an enemy?

PH   A loved one destroys me against my will and against his.

NUR   Has Theseus wronged you?   320

PH   May I never be seen wronging him!

NUR   What then is this terrible thing that urges you on to die?

PH   Leave me to my error. I'm not wronging you.

NUR   Not on purpose, but you will make me a failure.

      *The nurse falls at Phaedra's feet and takes hold of her
      hand in a gesture of supplication.*

PH   What are you doing? Using force? Gripping my hand?   325

NUR   *taking hold of her knees*

      And your knees, and I will never let you go.

PH   All this will seem evil to you too, woman, if you learn about it -- evil!

NUR   What evil is greater for me than not reaching you?

PH   It will ruin you. And yet it brings me honor.

NUR   Then why do you hide it, if I am begging for your own good?   330

PH   Out of shameful things I am making noble ones.

NUR   If you tell, won't you appear more honored?

PH   Go away, by the gods! Let go my right hand!

NUR   Certainly not, since you don't give me the gift you should.

pause

PH   I will give it. For I yield in reverence of your suppliant hand.   335

NUR   Then I'll be quiet. It's your turn to speak now.

pause

PH   O my wretched mother, what a love you loved!

NUR   The one she had for the bull, child? Or what is this you say?

PH   And you also, my luckless sister, bride of Dicnysus!

NUR   Child, what's happened to you? Are you slandering your relatives?   340

PH   And I a third! How miserably I am perishing!

NUR   I'm stunned. Where is this talk leading?

PH   My misfortune comes from them and is no recent thing.

NUR   I still know no better what I want to hear.

PH   If only you could say for me the things I have to say.   345

NUR   I'm no seer to know obscure things clearly.

PH   What is meant when they say people love?

NUR   Pleasure, child, but also pain at the same time.

PH   It's the latter I feel.

NUR   What are you saying? Are you in love, child? With what man?   350

PH   Whoever he is...the son of the Amazon...

NUR   Hippolytus, you say?

PH   You heard it from yourself, not me.

NUR   *distraught*

No! No! What do you mean child? You have destroyed me!

to the chorus

Women, this is unbearable! I can't bear
living! Hateful is the day and hateful the light I see!   355

throwing herself to the ground

I will throw myself down -- hurl away my body. Dying, I will
free myself from this life. Farewell! I'm already dead.
For virtuous people love evil things -- against their will,
but nonetheless they do! Cypris was no god,
but something greater than a god, if such there be,   360
who has destroyed this woman, myself, and the household.

CH-L   *singing to another member of the chorus*

Did you hear?
Did you hear
these unspeakable things
that the queen shrieked aloud -- her wretched misfortunes?

to Phaedra

I would rather die than ever have
feelings like yours, dear lady.   365

groaning sadly

O troubles that rear mortal men!
O woman luckless with such sorrows!
You are ruined; you have revealed your troubles to the light.
What awaits you in the course of this day?
Something terrible will happen to this house.   370
No longer is it unclear where the fatal star
of Cypris wanes and sets, O luckless child of Crete.

*Having risen from her bed, Phaedra approaches the chorus and
calmly addresses its members.*

PH   Women of Trozen, you who live on this
        furthest threshold of Pelops' land,
        already and in other circumstances during the long hours of the night 375
        I have pondered how the lives of mortals are ruined.
        It doesn't seem to me that they fail
        because of the way they think, for most men think rightly
        enough. But this is how it must be seen:
        we understand and recognize what is good,   380
        but we don't carry it through; some from laziness,
        others by giving preference not to virtue but to some other
        pleasure, and life has many pleasures, such as
        long gossiping and leisure -- a delightful evil --
        and shame, which is of two kinds, one harmless,   385
        the other a burden on the household. If every case were clear,
        there would not be two kinds with the same name.
        Since this is what I think,
        not even a magic charm could have made me change
        and fall into the opposite way of thinking.   390

I will tell you the path my thoughts have taken.
When love first wounded me, I looked to see how
I might best bear it. I began by
keeping silent about my illness and hiding it.
For the tongue is not to be trusted; it knows   395
how to advise the thoughts of other men,
but when it speaks for itself it gets only trouble.
Second, I planned to bear my senseless passion properly
by overcoming it with virtuous restraint.
And third, since I did not succeed in conquering   400
Cypris by these means, I resolved to die --
the best of all plans, as no one will deny.

May it be my luck not to go unnoticed if I do good deeds,
and not to have many witnesses if I do shameful ones.
I knew that both the deed and the illness were disreputable,   405
and moreover I knew very well that I was a woman --
a thing hated by all. May she die a horrible death,
whoever was the first to shame her marriage bed
with other men. This began in noble houses
and then became an evil for all women.   410
For when shameful things seem right to the best-born,
they will certainly seem good to the base.
I hate women who talk virtuously
but commit daring crimes in secret.

glancing toward the statue near the door

How, queenly mistress Cypris, do they ever   415
look their husbands in the face
and not shudder at the darkness that shared their deeds
and at the walls of the house, fearing they might speak?
It is this that is causing my death, friends,
so I may never be caught shaming my husband   420
nor the children I have born. But may they live
in the famous city of Athens as free men
thriving amid free speech, with a good reputation from their mother.
For it enslaves a man, no matter how bold his spirit,
when he knows of his mother's or father's misdeeds.   425
They say that one thing lets you compete in life:
having a good and just mind.
For time sooner or later reveals base men,
setting its mirror before them as before a young maiden.
May I never be seen among them!   430

CH-L   What a fine thing virtue is in all our actions,
        and what a noble reputation it reaps among mortals!

NUR   Mistress, just now your misfortune
        suddenly gave me a terrible fright.
        But now I realize I was foolish. Among mortals   435
        second thoughts are somehow wiser.

It's nothing out of the ordinary or unreasonable that you've
experienced, and now the goddess's resentment has fallen on you.
You're in love. Is that any surprise? Many people are.
Are you going to kill yourself because of love?   440
A bad bargain for lovers
now and in the future, if they have to kill themselves!
Cypris is an unbearable thing when she comes in full flood.
She comes gently to anyone who yields,
but if she finds someone out of the ordinary and thinking big, 445
she seizes him, and you can imagine how she humbles his pride!
She passes through the sky; she lives in the waves
of the sea; Cypris gives birth to all things.
It is she who sows and gives desire,
and all of us on earth are her offspring.   450

Now those who possess writings of ancient authors
and themselves live with poetry all the time
know that Zeus once desired to marry
Semele, and they know also that radiant Dawn once
snatched Cephalus up among the gods,   455
because of love. But just the same they dwell
in heaven and don't flee from the other gods --
content, as I think, to be conquered by their fate.
Won't you endure yours? Your father should have begotten you
on special terms or with other gods as   460
masters, if you are not content with these laws.
How many completely sensible men, do you think,
see that their marriages are sick but don't seem to see it?
How many fathers help their erring sons
come by love? One of the wise things for   465
mortals is this: hiding what isn't respectable.
Mortals should not strive to achieve excessive perfection in life;
nor would you make the roof over a house
exactly perfect. In a situation such as
you have fallen into, how would you expect to swim out?   470
If you have more good things than bad,
you are doing quite well for a human being.
Dear child, stop this wicked thinking.
Stop being so proud. For your wishing to be greater
than the gods is nothing but pride.   475
Endure your love! A god willed it!
Since you are sick, find some good way to subdue your sickness.
There are incantations and charms that cast spells.
Some remedy for this sickness will come to light.
Men would be late indeed in finding a way   480
if we women cannot find one.

CH-L   Phaedra, what she says is more useful
in your present circumstances, but I praise you.
Yet my praise is more distressing than
her words and more painful for you to hear.   485

PH   It is this that destroys men's well-governed
cities and homes: these fine speeches!
One should not say what pleases the ears
but rather what will bring a good name.

NUR   Why these proud words? It's not nobly phrased speeches   490
that you need, but the man! Let's get to the point quickly
and speak the straight truth about you.
If your life were not in danger over this,
or if you were a virtuous woman,
I would never have gone so far for the sake of   495
love's pleasures. But the stakes are high --
saving your life. No one would begrudge this.

PH   What horrible things you're saying! Shut your mouth
and don't let out such shameful words again!

NUR   Shameful, but better than virtuous words for you.   500
And the deed is better, if it saves you,
than the mere name for which you die so proudly.

PH   Stop! I beg of you in the name of the gods. You speak too cleverly
about shameful things. Don't go further! I'm overwrought
with desire, and if you continue to use fine words about shameful
deeds,   505

    I'll be consumed in what I now flee.

NUR   If that is how it is...
                    You shouldn't have gone astray,
but since you have, obey me. That favor is second best.
At home I have magic charms
for love (I just remembered them).   510
They will end your illness with no shame
or harm to your mind -- if you don't turn coward.
But we need something from the man you desire,
some token -- either a lock of hair or a scrap of his cloak --
to take and join the two for one good end.   515

PH   Is the charm a salve or a drink?

NUR   I don't know. Try to profit by it and don't ask questions, child.

PH   I'm afraid you may turn out to be too clever for me.

NUR   You're afraid of everything! What are you worrying about?

PH   That you might pass any of this on to Theseus' son.   520

NUR   Enough, child. I'll arrange everything -- very well.

    moving toward the door, and addressing the statue of Aphrodite

All I ask, queenly mistress Cypris,
is that you be my helper. The other things I have in mind
need only be told to my friends within.

Exit into the house.

CH *singing and dancing, at first solemnly, but with increasing
     agitation in the second strophe and antistrophe*

STROPHE 1

    Eros, Eros, you who distill desire   525
over the eyes, bringing sweet
delight to the hearts of those against whom you campaign,
may you never bring harm when you appear to me,
or ever come with discord.
For neither the shafts of fire nor those of the stars are more
                                 powerful   530
than the arrow of Aphrodite, shot from the hands of
Eros, child of Zeus.

ANTISTROPHE 1

    In vain, in vain by the Alpheus   535
and by the Pythian temple of Phoebus
the Grecian land increases its slaughter of cattle,
while Eros, the tyrant of men,
door-keeper of Aphrodite's
dearest bridal chambers, goes unworshipped by us,   540
although he ravages mortals and hurls them through all disasters
when he comes.

STROPHE 2

    The girl of Oechalia,   545
a filly unyoked before,
manless and unwed, was yoked by Cypris
from the palace of Eurytus,
and like a running nymph or bac-   550
    chante, amid blood and smoke,
she was given to the son of Alcmena
in a marriage filled with murder. O
    unhappy bride!

ANTISTROPHE 2

    O holy wall   555
of Thebes, O mouth of the fountain of Dirce,
you also could tell how Cypris comes.
For to the fork-flamed thunder

she gave in marriage the mother-to-be of twice-born Bac-   560
   chus and bedded her down
to a murderous fate.
Cypris blows furiously upon everything, and like a bee
   she flies about.

*Phaedra, standing near the palace doors and listening to
voices which begin to be heard within, addresses the chorus.*

PH   Silence, women! We are ruined, completely ruined!   565

CH-L   What's going on inside, Phaedra, that terrifies you so?

PH   Quiet! Let me hear what they are saying inside.

CH-L   I'll be quiet. But this is a bad beginning.

PH   *screaming*

        O wretched me, what must I suffer?   570

CH-L   *chanting or singing excitedly*

        What are you screaming about? Why are you shrieking?
        Tell us, woman, what you have heard that rushes upon your mind
        and terrifies you so.

PH   It's all over. Come over here by the doors   575
        and listen to the shouting that rises in the palace.

CH-L   *chanting or singing excitedly*

        You are by the doors. You should report
        any words from the palace.
        Tell me, tell me, what is the matter?   580

PH   Hippolytus, the son of the horse-loving Amazon,
        is shouting and cursing my servant.

CH-L   *still chanting or singing*

        I hear voices, but nothing clear.   585
        You can hear better, where the shouting
        comes to you through the doors.

PH   Yes, I can hear clearly now; he calls her "wicked
        matchmaker," "betrayer of your master's bed!"   590

CH-L *chanting or singing*

How terrible! You've been betrayed, my friend.
How can I help you?
Your secrets are revealed; you are ruined!

moaning

Betrayed by your friends!   595

PH   She has ruined me by telling of my troubles; as a friend would,
she tried to cure my illness, but she didn't do it well.

CH-L *calmer now*

Now what will you do in this impossible situation?

PH   I don't know, except for one thing; die as quickly as possible!
This is the only remedy for the disaster now upon me.   600

*Hippolytus rushes from the house onto the stage followed by
the nurse who attempts to restrain him. Phaedra retires to
one side of the stage and listens.*

HIP   *shouting*

O mother earth and spreading light of the sun,
what unspeakable words I have heard!

NUR   Be quiet, child, before someone hears you shouting.

HIP   No! I have heard terrible things and cannot be silent.

NUR   *grasping at his hand and then falling at his knees in an
attempt at supplication*

Yes! I beg you by this right hand and its strong arm.   605

HIP   Keep your hand away and don't touch my clothes.

NUR   By your knees I implore you, don't ruin me.

HIP   What do you mean, if, as you say, you have said nothing bad?

NUR   This story, my child, is not for everyone to hear.

HIP   But surely fine things are better told to the multitude.   610

NUR   My child, don't dishonor your oaths.

HIP   My tongue swore; my mind took no oath.

NUR Child, what will you do? Ruin your friends?

HIP "Friends?" I spit out the word! No wicked person is a friend of mine.

NUR Try to understand and forgive; to err is human, my child.   615

HIP *turning away from the nurse and raising his face and hands*
     to the sky

    O Zeus, why did you send women -- a counterfeit coin
    and a bane for men -- to live in the light of the sun?
    If you wanted to sow a mortal race,
    you should not have had it come from women.
    Instead, mortals should go to your temples and pay   620
    bronze or iron or a weight of gold
    to buy the seed of children, each man paying
    according to the worth of his estate, and they should
    live at liberty in their homes without women.   624

   soliloquizing

    It is clear from the following that a woman is a great evil: 627
    the father who begets her and rears her adds
    a dowry and sends her from home -- to be rid of an evil!
    Her husband in turn takes the ruinous creature into his house 630
    and rejoices. He puts jewelry on his idol
    (fine things for the wicked) and dresses her up with pretty clothes:
    the poor wretch, undermining his own prosperity.   633
    It's easiest to have an empty-headed woman, but even she is 638
    worse than useless, enshrined at home in her silliness.
    And I hate the clever one. May my home never have a woman
    who thinks bigger than a woman should.
    Cypris spawns more wickedness
    in clever women, while the mindless woman's
    stunted wits keep her out of trouble.
    And no servant should ever go in to a woman,   645
    but voiceless, biting beasts should dwell with them
    so that they would speak to no one
    and hear no voices in reply.
    But as it is, wicked women make wicked plots indoors
    and their servants bring them out into the open...   650

   to the nurse

    just as you have come to me about my father, you evil creature,
    to arrange an affair in his untouchable marriage bed.
    I'll clean these things away with streams of pure water,
    and wash out my ears. How could I ever be wicked,
    when I feel defiled merely hearing such things?   655
    Be sure that it is this same piety of mine that saves you, woman.
    If I had not been caught off guard and trapped into oaths by the gods,
    I would never have been kept from telling all this to my father.

But now I will leave home for as long as
Theseus is out of the country, and I will remain silent.   660
But I will come back when my father returns, and I will be watching
to see how you look at him -- both you and your mistress!   662

*The above words are spoken with a glance toward Phaedra as
Hippolytus moves toward the side of the stage to depart.
Before he exits, he delivers a last tirade.*

May you both perish! I will never have my fill of hating   664
women, not even if people say I am always talking about them -- 665
for they are always evil!
Let someone teach them restraint,
or let me trample them under foot forever!

*Hippolytus exits, and Phaedra, who has been listening in
silence, moves forward and sings the following lament.*

PH   *singing sorrowfully*

ANTISTROPHE

    Oh, how miserable   669
    and unfortunate
    are the destinies of women!
    What means do we have, or what words can we use   670
    to loosen this knot of words, now we are snared and have fallen?
    We have gotten what we deserved. O earth and light of day!
    Where can I escape from what's happened?
    How can I conceal my misery, friends?
    What god or mortal would be seen aiding me,   675
    sitting beside me, or helping me cope with these unjust deeds?
    My suffering carries me across
    the hardest of all crossings to the other shore of life.
    I am the most unfortunate of women.

CH-L   *sorrowfully*

    It's all over. Your servant's schemes,   680
    mistress, did not succeed. Everything's gone wrong.

    to her nurse

    O wickedest of women and corrupter of your friends,
    see what you've done to me! May Zeus, my grandfather,
    strike you with his fire and destroy you root and branch!
    Didn't I see what was in your mind? Didn't I tell you   685
    to keep silent about these things which now disgrace me?

But you had no restraint, and so I will no longer die
with a good reputation.
                         I need new plans now.
For he, now that his mind is whetted with rage,
will denounce me to his father for what you did wrong,   690
and fill the whole earth with shameful tales.   692
I wish you were dead -- both you and whoever else is eager
to help friends by evil means -- and without their consent!

NUR   Mistress, you can blame me for my mistakes,   695
        for shock overpowers your judgment.
        But I can speak against these charges, if you will listen.
        I brought you up and am fond of you. I sought a remedy
        for this sickness of yours, but found ... something I hadn't intended.
        If I had succeeded, I would certainly have been counted among the
                                                              wise.   700
        It's by our luck that we get known for intelligence.

PH   Do you think this is fair and what I deserve --
        wounding me and then smoothing it over with words?

NUR   We're talking too much. I didn't act wisely.
        But there is a way to save you even now, child.   705

PH   Stop talking! You did not advise me well
        in the past, and you set your hand to evil deeds.
        Get out of my way and try...thinking about yourself.
        I will arrange my own affairs, and I'll do it well.

        Exit nurse.

PH   *to the chorus*

        And you, noble daughters of Trozen,   710
        grant me this request:
        cover with silence what you have heard here.

CH-L   I swear by holy Artemis, Zeus' daughter,
        never to reveal any of your troubles to the light of day.

PH   Thank you. There is one thing more I have to say: 715
        I have thought of something for my misfortunes,
        something to give my children a reputable life
        and to benefit myself even as things have turned out.
        For I will never shame my Cretan home
        nor will I come to face Theseus   720
        amid shameful deeds because of one life.

CH-L   What are you about to do? What incurable evil?

PH   Die. But how, is something I will decide.

CH-L   Hush! Use words of good omen!

PH   And you, give me good advice!

turning to the statue by the door

I will delight Cypris, who is destroying me,   725
when I depart from life this very day,
and a bitter love will have conquered me.
Yet will I give trouble to someone else
when I die, so that he will know not to be haughty
over my troubles. When he shares equally in this sickness of mine, 730
he will learn restraint.

Exit into the palace.

CH   *singing and dancing*

STROPHE 1

I wish I were among the steep rocks in sheltering recesses
and that a god
would make me into a feathered bird
    among winged flocks.
I wish I were lifted up over the sea-   735
waves of the Adrian
shore, and over Eridanus' water,
into whose dark swell
    the wretched girls
lamenting in grief for Phaethon drip their tears'   740
amber-gleaming radiance.

ANTISTROPHE 1

I wish to end my journey on the shore, sown with apples,
where the Hesperides sing,
where the sea-lord
    of the dark shallows
no longer gives passage to sailors,   745
but sets the sacred boundary of
heaven, which Atlas holds,
and where ambrosial springs flow
    near Zeus' marriage bed,   750
and holy earth, abundantly bountiful,
increases the gods' happy lot.

STROPHE 2

Oh white-winged Cretan
    ship, who through the briny
    salt-crashing sea wave

ferried my queen from her bountiful home,   755
and gave her the gift of a disastrous marriage!   Truly it flew
a bird ill-omened for both sides,
    from the land of Minos to famous Athens.   760
    On the shores of Munichus
    they bound fast the twisted rope-ends,
    and stepped onto the mainland.

ANTISTROPHE 2

And for this an unholy desire,
    the terrible sickness of Aphrodite,   765
    crushed her inside.
Now she, foundering in her hard misfortune,
will fasten a hanging noose to beams of her bridal chamber   770
fitting it around her white neck,
    ashamed of her hateful lot,
    choosing instead a good
    reputation, and ridding her heart
    of its grievous passion.   775

*Phaedra has hanged herself inside the palace, and one of her
servants shouts for help.*

VOICE OF SERVANT FROM INSIDE THE PALACE

    screams, then

    Come and help -- everyone who's near the house!
    She's strangled in a noose -- the queen -- Theseus' wife!

CH-L   *sorrowfully*

    It's all over. The queen is
    alive no longer; she hangs, suspended in a noose.

VOICE OF SERVANT FROM INSIDE THE PALACE

    Won't you hurry? Won't someone bring a double-edged   780
    sword to loosen the knot from her neck?

ANOTHER MEMBER OF THE CHORUS

    to her companions

    Friends, what should we do? Do you think we should enter
    the house and free the queen from the tight noose?

CH-L   *in reply*

Why? Aren't there young servants near by?
Meddling doesn't make for a safe life.   785

*The queen's body has been lowered from the noose and is
being arranged, perhaps on the same bed on which she was
brought out from the house earlier in the play.*

VOICE OF THE SERVANT FROM INSIDE THE PALACE

to other servants inside

Lay out her body and straighten her limbs.
This is a bitter housekeeping for my masters.

CH-L   She is dead then, I hear, the poor woman,
for they are already laying out her body.

*Enter Theseus, just arrived from Delphi, where he has been
consulting the prophetic god Apollo. As he comes on stage,
his head is wreathed with garlands that indicate a favorable
reply from the oracle.*

TH   Women, do you know why they are shouting in the house?   790
What is the noise that I hear through the doors?
My house does not see fit to open its doors
and address me graciously as an envoy from the god.
Nothing wrong has happened to aged Pittheus, has it?
His life is already far along, but nonetheless   795
it would grieve me if he left us.

CH-L   What has happened to you here does not concern old people,
Theseus; it is the young that are dead and bring you grief.

TH   *anguished*

Surely my children haven't been robbed of their lives?

CH-L   They live, but their mother has died -- most painfully for you. 800

TH   What are you saying? My wife is dead? How did it happen?

CH-L   She fastened up a noose and hanged herself.

TH   Frozen with grief, or what happened to her?

CH-L   That's as much as we know, for we, too, have just now come
to your house, Theseus, to mourn your ills.   805

TH   *tearing the garlands from his head and speaking sorrowfully*

Why is my head wreathed with these
woven leaves? Disaster has struck me -- just as I return from the oracle!

Unbar the doors, servants; undo the bolts,
so that I may see the bitter sight
of my wife, whose death has destroyed me.   810

The doors are opened; Phaedra's body, laid out on the bed,
is brought onto the stage; a tablet hangs from her wrist.

CH   *singing pitifully*

Miserable woman and piteous woes!
You have suffered and done
enough to confound this house;
What recklessness was yours! --
a violent death in an unholy
    act, through the wrestling of your own piteous hand!   815
Who, miserable woman, has darkened your life?

TH   *lamenting in agitated song which alternates with restrained*
speech

    STROPHE

        Oh what troubles are mine! I have suffered, miserable that I am,
            the greatest of my ills! O misfortune!
        How heavily you have descended upon me and my house --
        some unexplainable pollution coming from a vengeful power.   820

        A destruction of life that I cannot survive;
            miserable, I behold a sea of troubles
        too great ever to swim back out of,
        or ever to cross its waves of disaster.   824

        How can I, so miserable, explain your fateful calamity   826
            and speak the truth, my miserable wife?
        For like a bird you have vanished from my hand,
        rushing to Hades with a swift leap.

    anguished

        Piteous, piteous are these sufferings.   830
        From some time long ago I must be gathering upon myself
        this god-sent calamity because of the sins of someone before my
                                                                      time.

CH   *speaking calmly*

You are not the only one to whom such woes have come, king;

                many others have lost their dear wives.   835

TH   *continuing his lament*

       ANTISTROPHE

            I wish I were under the earth, in the gloom under the earth,
               dwelling in darkness, dead myself, wretched as I am,
            bereaved of your dear companionship:
            for you have destroyed me even more than yourself.

            What happened? How did such a   840
               deadly misfortune come to your heart, wretched woman?
            Won't someone tell me what happened, or does the mob
            of my servants guard their ruler's house in vain?
              844
            Wretched me, what grief I see in my house!   845
            Unbearable and unspeakable! Oh, I am ruined!
            My house is empty, my children orphaned!

       anguished

            You have left, you have left us,
            O my dear, the best of all women whom the light of the sun
            and the star-faced brightness of night beheld!   850

CH   *singing*

            O wretched man, what trouble your house has!
            My eyes moisten and
            flood with tears over your misfortune.
            But I have long shuddered with fear of the calamity to follow.   855

       *The chorus and Theseus notice the tablet attached to Phaedra's
       wrist. Theseus, speaking more calmly now, takes it in his hands.*

TH   Ah!
       What is this tablet fastened to her hand?
       Does it mean to tell me something new?
       Did she write me a letter to plead with me
       about remarriage and the children, poor woman?
       Be assured, wretched wife. There is no woman   860
       who will enter Theseus' bed and home.

       inspecting the tablet

            These marks of the hammered gold seal that belonged
            to my wife, who no longer lives -- they revive my affection.
            Come, let us unfold the sealed coverings
            and see what this tablet has to tell me.   865

CH   *singing*

Here is a new evil that a god sends in upon us
to take the place of the old ....
....
Ruined, destroyed, I say,
is the house of my rulers.   870

TH   *speaking*

Another disaster added to disaster!   874

CH-L   *speaking*

What is it? Tell me, if I may know.   876

TH   *singing*

It cries aloud, this tablet cries aloud abominable things!
How can I flee the weight of my woes? I am dead! I am gone!
Such a song -- such a song of woe I have seen given voice
in these words! Wretched me!   880

CH-L   *speaking*

Your words are the beginning of trouble.

TH   *first singing and then speaking*

I can no longer hold back this ruinous woe
in the gates of my mouth, painful as it is to let out.

*shouting to summon citizens to witness the denunciation and
cursing of his son*

Ho! City!

A group of men gathers and listens.

Hippolytus has dared touch my bed   885
by force, dishonoring the sacred eye of Zeus.
Now, O my father Poseidon, with one of the
three curses that you once promised me,
destroy my son, and may he not escape
this day, if you really gave me true curses.   890

CH-L   King, pray to the gods and take back your words.
        In time you will know you have made a mistake, believe me.

TH   Impossible! And furthermore, I will drive him out of this land.
        He will be struck by one of these two fates.
        Either Poseidon will send him dead   895

to the house of Hades, honoring my curses,
or wandering in exile from this land
he will scrape together a wretched life on foreign soil.

CH-L   *seeing Hippolytus approach*

Here he is now, your son himself coming just in time,
Hippolytus. Relax your harsh anger, king   900
Theseus, and consider what is best for your house and family.

HIP   *rushing onto the stage followed by his companions*

I heard your shout and came right away,
father. I don't know what made you
shout, and I wish you would tell me.

catching sight of Phaedra's body

Hey! What is this? I see your wife, father,   905
but she's dead. What a great surprise this is,
for I left her just now, looking on the light
of this very day -- only a little while ago!
What happened to her? How did she die?

perplexed at his father's silence

Father, I want to know, and from you!   910
Why are you silent? Silence is no help in troubles.   911
It certainly isn't right to hide your misfortunes from   914
your friends, father, and from those who are more than friends. 915

TH   *soliloquizing and refusing to look at his son*

O men, you who make many mistakes and all for nothing,
Why do you teach thousands of skills,
contriving and discovering all things,
while there is one thing you don't understand and have never tracked down:
teaching brainless people how to think.   920

HIP   *perplexed yet further at his father's behavior*

You're speaking of a terribly clever person, if he could
pound thought into the thoughtless.
But this is no time for theorizing, father.
I fear your tongue is running wild in your troubles.

TH   *continuing to soliloquize*

Men should have been given some sure sign   925
of their friends and a means of judging their minds:
to know who is a true friend and who is not.
And all men ought to have two voices,

one honest and the other whatever it happened to be,
so that a tongue plotting unjust deeds might be refuted   930
by the honest one, and we would not be deceived.

HIP   *still perplexed*

Has one of my friends slandered me to your ears,
and am I in trouble, although in no way to blame?
I am astonished, for your words dumbfound me
by straying so far from the seat of intelligence.   935

TH   *still soliloquizing and looking away from his son*

The mind of man! How far will it go?
What limit will there be to its daring and recklessness?
For if it swells up throughout a man's lifetime,
and he who comes after will be more villainous
than he who went before, then the gods   950
will have to cast another land alongside this earth
to receive those men who are unjust and born evil-doers.

*Theseus turns toward his son and gestures with the accusing
tablet. As Theseus speaks the following lines, Hippolytus
hides his face in shame.*

Look at him there! Although begotten by me,
he shamed my bed and is clearly convicted
by the dead woman of being utterly evil.   945

addressing Hippolytus for the first time

Look at me now! Since I am caught up in your pollution
anyway, you can look your father in the face.

confronting his son directly

So you consort with the gods as if you were more than
man? You're chaste and untainted by evil?
No boasting of yours would induce me   950
to make the mistake of attributing such ignorance to the gods.
Keep your pretentions! Put on a good show
with your vegetarian diet, and let Orpheus lead you in your
frenzied dances as you bow down to the smoke of wordy doctrines!
For you are caught! I proclaim to everyone: shun   955
such men! For they hunt you down with saintly words
while concocting shameful deeds.

This woman is dead. Do you think this will save you?
It convicts you most of all, you wicked man.
For what oaths, what words would have more effect   960
than this woman and allow you to escape blame?
Will you say she hated you and that the bastard

is a natural enemy of legitimate children?
You make her a poor bargainer in life
if she gave up what was dearest to her out of hatred for you!   965
Or will you say that promiscuous behavior is natural for women
but not for men?   I know young men
who are no more stable than women
when Cypris stirs up their young hearts,
and the fact that they're men helps too.   970

But now why am I competing with your words,
while the body is here as the clearest witness?
Get out of this land as fast as you can, and go into exile.
And don't go to god-built Athens
nor to the frontiers of the land my spear rules.   975
For if I give in to you after you have done this to me,
Sinis of the Isthmus will never acknowledge
that I killed him, but he will call it an empty boast.
Nor will the Scironid cliffs bordering the sea
say that I am hard on evil-doers.   980

CH-L   I don't think I could call any mortal
        really fortunate, when even the foremost are overthrown.

HIP   Father, you are angry and under a terrible
        strain.   But this affair, which looks so reasonable,
        will look quite different if you spread it out and examine it.   985
        I am not clever at making speeches before a crowd
        but am better before a few people of my own age.
        This is perfectly natural, for those who make a poor showing
        among the wise speak more to the tune of the crowd.
        However, since this calamity has come, I must   990
        speak out.   I will begin with your first point,
        when you attacked me and thought you could destroy me
        without my answering back.   You can see this sunlight
        and this earth; they contain no man -- even if you deny it --
        with a more virtuous nature than mine.   995
        For first I know how to reverence the gods
        and to have friends who do not try to do wrong
        and who would be ashamed to commission evil deeds
        or return like for like to those who do shameful things.
        I don't laugh at my companions, father,   1000
        but am the same to my friends both present and absent.
        And I have never touched the one thing in which you think you have
                                                        caught me now.
        Up to this minute my body is pure of sexual love.
        I know nothing of the act itself except what I have heard people say
        and seen in pictures.   And I am not eager to look   1005
        at them, since my soul is virgin.

Theseus winces with disbelief.

But my chastity doesn't persuade you; go on, then,
you must show how I was corrupted.

Was her body more beautiful than
those of other women? Or did I hope to receive   1010
an inheritance along with her bed and thus dwell in your palace?
Then I was a fool and not in my right mind.
Or is ruling pleasant for sane men?
Not at all, unless the monarchy that pleases them
has first of all destroyed their common sense.   1015
I would like to be first as victor in the Greek games,
but second man in the city,
always living happily with the best men as my friends.
For the power to act is there, and the absence of danger
gives more pleasure than any ruler has.   1020

Theseus attempts to break in.

One of my points has not been mentioned; you have all the others.
If I had a witness to attest to what I am,
and if I were making my plea while this woman still saw the light of day,
you would know the wicked by examining their deeds.
But now I swear by Zeus, protector of oaths, and by the ground beneath
                                                       our feet 1025
that I have never touched your wife
nor wanted to nor even had it in mind.
May I perish without fame or even memory of my name,   1028
and may neither sea nor earth receive my dead
flesh, if I am evil by nature.
I don't know what it was she feared that made
her end her life; for it is not right for me to speak further.
She acted virtuously though she had no virtue,
While I, having virtue, did not use it well.   1035

CH-L   You have said enough to turn aside his accusation,
        and have added oaths by the gods; no small pledge of good faith.

TH   Isn't this fellow a born charlatan and spell-binder,
        who is so sure his smooth manners will
        overpower my spirit, after he has dishonored his father?   1040

HIP   And I am amazed at the same thing in you father.
        For if you were my son and I were your father,
        I would have killed you and not punished you with exile
        if you had thought fit to touch my wife.

TH   A fitting suggestion! But you will not die   1045
        according to this law you have decreed for yourself.
        For a quick death is easy for a man in misfortune.
        Instead, you will wander in exile from your fatherland
        and scrape together a wretched life on foreign soil.   1049

HIP   What are you going to do? Won't you wait for time
        to proclaim the truth about me? Will you drive me from the land?

TH   Beyond the Pontic Sea and the regions of Atlas,
       if I could. I hate your presence so much!

HIP   Will you test neither my oath nor my pledge nor yet   1055
       what the prophets say? Will you throw me out of the land without trial?

TH   *holding out the tablet*

       This tablet doesn't need any drawing of lots to
       condemn you on good evidence. As for the birds flying
       above our heads -- I bid them a fond farewell!

HIP   O gods, why don't I open my mouth,   1060
       I who am being destroyed by you whom I reverence?
       No, that's not it. I would not persuade those whom I must,
       and I would break my sworn oaths for nothing.

TH   Oh, how your saintliness kills me!
       Won't you get out of your fatherland as fast as you can?   1065

HIP   Where will I turn in my misery? What
       friend's house will I enter, exiled on this charge?

TH   Whoever enjoys entertaining friends who violate wives
       and share in corrupting households.

HIP   Alas, this cuts to the quick! It brings me close to tears,   1070
       if indeed I appear corrupt and seem so to you.

TH   Then was the time to groan, and you should have thought ahead
       before you dared violate your father's wife.

HIP   O house, if only you could speak
       and witness whether I have a corrupt nature.   1075

TH   How clever of you to flee to voiceless witnesses.
       But the deed itself needs no speech to proclaim you wicked.

HIP   If only I could stand apart and look at
       myself, so that I could cry over what I suffer.

TH   You have always practiced worshipping yourself far more   1080
       than being just and acting piously toward your parents.

HIP   O wretched mother, O bitter childbirth!
       May none of my friends be a bastard.

TH   Won't you drag him off, servants? Didn't you hear
       me proclaiming him an exile long ago?   1085

HIP   If any one of them touches me, he'll be sorry!
       Do it yourself, if that's what you want. You throw me out of the land!

TH   I'll do it, if you don't obey my commands.
For no pity comes over me for your exile.

Exit.

HIP   *soliloquizing*

It is all settled, apparently. O wretched me!   1090
I know what this is all about, but I know no way to reveal it.

addressing the statue of Artemis

O maiden daughter of Leto, my dearest goddess,
my comrade, my fellow-hunter, we will indeed be exiled
from famous Athens. *(looking into the distance)* Farewell city
and land of Erechtheus. *(to the landscape around him)* O plain of
                                            Trozen,   1095
what divine happiness you hold for those who grow up here!
Farewell! This is the last time I will look at you or speak to you.

to his companions

Come along, my young companions of this land,
speak to me and send me forth from this soil.
You will never see another man more virtuous,   1100
even if it doesn't seem so to my father.

Exit.

CH   *singing and dancing*

STROPHE 1

Whenever I think of how the gods care for us,
my sorrow is greatly lightened. Inside of me lies hope of under-
                                         standing, 1105
but it deserts me when I look at what happens to men and at their deeds;
for things come and go by turns. Men's lives change course
and wander about forever.   1110

ANTISTROPHE 1

And thus I pray that divine fate grant me
a prosperous good fortune and a heart unbroken by grief.
May my opinions be neither rigid nor counterfeit.   1115
May I have an easy disposition changing always with tomorrow's time,
and in this way may I live my life happily.

STROPHE 2

My mind is no longer clear; what I see is contrary to my hopes.   1120
We have seen the brightest star of Hellenic Athens,
seen him sent forth to another land
by his father's anger.   1125
O sands of our city's shore!
O mountain woods, where he used to kill
wild beasts with his swift-footed dogs,
accompanying holy Dictynna!   1130

ANTISTROPHE 2

No longer will you mount your chariot with its Venetian fillies
nor keep to the track around the lagoon with your well-trained horse.
The sleepless music from the strings of your lyre   1135
will cease in your father's house.
The resting places of Leto's virgin daughter
will have no garlands throughout the thick green meadows.
The young girls' competition for your wedding bed   1140
is ended by your exile.

EPODE

And for your misfortune
I will live out my ill-fated fate
    in tears.   O miserable mother,
you bore a child for nothing!
I rage at the gods!   1145
Graces, you with your hands linked together, since this
wretched man does not deserve his doom, why
do you send him away from his home and fatherland?   1150

CH-L   *in normal speaking tones*

I see one of Hippolytus' companions looking sad
and hurrying earnestly toward the palace.

COMP   *entering from the side of the stage*

Where should I go to find Theseus, the king
of this land, women?   If you know,
tell me.   Is he inside the palace here?   1155

CH-L   Here he is himself, coming out of the palace.

COMP   Theseus, I bring a message that deserves your attention
and that of the citizens who live in the city of Athens
and within the boundaries of the Trozenian land.

TH   What is it? Has some strange calamity   1160
         seized upon our two neighboring cities?

COMP   Hippolytus no longer lives -- or almost so.
         He still sees the light of day, but his life is poised on a slim balance.

TH   From what? Did he make someone his enemy
         by dishonoring his wife, just as he violated his father's?   1165

COMP   His own team of horses destroyed him --
         and also the curses that you called down upon your son with your own mouth
         when you prayed to your father who rules the sea.

TH   O gods -- and Poseidon! You really were my
         father, for you listened to my prayers!   1170
         How was he destroyed? Tell me! How did the dead weight
         of Justice's trap strike him for disgracing me?

COMP   We were near the wave-beaten shore
         currying the horses' hair with combs,
         and we were weeping, for someone had come and told us   1175
         that Hippolytus would never again set foot in this land
         since you sentenced him to a miserable life in exile.
         And he came to us on the shore with the same
         tearful tale, and an immense group
         of friends and companions was following along behind him.   1180
         And finally, when he had stopped groaning, he said,
         "Why am I so upset? My father's words must be obeyed.
         Get the horses yoked and ready for the chariot,
         servants, for this is no longer my city."
         Then each man hurried,   1185
         and quicker than you could say it we had harnessed
         the colts and brought them to stand right next to our master.
         He seizes the reins from the chariot rail
         and fits his feet right into the shoe frames.
         Then, opening his hands to the gods,   1190
         he prays, "Zeus, may I no longer live if I am an evil-natured man.
         May my father come to see how he has dishonored me,
         whether I die or continue to see the light of day."
         With this, he took the goad into his hands and struck it
         against all the colts at the same time. We servants followed   1195
         our master beside the chariot near the bridles,
         along the road straight to Argus and Epidaurus.

         When we entered open country,
         there was a certain promontory
         lying just beyond this land toward the Saronic Sea.   1200
         At that moment an earthly rumble like Zeus' thunder
         rose into a mighty roar, horrible to hear.
         The horses pricked up their heads and ears
         toward heaven, and we were terribly afraid over
         where the noise was coming from. Looking off   1205

toward the sea-beaten shore, we saw an awesome
wave standing fixed in the sky, so that my eye could not
see Sciron's shore, and the Isthmus
and the rock of Asclepius were hidden.
And then it swelled up and bubbled deep   1210
foam all around, and as the sea spurted high
the wave comes toward the shore where the four horses were drawing the
                                                                    chariot.

And as it broke with a triple surge,
it gave forth a bull -- a fierce monster.
The whole earth was filled with his roaring,
and the echoes made you shudder. And for us who saw it,
the sight was more than our eyes could stand.
Instantly a terrible fear gripped the fillies,
and our master, thoroughly at home with the ways
of horses, snatched the reins in his hands   1221
and pulled like a seaman on an oar,
hanging his body backward against the reins.
The fillies clamped their jaws on the forged bits
and bore him along in spite of his efforts, heeding neither the hand
of the helmsman, nor the reins, nor the   1225
well-built chariot. Whenever he gripped the tiller
and set his course straight toward smooth ground,
the bull appeared in front to head them off,
maddening the four horses with fear.
Whenever they rushed with raging spirits toward the rocks,   1230
the bull approached in silence and followed alongside the chariot's rim
until he tripped it and tossed it
by smashing its wheels against a rock.
Everything was thrown together. The wheel hubs
and the axle pins leaped up in the air,   1235
and he himself, the wretched man, tangled in the reins,
is dragged along bound in a knot hard to loosen.
Battering his head against the rocks
and ripping his flesh, he shouted with terror in his voice,
"Stop! You were raised in my own stables!   1240
Don't destroy me! Damned curse of my father!
Don't any of you here want to save me, the best of men?"
Many of us wanted to, but our feet could not keep up
and we were left behind. And yet somehow or other
he was freed from the cut leather thongs that bound him,   1245
and he fell, breathing only a little bit of life now.
His horses and that monster of a
bull that brought such misery were hidden somewhere in the rocky earth.

after a pause

I am only a slave in your palace, king,
but I will never be able to believe   1250
that your son is evil,
not even if the whole race of women hanged themselves
and if someone filled all the pinewood on Mount Ida

with writing.   For I know that he is good.

CH-L   *mournfully*

A new disaster has taken place   1255
and there is no escaping fate and what must be.

TH   In my hatred for the man who has suffered these things,
I was pleased with this report.   But now, out of respect
for the gods and also for him (since he is of my blood),
I will neither rejoice nor be distressed at what has happened.   1260

COMP   Well then, should we bring him in, or what should we do
with the wretched man to please you?
Think about it.   If you want my advice,
you won't be hard on your unfortunate son.

TH   Bring him in!   So that I may see with my own eyes
the man who denies he violated my bed,   1265
and so that I may refute him with words and with this god-sent disaster.

Exit companion of Hippolytus.

Theseus waits while the Chorus sings a hymn to Aphrodite.

CH   You subdue the unbending will of gods and mortal men,
Cypris, and along with you
        the bright-feathered one attacks from all sides   1270
with swiftest wing.
He flies about over the earth and the echoing
        salt sea.
Eros enchants those on whose maddened hearts
he rushes gleaming with his golden wings --   1275
young creatures of the mountains and the seas,
        and all those whom earth nurtures,
and those the blazing sun beholds,
and men.   Over all of these you hold the honor of a queen,   1280
Cypris, and alone wield power.

*Artemis suddenly appears above the palace, moved into sight by
a mechanical contrivance.   She carries her bow and arrows.*

ART   *addressing Theseus, first declaiming and then speaking*

You, the nobly born son of Aegeus, I command
to listen:
I, Artemis, the maiden daughter of Leto, address you.   1285
why, wretched Theseus, are you pleased at these things,

when you have impiously slain your son
and believed the lying stories of your wife
while things were unclear? Clear is the ruin you have gotten now.
Why don't you hide your body in the depths of earth,   1290
in shame,
or take wing and soar to a life in the sky,
lifting your foot out of this trouble?
For among good men there is no
    possible place in life for you.   1295

Hear, Theseus, the state of your woes.
I will carry the matter no further, but I will cause you grief.
Now I have come for this: to reveal your son's honest
mind, so that he may die with a good name,
and to reveal your wife's mad passion, or, in a way,   1300
her nobility. For the goddess most hated
by us who take pleasure in virginity
stung her with goads, and she fell in love with your son.
While trying to overcome Cypris by the power of her will,
she was ruined by what her nurse did without her consent.   1305
For she put your son under oath and told him about Phaedra's sickness.
As was right, he did not take up
her suggestion, nor again when you called him wicked
did he retract his sworn pledge, since he was pious in his very nature.
And she, fearing to face a cross-examination,   1310
wrote a lying letter and destroyed
your son with treachery which, though false, persuaded you.

Theseus groans.

Does the tale sting you, Theseus? Quiet now,
so that you can hear the rest and groan yet more.

You know the three powerful curses your father gave you?   1315
You took one of them, O most wicked man,
for use against your son, while it could have been used against an enemy.
Your father, the sea-god, though wishing you well,
granted your prayer as he had to, since he had promised;
it is you who have clearly done wrong against both him and me. 1320
You did not delay over the pledge or await the voice
of prophets, nor did you refute him, nor permit time to make
a lengthy examination. Instead, acting faster than you should have,
you sent curses upon your son and killed him.

TH   Mistress I wish I were dead!

ART   You did terrible things, but nonetheless 1325
          you can still receive pardon even for them.
          For Cypris wished these things to happen,
          to glut her anger. This law holds among the gods:
          no one of us wishes to oppose the will

of a god who wants to do something, but we always stand aside.   1330
For you can be certain that if I had not feared Zeus
I would never have come to this degree of shame
and let one who is dearest to me of all mortals
perish. First, your ignorance of your
mistake releases you from baseness.   1335
And then your wife in dying took away
the chance of refuting her words; so your mind was persuaded.
These evils have broken forth upon you most of all,
but I also have my grief. For gods do not rejoice
when pious men die, but we destroy wicked men   1340
entirely -- themselves, their children, and their homes.

CH-L   *declaiming*

Here comes the wretched fellow,
his youthful flesh and blond head
battered. O troubles of the house!
A double misfortune has come about,   1345
sent by the gods to seize upon this roof.

Hippolytus enters, staggering and supported by his servants.

HIP   *first screaming with pain, then declaiming, and finally
       breaking into song*

Wretched I, battered by the
unjust curses of an unjust father.
   I am dead, wretched I!   1350
Pains rush through my head,
and spasms leap in my brain.

to his servants

Stop! Let me rest my tired body.

He moves again and groans with pain.

O hateful team of horses,   1355
reared by my own hand,
you destroyed me, you killed me.

scream of pain

By the gods, gently, servants,
when you touch my wounded flesh with your hands.

making an effort to see

Who stands to the right of my body?   1360
Lift me gently and pull me along carefully --

me, the ill-fated and cursed,
through my father's errors. Zeus, Zeus, do you see this?
Here I am, the pious and god-fearing,
the one who surpassed all in virtue,   1365
I am walking to a death I foresee, my life
destroyed completely, and for nothing
have I struggled at works
        of piety toward men.

Hippolytus screams with pain and then sings.   1370

And now pain, pain comes over me.
Let me go, wretched me,
and may healing death come to me.
Destroy me completely, destroy me the ill-fated one.
        I long for a double-edged sword   1375
to cut through
and put my life to rest.
O wretched curse of my father!
Some murderous evil inherited
from ancient ancestors   1380
        is spilling over against me
and doesn't stop.
It comes upon me -- why me?
        I deserve no evil!

groans of pain

What should I say? How can I   1385
        release my life and free it from the pain
        of this suffering?
May the night-black
        force of Hades put ill-fated me
        to rest!

ART *addressing Hippolytus*

Unhappy boy, yoked to such a misfortune!
The nobility of your mind has destroyed you.   1390

HIP *recognizing the voice and presence of Artemis*

O divine breath of fragrance! Even in my troubles
I feel your presence, and my body's pains are eased.
The goddess Artemis is present in this place.

ART Unhappy boy! She is indeed, the goddess you love the most.

HIP Do you see me, mistress, how miserable I am?   1395

ART I see. But it is not lawful to shed tears from my eyes.

HIP   Your master of hunting dogs and your servant no longer lives.

ART   No. And yet you die still dearest of all to me.

HIP   Your keeper of horses and the guardian of your statues no longer lives.

ART   For Cypris, who would do anything, schemed it all.   1400

HIP   Alas, well do I know the goddess who has destroyed me.

ART   She blamed you for not honoring her, and she was angry at your chastity.

HIP   One goddess, I realize now, has destroyed the three of us.

ART   Yes, your father, you, and his wife as the third.

HIP   I begin to pity my father, too, for his mistakes.   1405

ART   He was tricked by a goddess's plans.

HIP   How miserable you are over what has happened, father.

TH   I am ruined, my son, and have no pleasure left in life.

HIP   I grieve more for you than for myself, because of your mistake.

TH   If only I might die instead of you, my son.   1410

HIP   O bitter gifts from your father Poseidon!

TH   I wish they had never come to my lips!

HIP   Why? You would have killed me anyway, since you were so angry then.

TH   My judgment was overturned by the gods!

HIP   Alas! If only the human race could curse the gods!   1415

ART   Enough! For even in the darkness of earth
        this willful wrath of the goddess Cypris
        will not fall upon your body unrevenged,
        thanks to your piety and noble mind.
        For with my own hand I will take vengeance on another man,   1420
        whoever happens to be the dearest of mortals to her,
        with these inescapable arrows.
        And to you, wretched youth, to make up for your misfortune,
        I will give the greatest honors in the city of Trozen.
        Unwed maids before their marriages   1425
        shall shear their locks for you, and through the long ages
        you will enjoy their fullest mourning and tears.
        And the maidens will always think of you when composing their
        songs, and Phaedra's love for you

will not fall nameless into silence.   1430
And you, son of aged Aegeus, take
your son into your arms and draw him close to you.
For you killed him without knowing what you did, since it is natural
for men to make mistakes when the gods so grant.
And I advise you not to hate your father,   1435
Hippolytus, for you have your lot in life and perish with it.

Farewell; it is not right for me to behold the dead
nor defile my sight with the last breaths of the dying:
I see that you are already close to that misfortune.

HIP   *to Artemis, as she departs*

Farewell as you leave, blessed maiden.   1440
You leave our long companionship with ease.
I will stop quarreling with my father, since you want me to.
For I always obeyed your words in the past.

turning toward his father

Alas, alas, darkness is already coming over my eyes.
Take hold of me, father, and straighten up my body.   1445

TH   *supporting his son*

Alas, child, what are you doing to me, the ill-fated?

HIP   I have perished and see the gates of the underworld.

TH   Leaving behind my blood-defiled hands?

HIP   No, no, for I free you from this murder.

TH   What do you say? Do you release me and free me from guilt?   1450

HIP   I call to witness Artemis who kills with her bow.

TH   Dearest son, how noble you have shown yourself to your father! 1452

HIP   Pray that you may have such luck with legitimate sons!   1455

TH   Alas, your pious and noble mind!   1454

HIP   Goodbye -- a fond goodbye, father!   1453

TH   Don't abandon me now, son, but endure.   1456

HIP   My enduring is over. I am dead, father.
        Cover my face with robes as quickly as possible.

TH   O famous boundaries of Athens and Pallas,
     you will regret the loss of this man! O wretched me,   1460

addressing the statue of Aphrodite as he exits into the palace.

how fully will I remeber your evil deeds, Cypris!

Exit.

ROMAN COMEDY TEXTBOOKS

PHORMIO
A Comedy by Terence
Elaine M. Coury

xxxiii + 224 pp (1982, Reprint 1984) Paperback, ISBN 978-0-86516-014-9

This unique textbook features a reproduction of the *Phormio* of the Bembinus Manuscript. Each of the 50 pages faces with a description to enable the students to experience the novelty and pleasure of reading a fourth-century manuscript. The text contains an edited version of the play, notes, and vocabulary.

PLAUTUS' MENAECHMI
Gilbert Lawall, Betty Nye Quinn

200 pp (1978, Reprint 2002) Paperback, ISBN 978-0-86516-007-1

Designed to offer a first reading of Plautus to second-year Latinists, this book's approach to vocabulary is to include familiar words in a general vocabulary at the end of the book, while new words are displayed opposite the text. The book also includes a lexicon of words prescribed by the second-year College Boards Examination and helpful questions concerning evaluation of interpretation of the scenes.

LATIN LAUGHS
A Production of Plautus' Poenulus
Christopher Brunelle, et alli, John H. Starks, Jr., Matthew D. Panciera

Student Text: 129 pp (1997) Paperback, ISBN 978-0-86516-323-2

Teacher's Edition: 89 pp Paperback, ISBN 978-0-86516-347-8

Video: ISBN 978-0-86516-324-9

Kidnapping, romance, and a contest between lover and *leno* form the plot of Plautus' *Poenulus*, an ancient comedy that provides a rollicking good time for modern readers and audiences. Scripted in the original Latin and laced with modern props and jokes, the University of North Carolina's rendition captured the attention of both general and classical audiences.

A complete set of materials for teaching, reading, viewing and staging Plautus' *Poenulus* is now available in a user-friendly format that will breathe new life into the Latin classroom.

BOLCHAZY-CARDUCCI PUBLISHERS, INC.
WWW.BOLCHAZY.COM

GREEK DRAMA IN TRANSLATION

AESCHYLUS: Seven Against Thebes

Translated by Robert Emmet Meagher

x + 44 pp (1996) Paperback ISBN 978-0-86516-337-9

Seven Against Thebes captured first prize for its playwright in its premier performance at the 467 BC Athenian drama festival.

THE ESSENTIAL EURIPIDES
Dancing in Dark Times

Translated by Robert Emmet Meagher

xii + 556 pp (2001) Paperback ISBN 978-0-86516-513-7

Two monographs ("Mortal Vision" and "Revel and Revelation") combine with translations of five Euripidean plays (*Hekabe, Helen, Iphigenia at Aulis, Iphigenia in Tauris,* and *Bakkhai*) in a one-of-a-kind volume: a rich selection of core plays along with a substatial, engaging introduction to the full scope of the Euripidean corpus.

EURIPIDES: Bakkhai

Translated by Robert Emmet Meagher

vi + 97 pp (1995) Paperback ISBN 978-0-86516-285-3

Eurpides' *Bakkhai* presents the inner conflict between the untamed, irrational side of man, represented by the god Dionysos, and the rational side, represented by the god Apollo.

EURIPIDES: Hekabe

Translated by Robert Emmet Meagher

vii + 55 pp (1995) Paperback ISBN 978-0-86516-330-0

Euripides' *Hekabe* presents a spectacle of suffering, rage, and revenge that offers compelling witness to the courage and desperation of those victimized by violence.

EURIPIDES
Iphigenia at Aulis and Iphigenia in Tauris

Translated by Robert Emmet Meagher

176 pp (1993) Hardbound ISBN 978-0-86516-266-2

The story of Iphigenia's sacrifice and her legendary rescue is a story for our time as much as any other.

We need playwrights like him.

– Irene Papa, Actress

He renders Euripides not only readable but extremely actable.
– Michael Cacoyannis, Director, Author, Translator

BOLCHAZY-CARDUCCI PUBLISHERS, INC.
WWW.BOLCHAZY.COM

SENECA'S MORAL EPISTLES
Anna Lydia Motto

224 pp (2001) Paperback ISBN 978-0-86516-487-1

Seneca's Moral Epistles offers an intriguing selection in Latin of 40 letters of Seneca on philosophical and practical topics ranging from the lofty ("On Integrating Knowledge" and "God Within You") to the nitty-gritty: debauchery at resort baths ("Baiae and Vice") and the woes of over-training ("Against Strenuous Physical Exercise").

These letters provide a fascinating glimpse into the daily life of Rome in the Empire and one man's contemplation of it. Seneca's is a Roman voice not often heard: He condemns slavery, and denounces the gladiatorial combats and the excesses for which the Roman Empire became notorious. Living in an era of corruption and tyranny, Seneca came forth as a "physician of souls," eager to impart ethical and moral precepts that would enable his fellow men to overcome their weaknesses and attain true happiness.

As a representative of stoicism, Seneca is the precursor of Paul's ethical system, vocabulary, and analogies.

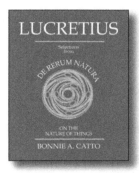

LUCRETIUS
Selections from *De rerum natura*
Bonnie A. Catto

304 pp (1998) Paperback ISBN 978-0-86516-399-7

Catto's text of Lucretius provides 53 passages in 1294 lines, spanning all 6 books of the epic. Each section features a short introduction, discussion questions, vocabulary and extensive line-by-line notes on facing pages and a wide variety of illustrative quotations from both ancient and modern sources.

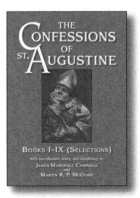

THE CONFESSIONS OF ST. AUGUSTINE
Selections from Books I–IX
By J. M. Campbell, M. R. P. McGuire

267 pp (1931, Reprint 2001) Paperback ISBN 978-0-86516-058-3

This illustrated edition features passages that show the grandeur and significance of the work and includes a section on grammar and style, vocabulary, a summary of innovations in the development of the Latin language, and a useful bibliography.

BOLCHAZY-CARDUCCI PUBLISHERS, INC.
www.BOLCHAZY.com

AURAL LATIN FOR VARIETY

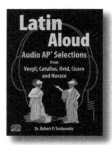

LATIN ALOUD: Audio AP* Selections
from Vergil, Catullus, Ovid, Cicero, and Horace
By Robert Sonkowsky

Audio CD (2007) UPC 00007

Latin Aloud presents 101 Latin masterworks—over 5 hours—on CD (converted to MP3), dramatically interpreted in Restored Classical Pronunciation by Dr. Robert P. Sonkowsky. Plays on any computer and most contemporary CD and DVD players. Included are AP* selections from Vergil (*Aeneid*, plus bonus selections from *Georgics* and *Eclogues*), *Catullus* (34 Poems, including Poem 64), Ovid (*Amores, Metamorphoses*), Cicero (*de Amicitia,* entire *Pro Archia*), and Horace (17 Odes, Satire 1.9).

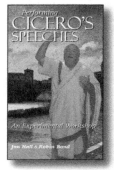

PERFORMING CICERO'S SPEECHES
An Experimental Workshop
By Robin Bond, Jon Hall

Video Cassette (2003) ISBN 978-0-86516-488-8

How exactly did Cicero perform his speeches? This video uses guidelines on voice and gesture from rhetorical treatises to reconstruct Cicero's oratorical delivery in a theatrical workshop environment. Passages discussed and performed are drawn from Cicero's *Pro Caelio, Pro Milone, Pro Ligario, Pro Archia,* In *Catilinam* 2, and *Philippic* 6. Bring Cicero's speeches alive! Includes a booklet of the Latin text and translation of all passages.

VERGIL'S DIDO AND MIMUS MAGICUS
By Symphony Orchestra of the Bayerischer Rundfunk
Composed by Jan Novak; Conducted by Rafael Kubelik

Audio CD and 40 pp/ libretto (1997) CD ISBN 978-0-86516-346-1

Composer Jan Novak's haunting choral rendition of Vergil's ancient poetry commences with the voice of Dido the queen, foreshadowing a tragic tale of love and duty. Widely acclaimed in Europe, Novak's *Dido and Mimus Magicus* is now available to American audiences in a CD recording and a 3-language libretto.

ROME'S GOLDEN POETS
By St. Louis Chamber Chorus

Audio CD ISBN 978-0-86516-474-1

With its chronological, cultural, and ethnic diversity of composers, this recording testifies to the timeless power of the Golden Age of poetry. Selections from Catullus, Vergil, and Horace are performed by the St. Louis Chamber Chorus under the direction of Philip Barnes.

*AP is a registered trademark of the College Entrance Examination Board, which was not involved in the production of, and does not endorse, this product.

BOLCHAZY-CARDUCCI PUBLISHERS, INC.
WWW.BOLCHAZY.COM